LIFE STORY
THE BOOK OF *LIFE GOES ON*
TV'S FIRST AND BEST
FAMILY SHOW OF CHALLENGE

BY HERBIE J PILATO

FOREWORD BY MICHAEL BRAVERMAN

Dedicated to the positive power of popular television.

Published in the USA by:
BearManor Media
P O Box 71426
Albany, Georgia 31708
www.bearmanormedia.com

ISBN 1-59393-085-2

Printed in the United States of America.
Book design by Brian Pearce.
Cover design by Matt Hankinson.

TABLE OF CONTENTS

FOREWORD

All television series are accidents. *Life Goes On* was just a fortuitous accident. It was merely a weird cosmic conflux of serendipitous circumstances that were neither predictable nor anticipated and surely not repeatable in today's television atmosphere. And, truthfully, no one was more surprised than I was when the *Life Goes On* pilot was picked up by ABC-TV for filming in the spring of 1989.

Our Thacher family had no sex, no violence, no cops, lawyers, cowboys or doctors. We had no car chases, no explosions, no action to speak of, and none of the delicious maliciousness and intrigue of incredibly wealthy families like the Ewings on *Dallas* or the Carringtons of *Dynasty*. What we had was a lower-middle-class family in which one of the three children, Charles Corky Thacher, happened to have Down syndrome. To completely stack the deck against us, Chris Burke, then a novice actor who actually happened to have Down syndrome in real life, was playing Corky.

The premise was intensely personal for me. Corky is the embodiment of my nephew, Charles, an incredible young man who also happens to have Down syndrome. My desire, but never my stated goal, was to expose the profound humanity of people with Down syndrome. I wanted to focus on the normality of the Corky Thachers of the world, not the abnormality. I wanted to demonstrate that people with differences — all people with all differences — are "different" only by perception. I wanted to create a legacy for my nephew to reflect upon. I wanted to create a world where people could be different and have it not matter. If that perception can be altered or (do I ask too much?) erased, the differences perish from our consciousness.

We later added the character of Jesse McKenna (in an Emmy-winning performance by Chad Lowe), who was diagnosed as HIV-positive (and who later developed full-blown AIDS), and the central theme of the show was expanded — with occasional controversy. Consequently, my initial desire went on to consume nearly five years of my life, both professionally and personally. It took its toll on my health and severely strained (but didn't permanently injure) my family life. It was, at times, agonizingly difficult to maintain, but it was also equally exhilarating and rewarding, making every minute of those five years worthwhile.

Did *Life Goes On* ultimately change the common perception of Down syndrome? Did the show help to knock down stereotypes and put a face on those with AIDS? Did it make people think differently about these issues, if only for one hour every Sunday night?

Yes, I believe it did, and this book is a testament to that.

Michael Braverman

PREFACE

There is an increased mainstream acceptance, general employment and social interaction of those with disabilities, various backgrounds, cultures and heritage. There also remains much prejudice in the world, leaving some to still wonder if we are created equal or if we can unconditionally love or dare embrace a person who is perceived as different.

From September 12, 1989 to May 23, 1993, the television series, *Life Goes On*, addressed these issues and more. This ground-breaking one-hour drama managed to present, weekly, engaging and often-time entertaining characters who were confronted with serious challenges: Down Syndrome (also known as Down's Syndrome) and AIDS.

Life Story: The Book of Life Goes On: TV's First and Best Family Show of Challenge discusses in detail the delicate topics at *Life's* — and life's — core. Linking the television tome with the academic reference, this book acts as an educational TV guide, serving as an affectionate and informative literary companion to a small-screen series that refused to take the easy way out. It tells the inside story of a show whose phenomenal success — which continues in syndicated reruns — remains a big surprise even to its creators.

As an intimate reflection, and prepared with the full support and cooperation of those associated with the series, *Life Story* profiles a group of actors, producers, writers, directors and various behind-the-scenes personnel whose personal warmth, vitality and camaraderie created a strong sense of family, not only amid the characters, but between the program itself and the viewers at home. It furnishes choice commentary from the show's actors, such as, Bill Smitrovich, Chris Burke, Kellie Martin, Chad Lowe, Tracey Needham, as well as series creator and executive producer Michael Braverman, co-executive producer Rick Rosenthal, producer/writer/director Michael Nankin, and many more, all of whom granted exclusive, in-depth interviews.

While *Life Goes On's* diverse eye on the family remains wide-open, *Life Story* is here to chronicle the entire journey. It puts to print a piece of TV wares that has set the standard for quality, educational and entertaining programming — a series that, while managing to cross all culture lines, has become the most prevalent family show since *The Waltons* (arriving long before *7th Heaven* and *Everwood*).

Life Story profiles a television series that goes on to say more than, *I'm okay, you're okay.* But rather, *I'm great, so are you, and together we'll make it.* It explores the various aspects of *Life*, with chapters that detail the show's creation, deciphering the theatrical methods, techniques and philosophies employed by the program's skillful on-screen performers, and capturing the visual, audio and technical procedures executed by the show's equally talented off-camera production team. Other chapters address the show's metamorphosis over its original four-year session and its general message. They present keys to its popularity and display how the series has influenced viewers in positive ways. There's even an itemized episode guide (with behind-the-scenes anecdotes for each segment) that closes the book in appendix form.

So, turn the page and begin to celebrate *Life*. Enjoy the entire spectrum of what it required to bring life to *Life*. Explore what made the whole *Life* experience so uniquely true for those in front of and behind the cameras, as well as for all of those at home. Embrace how it somehow bonded the reel and real worlds with a balanced blend of fact and fiction, artistry and appreciation, and aesthetics and communication, creating a colorful, meaningful, authentic media mosaic — one at which to gaze upon, one from which to walk away with respect, feeling both breathless and inspired.

ACKNOWLEDGMENTS

I am grateful to all of those who contributed to this *Life Story*, in the form of countless interview hours and commentary, research, editorial and graphic design, photos, moral support and encouragement.

First and foremost, I would like to thank Michael Braverman and Chris Burke, without both of whom there would have been no *Life Goes On*, let alone any *Life* Story.

I would also like to thank: Chad Lowe, Tracey Needham, Andrea Friedman, Kelli Martin, Tommy Puett, Ray Buktenica, Michelle Matheson, Adam Carl, Tanya Fenmore, Eric Welch, Al Ruscio, Penny Santon, Martin Milner, Leigh Ann Orsi, David Byrd, Troy Evans, Charles Frank, Dorothy Lyman and Michael Goorjian; Michael Nankin, Rick Rosenthal, R.W. Goodwin, Lorenzo DeStefeno, Michael Lange, Kim Friedman, E.F. Wallengren, Joe Pennella, William Olvis, Craig Safan, Linda Safan, Craig Schiller, Dee Dee Bradley, Chad Hoffman, Marshall Goldberg, Inness Weis, Marti Noxon and Kaley Hummel (for her endless supply of *Life Goes On* photos), and the many other actors, writers, directors, producers and additional members of the *Life Goes On* team, behind and in front of the camera.

Thank you, too, to the entire family of professionals at BearManor Media, especially to publisher Ben Ohmart for his loyalty and respect for all media things classic, and to his wife and executive assistant, Mayumi Ohmart.

Thank you, also, to graphic designer Matt Hankinson, who created the brilliant, eclectic cover of this book; entertainment historian Brendan Slattery for his fact-checking and impeccable research assistance; typesetter Brian Pearce; and an extremely special thank you to Jacki Garfinkel, for her dedication and concise editorial expertise in supervision over the entire content of this book.

Life Story would have never been properly told without any of you.

The Thachers: Patti Lupone, Bill Smitrovich, Chris Burke, Monique Lanier and Kellie Martin. *THE REGAL COLLECTION*

CHAPTER 1

AND NOW...*LIFE GOES ON*

"The opening hour of this ABC series was such lovely television..."
— Robert MacKenzie, *TV Guide*, January 27, 1990

Several weekly morality plays in the history of television feature strong, peerless and virtuous characters, many of whom are premised in the realms of science fiction, fantasy or mysticism; *Star Trek*, *The Twilight Zone*, *The Bionic Woman*, *Bewitched*, and *Kung Fu*, to name a few. These and other worthy programs (as well as other *otherworldly* shows) have referenced issues, such as strong work ethics, family values and common humanity, sometimes with a more realistic bent (*All in the Family*, *Maude*, *Good Times*). Some have singled out more eccentric, off-beat characters (*Twin Peaks*, *Northern Exposure*), while still additional shows introduced somewhat subtler characters enveloped within courageous, daring plots that contributed to a healthier, truer perspective on living (*St. Elsewhere*, *LA Law*, *NYPD Blue*).

Yet, no small-screen gem has balanced so well or catered so directly to the entire scope of TV as *Life Goes On* has so charmingly and meaningfully done. Still screened around the world, *Life Goes On* (periodically referred to from hereon as *Life* or LGO) continues to prevail with Chris Burke as Charles Corky Thacher, who has Down Syndrome (hereon periodically referred to as Down's), and Chad Lowe as Jesse McKenna, a young man who tests positive for the HIV virus, and who develops AIDS. Corky and Jesse suffer from the same pangs of discrimination as Elizabeth Montgomery's Samantha Stephens, a witch in the overwhelming mortal domain of *Bewitched*, or David Carradine's Kwai Chang Caine, an Asian in the closed-minded 1800s western territory of *Kung Fu*.

Like Samantha and Caine, Corky and Jesse are outcasts, and though they lack superior powers in the way of magic or martial arts to help them battle their turmoil (inside themselves, and from others), they are heroes, nonetheless. Heroes of the heart who are fearless against the odds. Heroes to those closest to them, in the face of objection, adversity, diversity and rigid distinction. Underdogs fighting the good-fight, with only the viewers knowing for sure how right they are. We, the outsiders at home, somehow bond with the *Life* outsiders on screen, who are inclusive or centrally involved within a working-class brood: The Thacher family.

This brave clan is headed by Corky's parents, Drew and Libby, expertly portrayed by vets Bill Smitrovich (once of *Miami Vice* and *Millennium,* and recently NBC's hit mini-series, *The '60s*) and Patti Lupone (the Broadway diva) with unwavering theatrical precision. There, too, is Corky's younger sister, Rebecca (a.k.a. Becca), embodied by the energetic Kellie Martin (later the star of the short-lived, but critically-acclaimed, 1993-94 CBS drama, *Christy*; once a featured intern on *ER,* today the star of the Hallmark Channel's hit series, *Mystery Woman*). Acting ingénues Monique Lanier (today in the real medical field, off-camera) and Tracey Needham (a former model and frequent featured actress of TV and film) shared the role of Paige, the free-spirited eldest sibling (from Drew's first marriage). Tommy Puett and Andrea Friedman round out the cast as Tyler Benchfield and Amanda Swanson. Tyler was there from the beginning; the jock with a heart and a brother with Down's. He's Jesse's rival for Becca's affections - the first apple of her eye who would later die due to a bad mix of booze, hurt feelings, and poor judgment. Amanda is the love of Corky's life. She arrived in the third season. She, too, has Down's. She, too, doesn't make it matter.

These characters confront with diligent intrepidity the anxiety and relief caused by a two-income household, the perils and pleasures of mid-life birthing and parenting, the complications facing the metamorphosis of the modern independent female, the dangers that ride along with teenagers who drink and drive, and the trials of any individual who is forced to face the emotional, physical, financial, psychological, sexual and even spiritual challenges of family life in contemporary times.

All were inspired performances acted within well-written, directed and produced episodes, encased with superior production values and credible, yet compelling stories. Each segment was initially presented with a sincere dedication to producing quality television. To LGO's credit, all of the Thachers, their friends and associates, are depicted as a working-class people who wrestle with everything from jobs to school to their own hearts and minds in an unassuming, authentic manner. They love and argue with each other. Nothing is held back. Just like real life. For this is series television at its best. It's open and truthful with its presentation of characters that display not only what it does mean, but also what it *should* mean to be a human being. Its ground-breaking premise illuminates the viewer's intellect and soul, while it refuses to ignore the benevolent seat of passion. The qualities of *Life* shine through from its very essence. As *TV Guide's* Robert MacKenzie reported during the show's first year, "The series, like a newborn world, has a glowing light at its center."

MacKenzie was specifically referring to Chris Burke as the tear-jerking but stoic high school student with several obvious unyielding tasks. Yet, the columnist may as well have been addressing the intent, content and high performance level of the entire series. As the first show to feature regular characters with Down's and AIDS, *Life* certainly presented unusual images for weekly television, a medium disreputably circumspect of presenting notions that viewers find jarring - more so during the show's initial run in the early 1990s, at the emergence of formal politically-correct behavior and communication.

When LGO debuted, *New York* magazine's John Leonard found it hard to "think of another TV series full of so much stress that doesn't resort to punch lines or punch-ups and yet is so comfortable with the long haul, that knows so well the annealing powers of commitment, as though for all those rainy days, [Corky's family] saved up graces. Imagine *A Year in the Life* [a short-lived series on NBC, 1988-1989] with people you care about - or a daytime soap without the lip gloss; or maybe the *Coping* column of the *Saturday Times*, except with sweat glands: making do instead of scoring."

People added: "*Life* is a warm, delightful, touching family show, the kind guaranteed to make you feel good to be drawing breath - the way the movie *It's a Wonderful Life* does. This well-cast and beautifully written show also treats women, blacks and the handicapped with dignity, which not enough TV shows do."

Time went as far as to submit *Life* as proof that popular small-screen entertainment can indeed be tutorial, while pointing out, too, that such programming does not usually receive the kind of support from its home-network, as, say, a more violent-ridden police series.

"Television bears a heavy burden. Unlike movies or books or plays, TV shows are expected to do more than just provide entertainment. They are asked to be socially responsible as well. Because they come into the home uninvited, network programs are supposed to uphold proper moral values and teach life lessons: drugs are bad, race discrimination is wrong, women would get breast exams early and often. Sometimes the second task tends to overwhelm the first: that is, a show is so busy doing good that no one bothers to notice whether it is good. The new season's prime example is ABC's *Life Goes On*."

Though LGO was never a super-hit on ABC, Sunday nights at 7:00 P.M., opposite the CBS powerhouse *60 Minutes*, it held its own, becoming the best-rated weekly show in that time-slot in the network's history. In reruns around the globe, it continues to reach beyond the realm of average entertainment, presenting itself as an affirmative alternative to mindless car-chases and blood-soaked murders, more than ten years after its debut. Though it took some doing, its educational quality (which diametrically opposes the widespread belief behind, *per se*, *Seinfeld's* historic *no-hugging* theory of series success) holds great positive influence, while tweaking the viewer's intellectual and aesthetic interest.

What more could a TV viewer want?

Life creator Michael Braverman. *MICHAEL BRAVERMAN*

CHAPTER 2
LIFE GENESIS

"I'm very proud of the pilot for *Life Goes On*."
— Michael Braverman, creator/executive producer, *Life Goes On*

The initial episode of *Life Goes On*, aptly titled, "The Pilot," is moving and well structured. It's the first example of a series that can never be classified as an average television production. Viewers catch more than a mere glimpse of the truth through the looking glass in their living rooms; they actually watch a program that uniquely mirrors a more deftly sketched state of being.

The first episode presented the story of a middle/working-class clan residing in the fictional town of Glenbrook, Illinois (mirrored after the real-life Glen*dale*, California; on *7th Heaven*, the setting is Glen*oak*). Both parents were employed because they had to be, not because they wanted to be. Here's a detailed, chronological summary of "The Pilot":

It's established that the Thachers live in a middle-class neighborhood. Their living room is filled with mementos and pictures. We meet Arnold, the dog, in the kitchen while Becca's in her room, which is decorated with rock 'n' roll idol posters. Drew and Libby's bedroom holds the exercycle that Drew never uses. Corky faces his initial day of academia, more of an ordeal than it is for most kids. Drew and Libby are making an attempt (not their first) to mainstream him into a regular high school (instead of one for *special kids*).

The combination of apprehension and optimism that Corky feels is more than evident on his face. In the early morning, Libby places her head round her son's bedroom door to wake him. She finds him on his bed, fully dressed, anxious and expectant. (A sequence effective enough to become part of the show's opening credits.)

In a vivid fantasy play (which would become a series trademark), Corky imagines school as a hostile environment, almost like a scene from Mel Gibson's *Mad Max* films. In another one of these arresting visions, he pictures himself and Rona, the best-looking girl in the class and Tyler's first love (played by Michele Matheson), as homecoming king and queen.

17

Ridiculed all of his life for being distinct, Corky (now eighteen), is placed in the same freshman class with his younger sister Becca, for whom he's a source of huge possible abashment. While she's tormented by the demands of peer pressure, his potential for not making it in a mainstream school have important implications for his financially- and emotionally-strapped siblings and parents, the latter of whom may have to resume paying for his

The Thachers celebrate *Life* in this shot from "The Pilot." THE REGAL COLLECTION

education. While Drew is on the verge of gambling $50,000 to start his own construction company with three partners, Libby is agonizing over of her imminent fortieth birthday. Of their two daughters, the eldest Paige is the most unsettled, though Becca is as confused, melodramatic and frustrated as any fourteen-year-old. Corky's simplistic honesty, however, cuts through the artificial status accorded to Becca's high-school cliques, and his unaffected warmth helps Paige return to the family (after a brief separation).

In a concluding sequence, Corky's asked by his incisive but kindly English teacher (Steven Keats) to hand in a test paper on which he's suspected of cheating. His body language reads fright and bafflement. He's asked to recite a stanza from Edgar Allan Poe's *The Raven*, over which (with his father's help) he labored long to learn.

It's an important moment.

Called to school, Drew and Libby sit with Corky and smile with pride as their son clears his name. When he hugs his dad in victory, a look of warm bliss suffuses Corky's face. He conquers the first of many trials to follow as an *average* high school student, as *Life Goes On* initiated its splendid victory in television entertainment.

The campaign to get "The Pilot" for *Life Goes On* on the air began approximately eleven years ago, after Chris Burke viewed actor Jason Kingsley (who has Down's) on an episode of ABC's *The Fall Guy*. Burke was so inspired by Kingsley, that he wrote a letter of praise to the young performer. Jason's mother, writer Emily Kingsley, responded to Burke's communication, and a pen-pal relationship was formed.

The Burke and Kingsley families met at an annual Kingsley picnic. Due to Emily's involvement with the entertainment industry (she was associated with *Sesame Street* and various TV projects), Warner Bros. Television contacted her for advice on casting a character with Down's for the tele-film, *Desperate* (which was originally broadcast on ABC in 1987), and produced in Key West, Florida, by Michael Braverman, creator of *Life Goes On*.

Desperate was loosely based on *Lord Jim*, the novel by Joseph Conrad (who authored the series of books that gave birth to the film *Apocalypse Now*, released in 1979). The story involved a ship's captain named Noah Sullivan (portrayed by John Savage), who sails from Miami to Havana. The boat flounders in a hurricane and the captain abandons it. But he's actually smuggling refugees, whom he then leaves to fend on their own. The ship, however, does not sink. The coast guard tows it to Miami. Yet, the young sea captain, whose heritage stems from a long line of traditional naval families, is dishonored and, as Michael Braverman relays, "he loses himself in drink and everything else in Key West. His fiancée leaves him, and an entire series of negative events begin to transpire."

One key establishment at which the captain inebriates himself is a bar owned by a character played by Meg Foster, who co-starred with Loretta (*M*A*S*H*) Swit in the original pilot for *Cagney & Lacey*, as well as with Perry King in the 1978 film *A Different Story* (a tale of a gay man and a lesbian who fall in love). It's Foster's character in *Desperate* who has the mentally challenged son, the role for which Emily Kingsley had in mind for Chris Burke.

Desperate was shot as a pilot and aired twice and, though it failed to make any big waves at ABC, the network was impressed with Burke. So much so that Braverman was asked to create a show for the actor. According to Chad Hoffman, ABC's then head of Drama Programming, Burke became a beacon of light. "We were all quite enthusiastic about Chris," he recalls.

In the summer of 1988, shortly after the airing of *Desperate* (and the end to a wicked writer's strike), Hoffman lunched with Braverman, with whom he had long wanted to develop series projects. "We talked about a couple of different ideas," Hoffman says, "one of which involved a show centering around Chris. I thought there might be something there and he agreed. So we started to think about some of the areas for it."

At first, Braverman suggested various ideas; one spring-boarded directly from *Desperate*, involving Captain Sullivan relocating to San Francisco with Burke's character, and becoming an investigator. The idea sank, but then surfaced *Life Goes On*, introductory material for which Braverman had presented to Hoffman the day after ABC's Emmy-triumph for *thirtysomething* as Best Drama, in the fall of 1988 (the first year the awards ceremony switched from a spring broadcast). The two met at a LA restaurant called Artie's. Basking in the joy of victory, Hoffman was ready to move full-speed-ahead with Braverman's idea, which Hoffman called "Great!" He gave the project the green-light, and said, "Let's develop it."

Soon after, Braverman penned the pilot for *Life* which, as Hoffman ascertains, "was quite good. When Michael first turned in the script, we did a couple of rewrites on them, but nothing severe. When it came time for pilot season, we liked it so much, that we placed an order to have it filmed." The show took the network by storm with a premise that Hoffman thought did not really have a voice on television at the time. "One of the things we always did at ABC," Hoffman says, "was to look around to see what wasn't on television. What ideas were *not* being addressed, with regards to the audience. The working-class did not have a series with which they could identify. That kind of show was simply not on the air."

With LGO, he continues, "We wanted to prove that this family could overcome the daily obstacles of life, that they would substantially establish that hope and love triumphs. Into that situation, we thought to add an extraordinary circumstance — that being a child with Down's. So we asked ourselves, *What would it be like for this person to function in the mainstream of society?* And *What would it be like for his family?* And we went from there."

Surely, it was not that easy to get a series pilot produced. In the late 1980s, it was not uncommon for the programming executives at the three major television networks to sit through literally five-hundred presentations or pitches of proposed new television drama series (comedies, variety shows, reality shows, etc. fell into a different category). Of these five-hundred pitches, the networks would each choose perhaps fifty ideas to go to script, that is, employ a television writer to write a full script of the pilot idea.

"So already the odds are 10-1 against," explains Michael Braverman. "Of the fifty scripts, the networks would choose possibly as many as ten to fifteen scripts to shoot pilot films. And of the fifteen pilot films, they would painstakingly select four or five to premiere each September as new television series. Some quick math, just using your fingers, tells you the odds of a dramatic television idea actually making it to series are about 100-1. If you also factor in that approximately 90% of new television drama shows fail, what were the chances of *Life Goes On*?"

Braverman was so certain that LGO had about as much chance of succeeding as "the Chicago Cubs winning a pennant," that he decided to hire someone else to write the first segment. At the time, he was committed to another pilot at NBC plus a TV movie for the same network. "My wife often…but affectionately…criticizes me for being single-task oriented," he says, "and I knew my work habits wouldn't allow me to do justice to all three projects so, abiding by the law of the TV jungle, I sacrificed the weakest of the litter. I spent a few days writing the pilot story and then handed it off to an extremely talented feature film writer to write the script. It was a rare exception in those days of television."

Therewith, as Braverman goes on to describe, "The heavens began to conspire in ways I still can't fully understand." One week after the feature film-scribe began penning the LGO pilot (then entitled *Northbrook*), she was given what Braverman calls a "very prestigious theatrical movie assignment. And, despite our contract, and abiding the law of the feature film jungle, she begged off the pilot. It was, after all, just television."

Now, the ball was back in Braverman's court - and the script was due in less than three weeks. Never having spoken to Braverman's wife about his "single-task orientation," the executives at Warner Bros., the studio responsible for financing and producing *Life Goes On*, persuaded the producer to pen the pilot himself. It wasn't a difficult decision. "Since the beginning," he admits, "I had always felt compelled to write it. Now I had no excuse."

Yet, his goal was merely to survive the next three months of production, in the face of several obstacles. The script he submitted to ABC, which was composed in less than 14 days (and now entitled *Glenbrook*), was eagerly accepted by Chad Hoffman and Mireille Soria, whom Braverman calls "two of the more gracious and enlightened network programming executives I have encountered in my twenty-five-year television journey." It was now Hoffman and Soria's job to read the material and offer suggestions for improvements, an often humiliating and invariably odious and destructive process known in the business as "giving notes."

"Chad and Mireille were the gatekeepers," Braverman says. "They possessed the authority to reject the script and, consequently, end the entire process right there. Or, they could give notes, wait for the rewrite and then make their decision. Ironically, although at their level of network executiveship they had the authority to say *no*, they did not have the authority to say *yes*. That privilege is reserved for the rank of entertainment president or higher, in this case, Bob Iger and Ted Harbert. The best Chad and Mireille could have done, given that they liked the script, was recommend it to Bob and Ted and lobby to keep it going in the pilot process."

So Braverman waited for notes. And waited. Yet the commentary was not forthcoming. So he, and the Warner Bros. executives, took this as a bad omen. No notes usually means no interest; what Braverman calls a television pocket veto.

What he had no way of knowing, at the time, was that the strange cosmic conspiracy had once again come into play on his and the studio's behalf. As the ABC executives in Los Angeles were evaluating the pilot script for LGO, the ABC executives in New York and Washington, D.C. were testifying before Congress and the Federal Communications Corporation (FCC) decrying the financial woes imposed upon them by the then-mandated family viewing hour.

ABC's position was that they could police themselves and program appropriate family material without Congressional interference. In fact, they contended, they had many such shows in development at that moment (though they really did not). And by the time the East Coast ABC suits returned to their phones, LGO suddenly became a serious contender. A few days later, Braverman was called into the ABC Century City offices for notes on the pilot script. "The network's script notes were minimal," he says. "Chad and Mireille asked me to change the title and alter a few minor story points… nothing significant nor substantially different than the original first draft. As is customary, the revised script incorporating the network's notes went in on a Friday, giving the executives the weekend to absorb my script and probably a dozen others. The following Monday we got the call: *Life Goes On* had been picked up for film. We were going to make the pilot. Except for the Warner Bros. executives, no one in Hollywood was more surprised than I. Now, of course, the real fight would begin…starting with the deal."

"It's called show business," Braverman goes on to explain, "but the real emphasis is on the business, not the show." Lou Race, his good friend and the 1st Assistant Director on LGO, constantly reminded him that film was just the by-product of the business. In other words, Braverman clarifies, "If they could find some way to eliminate the film and still have the business, they would."

Here's how it worked back then (when the business was more in favor of the producers and the studios; it has since shifted dramatically in favor of the networks over the last ten years): The network, in this case, ABC, licenses from the studio (Warner Bros.) the pilot and subsequent episodes for only two network runs - the original broadcast and one repeat airing. The network has no ownership in the series. The studio owns all the film. However, since the network is only licensing and not buying, they only pay for part of the production, known as the license fee.

The difference between the license fee - what the network pays, and what the film actually costs - is called the deficit. It is the studio's obligation to pay the deficit, often several hundred thousand dollars per episode. The studio makes back its deficit and, hopefully a profit, by selling the series into foreign markets and into the domestic syndication market (cable TV, local channels, etc.).

So Warner Bros. calls a meeting of their foreign and domestic sales executives. The question posed is: *How many markets and how much can we get for a series about a lower-middle-class family raising a son with Down Syndrome?* Braverman jokes: "Can you just hear the silence in the room? Although I was not, of course, privy to that meeting, I'm sure someone must have asked the obvious: *Is the father a cop?* No. *Is the mother a lawyer?* No. *Does the kid have super powers?* Again, no. *So what's it about? Well, it's about a closely-knit, loving, lower-middle-class family facing life with a kid who has a learning difference.* After another long silence, someone must have said, *You guys must be nuts.* We're not going to make a nickel on it."

Warner Bros., needless to say, was not inclined to put a lot of deficit money into the production of *Life Goes On.* Consequently, the show's network license fee and deficit finance package fell far short of what most other pilots being readied were getting. "We had no choice but to do our best with what we had," Braverman says. "Secretly, I agreed with the conventional wisdom…this pilot wasn't going anywhere."

"Then," he adds, "for whatever cosmic reason, the stars lined up again and again."

Within the large number of directors in the Director's Guild of America, there is a very small cadre of network acceptable pilot directors. These are the cream, the elite, the chosen few. And this was pilot season - everyone producing a pilot was going after the same directors. Braverman was no exception. He remembers having meetings and lunches and dinners and breakfasts with many of the chosen few. "With all of the offers they were getting for the hot new pilots that year," he says, "none, for obvious reasons, wanted to do my *Life Goes On* pilot."

Which obvious number one reason? Money. "It's called show business," Braverman reiterates. "If a director's pilot gets picked up for series, that particular director receives a royalty [in the vicinity of $5,000.00] for every subsequent episode in the series. Pilot directors bank on a series going three, four, five years or more. At 5,000 bucks a pop, that's a lot of royalty. And none of them saw *Life Goes On* going beyond the pilot. So who could blame them?"

Braverman was becoming desperate for an acceptable director when Norman Stephens, then the Vice President of Television Movies and Mini-Series for Warner Bros., asked him to lunch. He had a director in mind: Rick Rosenthal, a respected young man who was beginning to make a name for himself in the feature world, but who would also consider the appropriate TV pilot.

Still, Braverman asked: "Who's Rick Rosenthal?"

Stephens hesitated a few moments and finally said, "Well…he's actually my brother-in-law. But don't hold that against him."

Braverman did not. He looked at Rosenthal's sample reel, met with him, and found, to his absolute delight and joy, that the two saw the pilot exactly in the same way. "We were, as they say, in sync," Braverman deciphers.

Bill Smitrovich and Patti Lupone were cast as Drew and Libby Thacher. *THE REGAL COLLECTION*

CHAPTER 3

TEAMING WITH *LIFE*

"*Life Goes On* will always have meaning for me."
— Chris Burke

With Rick Rosenthal on board for the LGO pilot, the next big hurdle was casting. In a twisted irony found only in the television business, Chris Burke actually had to audition for the role of Corky in front of the very same network executives who asked Michael Braverman to design a show for him. "The first thing we did was talk about who we would cast in Corky's role," former ABC executive Chad Hoffman explains, "and the intention always was for it to be Chris."

Burke was sent the script. He came in to audition with his father and, according to Hoffman, "did a terrific job." Hoffman and Braverman were there, as was Donna Rosenstein, head of casting for Warner Bros. Television. "I'll never forget it," Hoffman relays, "because after Chris left, we kind of all had tears in our eyes. He was still in the building at that point, and we went down the hall and told him and his father [that he got the part]. He was absolutely ecstatic. It was one of those rare moments in the entertainment business where not only are you doing something you believe in, and something that you hope will be successful and good, but where you also feel like maybe you're doing something that was for the good of someone else."

As Burke puts to summary, "First, I did *Desperate*, and then ABC wanted to do a series with me in it, and *Life Goes On* was the result. From the beginning, I was very happy that I did the pilot. I loved working on it, and I'm glad they decided to continue with the series. It just got better and better."

One point was clear to most producers planning to introduce a new series idea to ABC: The network was not solely interested in casting big names in the leads. Or as Chad Hoffman explains, "We would always try to find the best people we could"— an integrity that was employed specifically during a quest for the actors who would play Drew and Libby, Corky's understanding parents.

A thorough star search for *Life's* mom and pop was begun by Michael Braverman in California, where a series of reading tests transpired with

several good actors. "Drew and Libby Thacher were both much more difficult to cast than I anticipated," Braverman explains. "There were dozens of
immensely talented actors and actresses in Los Angeles in that age range
[40-50], but for some reason, we couldn't find the right combination. Drew
Thacher needed a particular everyman quality that was so elusive. And for
the role of Libby, I needed someone, for lack of a better description, outrageous. She had to be the counterpoint to Corky."

Braverman says someone like Sada Thompson was more than suited as
the mother, Kate Lawrence, in the Mike Nichols-directed pilot for one of
ABC's other kindred shows: *Family* (a rare Aaron Spelling non-jiggle production that aired in the *Charlie's Angels* era from 1976 to 1980). Yet in order
to keep *Life Goes On* from falling into the maudlin pit, he required the exact
opposite of an apron-wearing, hand-wringing TV mom like Thompson's
Lawrence. "That was the *last* thing I wanted," Braverman emphasizes. "Sada
is a wonderful actress, absolutely brilliant at times. But basically, if you put
Sada and Patti in the same room, you will see that they are not twins."

Again, he required someone outrageous.

Donna Rosenstein then came up with the most shocking idea of all:
Patti Lupone. Lupone had just finished an extraordinary run as *Evita* on
Broadway and was toying with the idea of doing television again. She
had one failed TV pilot behind her and still had some lingering trepida-
tions with performing on the small screen. No matter. Braverman and Rick
Rosenthal were on a plane to New York the day after Rosenstein suggested
the actress. ABC had arranged for the use of the New York set and crew of
Good Morning, America to tape Lupone's audition. Braverman viewed the
America sets as too upscale, working against the half-dozen page line-read-
ings given for the actor. He had the set crew bring in a blue-sky background.
Yet that did not sit well with the NY casting director who, Braverman says,
"was just devastated that we were not using *America's* beautiful, marvelous
set."

There was also only a two-hour window in which the set would be available. "That's not a lot of time," Braverman admits. "There were many other
actors and actresses we wanted to audition as well who, because of the time
constraint, we decided to pass on."

One of whom Braverman and Rosenthal did not overlook was Bill
Smitrovich. "Rick and I were both big admirers of Bill's work on *Crime Story*
and *Miami Vice*," Braverman says of the two NBC police shows from the
mid-1980s. In the former, Smitrovich emerged regularly as Detective Dan
Krycek. In the latter, the actor appeared only in the pilot, playing Scotty
Wheeler, Don Johnson's ex-partner, who became corrupt for the sake of his
wheelchair-bound son. An image of lasting impressions. A vision of what
was meant to be.

"He brought a certain intensity with him to the audition," Braverman says of Smitrovich, ". . . the weight of the world on his shoulders, muddling through. He had that certain look and feel that seemed right for Drew. He just felt fatherly to me. So we took a gamble and paired him up with Patti for the first audition. And to be honest, I don't remember who auditioned after them. We had found our Drew and Libby." (For the record, some of the others who tried out for Drew and Libby included Max Gail, best known as Detective Wojohowicz from TV's *Barney Miller*, Charles Frank, who would later join *Life* as Tyler Benchfield's father, and Susan Anspaugh.)

Though sick in bed with the flu back in L.A., Chad Hoffman listened to Braverman's long-distance communicative screen-test update, and anticipated his return to the West Coast with the audition tape. "We got lucky," Hoffman admits. "We found two extremely talented actors who fit perfectly into the mother and father roles. It all just felt very natural. It felt right."

Bill Smitrovich's professional career began in New York City at the Harold Clurman Theatre, where he received his first big break, becoming the understudy for all 28 male roles in Arthur Miller's *The American Clock*. While at Smith College in Northhampton, Massachusetts, Bill became a founding member of the No Theatre Company (which is still in existence). He then went on to establish a lengthy course in film, and on the stage and TV (i.e., *Crime Story*, *Miami Vice*). At the time of his Drew-initiation, Smitrovich explored his own emotional intelligence, which included a desire to return to the theatre, following *Crime Story*. He began appearing in *Frankie and Johnny in the Claire Deloon*, a Terrance McNaulty play off-Broadway at the Westside Arts Theatre in New York. Soon after, his agent sent him the pilot script for *Life Goes On*. As the actor recalls, "I read it, and absolutely loved it. So I asked my agent to set up an audition, since both Patti and I were doing theatre in New York, where she was appearing in *Anything Goes* at the Lincoln Center, we couldn't get out to LA."

Soon following, he and Lupone auditioned on that little poor man's set belonging to *Good Morning, America*, which they used after the morning chat show had completed a day's taping. "After I did a few scenes with Patti," the actor explains, "I was given the rather dubious distinction of performing with Rick Rosenthal as Corky. It was a scene from the pilot where Drew realizes how proud he is of his son. I don't know what got into me, but I became caught up in the moment. I reached over and gently patted Rick on the cheek. He had *become* Corky in my imagination." Yet Rosenthal sported a beard, which kind of awakened Smitrovich from his surreal reverie. At that point, he stopped, and asked himself, *What the hell am I doing?*

As trained and experienced actors, however, he and Lupone knew exactly what they were doing. Like her soon-to-be-co-star, Lupone had chalked up an impressive list of credits. These ranged from musical leads on Broadway to starring roles in feature films (*Driving Miss Daisy*) and television movies (*LBJ: The Early Years*). As Michael Braverman has conveyed, she came to *Life* with a Tony Award for Broadway's top-shelf musical *Evita*, and had performed in London stage productions of *Les Miserables* (for which she originated the role of Fantine) and *The Cradle Will Rock*, both for which she received the Laurence Olivier Award for Best Actress in a Musical. For *Anything Goes*, she earned a Drama Desk Award, a nomination for the Tony, and an Outer Critics Circle Award.

Born in Northport, Long Island, New York, Lupone started tap dancing at age 4. She later began voice lessons, and fell in love with the stage during her initial appearance at a local elementary school. At that very young age, she knew she wanted to act. Upon high-school graduation, she was accepted as one of the original members of the newly-formed drama division (founded by John Houseman and Michael St. Denis) at the prestigious Julliard School. Her musical theatre experience notwithstanding, Lupone had won the role of *LGO's* Libby Thacher, a non-muse. As she told a reporter, "I left *Anything Goes* to do *Life Goes On*. My agent sent me the pilot script and I was moved and educated by it. The thing that I have always loved about my career has been the surprise in it. I sort of let it unfold. I never thought about television until it presented itself to me."

With Drew and Libby in place, other casting decisions still had to be made for the *LGO* pilot. Though it was Kellie Martin who ultimately played Becca, Corky's intellectual and spirited younger sister, several actresses auditioned for the role, including Tanya Fenmore (who would later be cast as Becca's best friend, Maxie) and Mayim Bialik (who later bloomed on screen as NBC-TV's *Blossom*).

Bialik was then a hot property due to her knockout portrayal of a young version of Bette Midler in the 1988 film, *Beaches*. She had also competed against Martin for many other roles, prior to *LGO*. "Mayim became kind of like Kellie's nemesis on the audition circuit," Michael Braverman divulges. "They may be good friends now, I don't know. But I do know that Bialik wanted to do a half-hour show, and in the long run, opted not to do *Life Goes On*. That's not to say that we would have gone with her, but that's what it came down to."

From the moment he conceived the character of Becca Thacher, however, Braverman admits he had Bialik in mind for the role. But when he met with the actress and her mother and described the part, he could sense more than the usual amount of negotiating hesitancy on her mom's part. "When you commit to a television pilot, you are also committing to the run of the series," he explains, ". . . it could run anywhere from a *thank you very much* failed pilot to a commitment of four, five or even ten years. It is, in essence, not only a career choice, but a life choice as well."

What's more, filming a series is a full-time job, even for child actors. Schooling, mandated by the state, is done in a dressing room trailer, between takes on the set. A child actor necessarily gives up a regular education. There are no football games, school dances, and classes with other kids. It's all private tutoring. Bialik's mother wanted her very talented and in-demand daughter to have a normal adolescence, and decided to forego a one-hour drama commitment in favor of the far-less time-consuming half-hour comedy stint. Subsequently, Mayim went on to star in her own sitcom, which stayed on the air for over five years.

Chris Burke and Kellie Martin came to *Life* as siblings Corky and Becca Thacher, while Bullet was cast as Arnold. *THE REGAL COLLECTION*

Meanwhile, *Life* was still without its Becca.

According to Rick Rosenthal, *LGO's* pilot director and co-executive producer (who would also go on to guide several segments — and act in "The Return of Uncle Richard"), ABC was high on Mayim Bialik from the onset, while Kellie Martin was a close second, with only Rosenthal as her main supporter. "I thought there was something there," he concedes. "There was something arresting about her."

Rosenthal introduced her to ABC's bigwigs, to get her approved. "She got it together for that audition, which was superb," Rosenthal recalls. "Just terrific. She walked in with those red glasses [a Becca staple; a Kellie reality], and ended up doing an improv that was an amazingly funny turn for a thirteen-year-old to sustain in front of a major network brass." She just blew everyone away." So much so that Rosenthal peered around the room and gushed, *I don't know about you guys, but I think we should go with Kellie and forget about any other actresses. They may be terrific, but if you're looking for someone who will have great longevity and grow, Kellie is our girl.*

"And there wasn't much dissent from that," he adds today.

Martin, of course, did go on to play the youngest Thacher, and though only in her early teens and considered the baby of the show, she had already amassed a full slate of credits, including spots for commercials, film and TV (including a debut on *Little House on the Prairie*). As she herself recalls about becoming Becca: "My first audition for the pilot was with the casting director. That's when I wore the red glasses. But with the network, I auditioned with the last scene in the pilot with Paige, where Becca's walking down the stairs. That's when I made everything up, because it said in the script that *she continues*, and there weren't any lines. So, of course, I *continued*, and just kept talking and talking and talking. I guess they liked it, and they also liked my red glasses. I think the red glasses are why I really got hired."

Martin admits to not recalling much about the *Life* test and the general audition process. "Because once I go in there," she says, "I try to go on autopilot, especially at networks. There are so many people. It's so frightening, that if you don't know how to just let the scene take over, you could really get nervous."

Yet, in recalling the *LGO* initial exam, she does point to one specific incident: Walking out the door, as part of the famous improv that helped her win the part. "I just left," she says. It was a good move for Becca, but Kellie "just wanted to get out of there."

While Kellie Martin was a veteran performer by the time she played Becca, novice actress Monique Lanier was cast as Paige, Becca and Corky's older sister (and Drew's daughter from his first marriage). New to the field of television acting, Lanier had only performed in regional theatre in Utah (her home state), but *Life Goes On* would be her small-screen premiere. As Warner Bros. casting director Dee Dee Bradley remembers: "I was in Utah casting for *Halloween V*, and basically saw every actress in Salt Lake City. Monique walked in my office, and we didn't have a part for her. But there was something interesting and remarkable about her. Then I was assigned to the pilot for *Life Goes On*, and I remembered her because she was fantastic. And it's not always easy to remember an actress, even if they are very good. When you cast a pilot, you tend to audition everyone in Los Angeles and in New York. For *Life Goes On*, I even contacted every agent in Chicago."

Still, Monique remained ingrained in Bradley's memory. She contacted Lanier's agent in Utah who, Bradley says, was approximately nineteen years old at the time. He readied a demo video reel and sent it to Bradley, who thought Lanier's performance was incredible. Bradley then introduced the tape to the *LGO* producers, and her Warner Bros. casting supervisor at the time, Marcia Ross, all of whom agreed that Monique was unique — a stellar talent. "We then brought her out to LA," Bradley explains, "took her to the network, and she ultimately ended up getting the part. She had no experience except for college theatre, but she was astounding."

Bradley is quick to clarify that, in the *LGO* pilot, "Monique had very little to do. But there was a charisma about her. There was this one look she gave, when Drew says something to Paige, and she just looks up at her daddy with this intense look in her eyes. It represented so perfectly what Monique is all about."

Also cast in "The Pilot" was Tommy Puett, who became Tyler — a role that earmarked the actor's signature carefree style. Puett had previously worked with Dee Dee Bradley but, as he recalls, he almost did not make the audition, let alone get the part: "One day, I just stopped in to say hi to Dee Dee, and she just looked at me with these eyes that could kill. She came storming up to me and said, *Tommy Puett, where have you been?!* I was like, *Uh?*"

To Puett's astonishment, Bradley had been attempting to contact him for weeks. She had left messages with his agent, who provided only a number of excuses regarding the actor's alleged unavailability; that he was sick, out of town, and so forth. The agent had even submitted other clients to Bradley. Everyone but Puett. "Come to find out," he says, "I was being blackballed by my agent."

Fortunately, Puett had time to audition during his random visit with Bradley, who was immediately impressed. "Perfect," she said. "I knew you would be right for this." From there, he met with *Life* producers, who were holding call-backs later that day.

His competition included five other actors, including Chad Allen, who previously appeared on NBC's *Our House* (with future *LGO* guest Shannen Doherty), and who would later be cast as one of Jane Seymour's adopted children on CBS's *Dr. Quinn, Medicine Woman*. While Puett remembers each of these actors as being incredible during their tryouts, it was just prior to his own *Life* audition when, in the men's room — of all places — he was really put to the test. "I started to rehearse my lines standing in the urinal," he recollects. "And there was this guy standing next to me, laughing." When the man asked, rather matter-of-factly, if Puett was reading for a part, the young thespian replied, *Yeah, just another damn part. But I'm probably gonna screw it up.*

No, no, no, the stranger returned. *Don't worry about it. You'll do fine. Just take it all with a grain of salt.* Upon exiting the restroom, Puett and the stranger parted in opposite directions. "Actually," the actor says, "I didn't see where he went. But when I returned to the audition, and they called my name, I walked into the office and, there sitting right smack in the middle of all these producers was that same guy I had just seen in the bathroom. It was Phillips Wylly, Sr., and he was still laughing."

Upon commencing his *LGO* trial, Puett recalls he became nervous, and started to tremble. "It was almost double the pressure," he says, "because I had just seen one of the producers in the bathroom. Plus, I didn't have that much time to prepare for the character. So later, I'm like, *Shit! I didn't get the part!*" Further frustrated, Puett jumped into his car (a convertible with a t-top thatch), and began driving on the freeway. He was so upset, that he tossed his script out of his roof window, and thought, *Man...I wasted my whole afternoon for this?*

Not exactly. That night, he received a startling telephone call. *Tommy*, a voice began over the line *...this is Philips Wylly...your pee partner.*

Puett "just about died," and assumed he left something in the office, like his watch or a jacket. But before Tommy had a chance to think of other reasons why Wylly had made the call, the producer continued with: *I would just like to inform you that you did a really good job today, and that we'd like you to be Tyler Benchfield on Life Goes On. We'll be seeing you on the set in about two weeks.*

Puett and Wyllie later became close friends — a bond which still remains today.

One more regular cast member who debuted in "The Pilot" was a canine performer named Bullet, who played Arnold, the semi-wonder dog. As Michael Braverman joked to *Television Chronicles* magazine in 1996, Bullet was a horse of a different color. He was a talented, but somewhat of an aloof performer with a secret. "I don't think we publicized the fact that he was a half-pit bull," Braverman said. "Pit bulls had such a bad rap! But he was an incredibly wonderful animal."

Chris Burke, for one, was thrilled to act beside Bullet. "I loved working with him and his trainer, Richard Calkins," Burke recalls. "He was a wonderful dog and I loved him very much. My aunt and uncle had a dog named Herbie Egan, and we had a very special relationship. But he died in an automobile accident, and I wanted to have that same story on the show, one in which Arnold got hit by a car. I wanted to see more of Corky's relationship with Arnold, and this idea would have helped to explore that. I thought it would have been a good story because a lot of people deal with that situation. But it never happened. The producers didn't want to do the story."

The promotional *Life* billboard on a street-side wall of Warner Bros. Studios in Burbank, California. *KALEY HUMMEL*

CHAPTER 4
EARLY *LIFE* ADJUSTMENTS

"Producing any television show is a challenge."
— Michael Braverman

When producing a TV pilot, series, movie, or even a feature film, you get up every morning and ask yourself the same question: I wonder what today's crisis will be? At least that's what Michael Braverman asked himself into the third days' shoot of "The Pilot" for *Life Goes On.* That's when he and a few Warner Bros. executives were summoned to ABC's headquarters in Century City, California for a serious sit-down to discuss some solemn issues. "Being the keenly perceptive individual that I am," Braverman exclaims with a slightly sardonic tone, "I had a nagging feeling that this wasn't going to be good."

In fact, it was worse. At the conclusion of each day's shooting, the exposed film is sent to the lab for processing and, after being synced to the soundtrack by the editor, the previous day's film is distributed the next morning to the producer, the studio and the network. As a result, the previous day's shooting is cleverly known as dailies. ABC, having a major investment in *LGO,* had been watching the dailies and they were not happy. Their problem was Patti Lupone. "She was too big," Braverman recalls, "...too over-the-top...too not motherly enough...too...outrageous." He told them he would speak with Lupone.

They told him to replace her, to cast a new actress and reshoot her scenes. "I don't remember exactly what I said," Braverman recounts, "but I said a lot, and I said it fast and passionately. I know I gave them my Sada Thompson speech."

Lupone is an incredibly talented Broadway diva. Her stage training demands that she be big in gesture, expression and projection. Yet, unlike the stage that swallows up small performances, film magnifies everything. A quickly and dramatically-raised eyebrow on stage flies off an actor's face on film. Braverman viewed the same dailies the ABC executives did, and he was absolutely convinced that Lupone was the perfect counterpoint to Chris Burke. "I just had to tone her down," he says, "that's all."

As a result, the producer urged, pleaded and cajoled the ABC execs, who finally conceded to give the actress a few more days. As Braverman sees it, "It was the best concession they have ever made." He journeyed directly from the ABC Century City offices to the *LGO* location site in L.A.'s prestigious suburb, Brentwood. When he arrived there, Lupone was on the set rehearsing a scene that was about to be shot. Braverman took her aside, and he sensed that she knew something was amiss. So he did the only honorable thing - he lied through his teeth. "Actors, like every other artist," he explains, "no matter how successful, are insecure about their work. I felt no driving need to make Patti even more insecure by telling her the crux of my ABC meeting."

Instead, with Rick Rosenthal at his side, Braverman relayed to Lupone that her performance was coming across somewhat larger than necessary. It was a little too…New York. She understood exactly what he meant, and her subsequent performances translated as substantially smaller. "From then on," Braverman reveals, "New York became our on-set code word for getting too big."

Following Patti Lupone's theatrical meltdown, there were still other technicalities to firm up before the airing of "The Pilot," some including the show's central moniker. The original working-title for the series was *Northbrook* (even before Bill Smitrovich had been handed the script called *Glenbrook* - which viewers would later come to know as the name for the Thacher's fictional suburban Chicago home-turf).

Yet, as Chad Hoffman explains, when it came time to actually shoot the show's igniting episode, Michael Braverman gave somewhat more serious consideration to what he wanted to name the series. Hoffman remembers a phone call from Braverman, detailing his choice for the name of the show: *Life Goes On.* Hoffman thought that was ideal, "because that's really what the series was about. How life goes on. How every day we all get up, and try again."

So, while the program's main nameplate was transposed to *Life Goes On* (and the individual pilot title changed to simply "The Pilot"), when it came time to create the graphics and scenes for the opening credits, Braverman's *Life* was limited. Only a modest amount of money was allocated to this area from the studio. The title sequence, now famous among *LGO* fans, involves a newspaper boy riding down the street on which the Thachers live, followed by a small-cased insignia of *Life Goes On.* A simple, yet effective image that was inexpensive to shoot and produce, which is the main reason it made the final cut.

There were other aspects of the show that he was more concerned with than the titles. The money-conscious, aesthetically-conscientious producer did not want to take the time or the funds to attempt a more detailed approach with animation or extensive graphics (some of which are displayed at the opening of, say, ABC's *The Practice* or CBS's *Early Edition*), and hire a company to design the show's opening visuals. Instead, one day on his home computer he, with a background in advertising, assembled the *Life* little-letter emblem himself. Braverman had a regular drawing graphics program in the system, one that, he thought, worked out quite well. Though he was unaware the similarity between *Life*'s logo and ABC's previously-aired *Family* fare. "That was a terrific series," he says of the latter program, "but I had no idea that our opening sequence was similar to what they used."

To match the *LGO* logo with an audio soundtrack, Braverman and company licensed the Beatles' tune, "Ob La Dee, Ob La Da," which includes the phrase, *life goes on.*

As Rick Rosenthal recalls, the song was acquired for sentimental reasons: "It was a very old-fashioned family drama, and we thought using The Beatles music would fit in well with the nostalgic feel that we were trying to present." Or, as Chad Hoffman puts it, "it was a nice way to lead up to the title."

By coincidence or inspiration, today's NBC family drama, *Providence*, also opens with a Beatle tune including the word, life, in its title – "In My Life"; while the show also mimics *LGO*'s use of fantasy/flashback sequences. Moreover, Jennifer Love Hewitt's now-defunct series, *Time of Your Life*, opened with a Beatle tune as well, and was a spin-off from *Party of Five*, with which several *LGO* veterans, on screen and off, are associated.

While the band played *On* (as in *Life Goes*), and though Michael Braverman remained his own harshest critic, the show's creator, executive-producer, and first-episode director was still extraordinarily pleased with the end result of "The Pilot." "Rick, the cast, and the editors," he explains, "had all locked into my vision and pictured the exact same film I saw in my head as I wrote the script. Everyone had delivered far more than I could ever have hoped for or reasonably expected. It was a cosmic convergence. And I was humbly grateful to all of the many talented people who made it happen. We turned the finished film over to the network in early May of 1989. We finished shooting the pilot on time, on schedule and on budget. The next six weeks were spent in post-production: editing, scoring, mixing, dubbing, and all the other things that transform raw footage into a wonderful film. And then it was over."

Or so it seemed.

Until recently, May was the great television migration month. All of the pilots that were ordered and filmed were sent to the New York headquarters of the major networks for final screening and selection. As they migrated east, so did hundreds of studio executives, West Coast executives, producers' agents and flocks of entertainment press follow them. Or as Braverman details, this is "when and where the hard-sell takes place. This is elbow-grabbing-in-your-face-drinks-are-on-me lobbying at its finest and most frenetic. This is where television stars are born, millionaires are made and acting careers can either take off or die quick and ignoble deaths. One by none, the pilots are screened for the respective networks sales departments and for the major advertising agencies to determine their basic worth and viability in the marketplace.

"Remember, it's a business. Art is for museums. Television is for advertisers. The business of television is delivering eyeballs to advertisers. Period. So, if the advertising gurus give their blessings, a pilot shoots to the top of the list. If they're the least bit dubious, it'll take a full frontal studio sales attack just to keep that pilot on life support. Going in, we all knew that *Life Goes On* had everything the advertisers didn't want and none of the things they did. For once, I agreed with the conventional wisdom: *Life Goes On* didn't stand a chance. Contemplating those overwhelming odds, I declined Warner Bros. generous offer to migrate East with them and, after cleaning up a few loose ends, I headed to Hawaii with my family where, if all went well, I could lie comatose on a beach for a few weeks."

The next day, when Braverman checked into what was formerly the Kahahal Hilton on Oahu, there was a message waiting for him from Norman Stephens in New York. It was six hours ahead there and Stephens called to report that the initial screening of *LGO* had gone much better than expected. "That didn't mean we were even in contention for a series pick-up," Braverman clarifies. "It just meant that what none of us had counted on was the fact that the audience for the pilot screenings also included many of the executives' wives and older children as well as female media buyers, female assistants and other support troops. When the lights came up after the initial *Life Goes On* screening, many of the women in the audience were openly weeping. They loved the show. This isn't a sexist statement, just a reality. The male executives in the audience were viewing the pilots from a practical point of view. But their emotional reaction to the film was not lost on their husbands and fathers."

Braverman had not yet finished unpacking when Stephens called again. He had just dined with a few ABC executives and they were contemplating giving *Life* a mid-season script order. Braverman was cautiously happy. Even though a mid-season script order was a euphemism for preparing three or four series scripts to be considered as a substitute or fill-in when one of their new fall shows inevitably fails, it was still an order nonetheless. "Or at least it wasn't a complete rejection," Braverman says. "So I went to the beach."

At 6:00 A.M. the next morning, the update-calls began coming in every half-hour. *LGO* was now actually being talked about for the fall schedule, but ABC had no idea where to program it in their line-up. At 10:00 A.M., Braverman was alerted to stand-by for a conference call.

It was the Warner Bros. and ABC executives asking questions about the direction of the series, and wondering what kind of stories he had in mind for future episodes. "I tap-danced around a few story ideas as best I could,"

Braverman recalls. "I was told to stay by the phone. I did, just sitting on my lanai staring out at the ocean."

An hour later the call came from Chad Hoffman: *Life Goes On* was being picked up for the fall season with an order for thirteen episodes. Braverman was shocked and dumbfounded. He thought, *Who would have figured?* Hoffman explained it this way: "We have no idea where it will fit on our schedule, but it's too damned good and there's no way we can justify not picking it up. Congratulations."

Finding the right spot on ABC's prime-time register was the next step in bringing *Life* to the air. During its formation, the series was envisioned as a family show created to air somewhere on the schedule at 8:00 P.M. - a time interval that was once known as the family hour. ABC had also decided early on that they needed to develop weekend programming that would be broadcast one hour earlier: on Sunday, at 7:00 P.M., opposite the CBS super-hit news program *60 Minutes*; a time period that *New York* magazine labeled *the suicide slot.*

Hoffman believed *LGO* fit into both categories, but that it would be more suited to 7:00 P.M., allowing it to invite and appeal to both children and their parents. But, as he admits, "It was a fight to get it on the air. There was substantial opposition at the network, amongst various people, not to the quality of the show, but that it would have a great deal of trouble attracting an audience. Fortunately, there were also those like myself who felt very strongly about it."

The network still took precautions. In order to have introduced the show to as wide an audience as feasible, the alphabet network broadcast "The Pilot" twice in one week, at 8:00 P.M., on Tuesday and Friday. The Tuesday debut proved victorious with a 29-share (29 percent of all homes with a television were glued to *Life*), and ranked in that week's Top Ten in the Nielsen ratings. The Friday viewing garnered a 24-share and also won its time slot.

Overall, the *Life Goes On* pilot was inspirited by above-level production standards and solid characters whose real-life acting counterparts, "seemed very familiar," says Michael Braverman. "They jumped off the screen. They seemed to have such an extraordinary chemistry. That usually happens maybe in the second season of a series, maybe fifteen episodes into a show. But these people had it during the pilot."

"The Pilot" "did something that you hope all pilots will do, but often don't," concludes Chad Hoffman. "When it was finished, it looked like it had been on the air for about a year and a half, or two. What that said to us is that we had a complete melding of the talent, writing and directing. We felt you would have never known that the project had just come together from the start of production to the end of delivery in only about eight weeks. It also made money for the network, and scored high marks with the Viewers for Quality Television. And the rest, as they say, is history."

Kellie Martin's Becca celebrates a milestone birthday, perceiving it may turn serious, with Tommy Puett's Tyler in this scene from "Sweet 16." Also pictured: actress Terri Ivens. *THE REGAL COLLECTION*

CHAPTER 5
LIFE CYCLES

"There's an old adage among us old pilot producers — the good news is your pilot's been picked up. The bad news is your pilot's been picked up. The good news speaks for itself; the bad news refers to the overwhelming amount of time, effort, work, strife and physical punishment it takes to produce an original network quality film week after week for twenty-two weeks. It took three months to make the pilot, now I had to make another one and another one every eight days. And I was so glad and grateful to have the opportunity to do it."

— Michael Braverman

The ratings slipped considerably when *Life Goes On* settled into its regular time slot on Sunday, at seven o'clock in the evening. It was not in the Top Ten, but ABC was pleased with the numbers. As it turned out, the show did very well at 7:00 P.M., and achieved the best ratings ABC had in that time period in years. Though *Life* consistently came in a strong second against *60 Minutes* (which the *LGO* cast nicknamed *The Terminator* because of its unbeatable ratings), and frequently was victorious against broadcast NBC and FOX fare, it was screened one hour prior to when the majority of watchers usually tuned into prime-time.

At the end of its first year, *Life* ranked 98 out of 124 weekly programs. Despite the low numbers, it was renewed for a full-second term when many higher-rated shows were gone from sight. In the long-haul, it reached beyond ABC's expectations, and typically garnered a 15 or 16 percent share.

Though the production quality of "The Pilot" was maintained throughout the show's four seasons, the series went through several modifications over this time, behind and in front of the camera. Some minor. Others, greater. A few were cosmetic, when it came to casting and presentation. A few more were intrinsic, and not as immediately obvious to the eye (as with regards to writing), and would be better perceived as the series continued.

Here's a general run-down of *LGO's* quad sessions:

In *Life's* first season, Corky, Becca, Paige, Libby and Drew are carefully presented to the audience with situations concentrating on their separate personalities. From this initial semester, there was "Break a Leg, Mom," in which Corky resolutely believes that the strong-willed Libby sacrificed her singing career due to him; and "Becca's First Love," in which the ordinarily discerning Becca becomes overtly captivated by a good-looking yet narcissistic 15-year-old rock singer named Gabe (portrayed by the single-named actor Andrew).

There are also two noteworthy segments from the freshman year that concentrate on Paige: "Paige's Mom," in which her birth mother (Lisa Banes), a famous, though self-absorbed actress, pays a visit and breaks her heart; and "Paige's Date," when she falls in love with a too-good-to-be-true courteous young gentleman (Johnny Haymer) to whom even Drew takes a liking.

Drew himself is showcased in two outstanding initial year episodes: "Ordinary Heroes," in which he resolves to leave his position as a construction worker and open his restaurant, while his friend (Louis Giambalvo) struggles with the birth of a child with Down's; and "Thacher and Henderson," which centers around an annual gathering of his high school football buddies, one with whom (James Cromwell) he shares a strong resentment.

In the second season, the Thachers win a two-episode vacation to Hawaii, within "Honeymoon from Hell" and "Corky and the Dolphins." The former features the family's intense doubts as to the luck of their excursion. The latter allows Drew a duet with island icon Don Ho, and Corky a chance to bond with dolphins, while he resents a popular surfer (Dean Cain) who also happens to charm Becca. Fear not, for Becca falls in love once more in "Head Over Heels," in which she has a major crush on her gymnastic coach (Whip Hubley).

An arc of sophomore episodes, beginning with "Libby's Sister," also proves insightful. "Sister" introduces visits from Libby's moody sibling, Gina (Mary Page Keller), and her precocious daughter, Zoe (Leigh Ann Orsi) — a continued storyline which makes for interesting family conflicts that stem from Libby's pregnancy: the need for additional household support. Gina and Zoe fit the bill, but provide two other mouths to feed, one of which (Gina's) frequently argues with Drew.

By the second-term finale, "Proms and Prams," Becca and Tyler's plans for the ball are derailed as Libby finally gives birth to a boy. Only days before that moment, Libby reflects on how life might have been with a former love (Ben Murphy), as Becca displays wisdom beyond her years when she tells a low-esteemed, academically-failed Tyler, "I'm not disappointed *in* you, but *for* you."

One of the most stand-out episodes from the show's second year involves a rare TV appearance by musical performer Leon Redbone in

"Corky's Travels." Here, Corky gets confused in Chicago, but finds his freedom. Failing to meet Paige for a rock concert, he boards a bus and ends up stranded, with only a mystical musical balladeer (Redbone), who serves as his spiritual godfather. Redbone is a drawling troubadour whose lyrical commentary celebrates the unpredictability of Corky's mishaps (mugging by a street gang, seduction and fleecing by a teen streetwalker). "With all its glories and all of its faults, it seems life is a bittersweet waltz," Redbone drones as the hour concludes (which may also be as true for Becca, who enlists Tyler to race to Corky's rescue).

"Travels" is significant for several reasons, mostly because it allows Corky a sense of being lost (without concentrating on the fact that he has Down's), and permits his wits to be about him. As when he returns home to his parents and heralds, "I'm just a ramblin' man." This line, alone, makes the episode worth watching.

By the show's trimester, Drew finds his success, hopes and dreams up in "Toast," an episode in which his restaurant is destroyed by fire shortly after the birth of his and Libby's new child (Nicky, later played by Kevin and Christopher Graves in the fourth year). Such a dire predicament, however, portends new insights for Libby, as Jerry Berkson (Ray Buktenica), her usually greedy advertising boss, is motivated to pay for the reconstruction of the Thacher establishment.

At once grateful and surprised, Libby asks Jerry (a man of the Jewish faith) to be godfather to her son at a Catholic baptismal. When he declines, Libby reminds him of a note that he thinks he anonymously delivered with the money to rebuild the restaurant. It reads: *Generosity of spirit is the measure of a man.* Jerry then agrees to the ceremony.

By the end of this fourth and final year of *Life*, a plethora of events have taken place. In "Bec to the Future," the first episode from this season, Becca makes new friends: Kathy Goodman (Kiersten Warren), an extreme extrovert who wants Becca to get a bigger slice of life; Harris Cassidy (Martin Milner), the storytelling boss and owner of the Nevermore bookstore where Becca now works with Goodman, and Eric (Ned Vaughn), the bookstore's young manager, who has the hots for Becca.

Meanwhile, Becca and Jesse became as intimate as possible in "Lost Weekend"("We went as far as it was safe to go," Becca relays, "and then we stopped"). He's beaten by gay-bashers ("Incident on Main"), and befriends a brave hospital room/soul mate with AIDS ("Bedfellows"). In the interim, Becca yearns for a regular adolescence, and flirts more intensely with Michael Goorjian's Ray ("Last Wish").

By now, too, Libby has long left her job with Jerry and has become a full-time mom to a two-year-old Nicky Thacher. Paige has removed herself from the welding industry and the wealthy, conservative Kenny (the son of her boss at the plant played by Steven Eckholtd) and her moody artist husband Michael (Lance Guest), and struggles in a romantic/platonic/business relationship with Artie (Troy Evans). For after she becomes pregnant by Michael (and they separate), Paige contemplates abortion ("Choices"), and it's Artie who convinces her that such an action may not be her best option.

Also, by the fourth semester, Corky has met and married Amanda (Andrea Friedman), a woman with Down's. They move into the loft above the garage (that was once housed by Paige, who offers the place as a wedding gift in "Windows"). Like Corky views any other newlywed couple, he complains about her cooking, she's interested in romance, and they both could not be happier (even in the midst of their final, honest realization that they will never have children — just as Paige reflects on her pregnancy).

In the show's final episode, "Life Goes On (And On…And On")," Becca and Corky graduate high school, we flash-forward thirteen years to find Becca speaking with her son about Jesse, and we are left to wonder if Jesse is the boy's father.

Beyond *Life's* basic structural changes from year to year, there were more specific on-screen/off-screen alterations throughout the show's four seasons.

For example, the Paige-to-Paige exchange — which took place during the program's second semester. In the fall of 1990, Tracey Needham stepped in as Drew's daughter Paige after Monique Lanier, near the end of the 1989-90 season, had returned to her home in Utah. The *LGO* producers decided to replace the same character with a different actress, as opposed to eliminating the part altogether.

"I remember Monique being like a flower-child," recalls Kellie Martin. "Everything was…really cool. She didn't want to work. She would have rather been meditating. I don't think she ever wanted to act. She didn't have any idea what she was getting into. She never worked [in TV] before. Though I think she's a great actress. Very interesting, and very different from anyone that I have ever worked with. The producers loved her unique qualities. But she never wanted to be on an episodic television show. So I'm glad that she got out of it, because that's what she wanted."

As Tanya Maxie Fenmore adds, Lanier's decision to leave *Life* came out of nowhere. "I heard that she simply did not want to do it anymore," Fenmore says. "She chose the life of Salt Lake City, instead of life on the Burbank lot." Casting director Dee Dee Bradley, who became close friends with the actress, says Lanier was unhappy in Los Angeles. "It was not the kind of life that she wanted. She was lonely. She missed her family. She missed her boyfriend. She just wanted to leave the show. Toward the end, and probably after the third episode, all she was thinking about was home. That's where she really wanted to be. Show business was just not for her."

For Tracey Needham, however, it was another matter. "Tracey really

A *Real Paige Turner:* Tracey Needham (top) replaces Monique Lanier as Paige — the-eldest-half-sister to Chris Burke's Corky and Kellie Martin's Becca — in *Life's* second season. *THE REGAL COLLECTION*

wanted to be Paige," Bradley concludes. But, even before that transpired, Michael Braverman and his team debated on whether or not to even replace Monique. "We thought the family lacked that other element of the older sister," he says. "So we cast Tracey, who was great in the role."

"I was actually only brought on for one episode to see if it would work out," Needham herself recalls. "When it did, they decided to keep me. But originally, I was billed as a guest star, and hired only in order to have the character sing her swan song. Then they decided that the transition worked. Usually they don't do that on prime time."

The actress also credits the writers for making smooth the Lanier/Needham shift: "They really helped to sustain the continuity. I was so green when I started on the show, and I would just use my own personality when acting as Paige. They were very supportive of that."

Down the line, however, there were certain character developments that the *LGO* scribes envisioned for Paige that Needham did not necessarily agree with, like her relationship with Artie (Troy Evans). "I thought that was a little weird," she says. "I loved the character of Artie and all, and I loved the relationship that he had with Paige, but when they tried to make it a sexual thing, I just thought it was a little off-base."

Coincidentally, by 1998, Needham had worked with Evans on a pilot in which she acted as his daughter. "I was kind of like doing in my head, *Oh, no…my dad, my lover, my dad, my lover*," she laughs. "Actually, I've done four different shows with him. I work with him all the time. I adore him."

Meanwhile, back in *Life* land, the viewer's response to the Paige trade was docile. "To my knowledge," construes executive producer Rick Rosenthal, "we never received one letter as to anyone wondering what had happened to the old Paige. Never. While this amazed me, there were several reasons why this occurred: First, this kind of thing happens on soap operas all the time. I think our audiences were similar, and they were used to such cast changes. Second, we made the switch from the first season to the second season, with several episodes airing without Paige, before she ever returned. Thirdly, both Monique and Tracey were blondes, who looked a little alike, but not much alike. They each captured the same quality of the character."

In essence, the decision to resurrect Paige became mandatory. "We had to bring back the character," Rosenthal relays. "We toyed with all sorts of other possibilities, but she was so integral to that family. We talked about sending her off to college. But in the end it seemed to work pretty well that we had her return home."

Other changes in *Life* transpired when Drew switched careers from construction worker to owning his own restaurant, and when Ray Buktenica, who played Jerry Berkson, exited the series. Bill Smitrovich comments on the former: "The producers came to me and said, *We want to give Drew another line of work.* I said, *Well, I'm comfortable with a restaurant.* I worked my way through college in restaurants. I was a manager, a bouncer, a bartender, a waiter, a cook. So we went with the restaurant."

Though Smitrovich felt at ease with Drew's career move to food-serving proprietor, the actor had embraced one particular aspect of Drew's position as a construction worker: a friend who happened to be African American in the guise of Eugene Clarke as Richter. "I missed that," Smitrovich relents. "I thought it was great that Drew had this close friend who was of an ethnic background. I figured he was going to have many different types of friends, because of Corky. It would have been ideal had we explored that a little more. It would have been the icing on the cake."

As to the Jerry withdrawal, Jerry departed the show in the third season episode "Jerry's Deli," in which his father passed away. We never saw the manic, comic-relieving Jerry again (ironically, just as we met his father). Buktenica is quite clear on how he felt about his character's permanent leave of absence. He believes *LGO*, in general, was straight-laced, when Jerry is excluded from the mix, and was crushed at Jerry's departure. "I found it very, very difficult to watch the show in the last year," he confesses. "Though I did a few times, because I still felt a certain loyalty to do so."

Buktenica surmises that his *LGO* egress may have had something to do with a complication that arose during the second season. At that time he was cast in *Cutters*, a sitcom starring Robert Hays (*Airplane!*), for which he filmed six episodes. "I had no binding contract with *Life Goes On*," Ray reveals, "so I became an indefinite commodity to them. They had to do what they had to do. They had to deal with who they had to deal with, and build their show. It's an extraordinary task to produce twenty-two episodes of a TV series. So after I did *Cutters*, they kind of just said, *Well...maybe we'll have to deal with this as a 'lost character' because we have no guarantee that the actor is going to be here. So we'll have to change the direction of what's going on.* And that's really what I felt had happened."

The explanation that Ray actually received, however, was that ABC was making extensive financial cutbacks on the show. And since the more youthful characters were becoming the thrust for the main storyline, there would not be much room for Jerry. So he was gone, and Ray missed being involved with *Life*. "From an objective standpoint," he says, "and if I may look at the show as a disinterested party — Jerry was the kind of guy who brought some sort of life to what came to be known as ongoing tragedies."

What added to the misfortune of Buktenica's absence was his potential, though unfortunately unrealized concept for a spin-off series featuring Jerry. One idea involved the character's return to Glenbrook, deejaying at Drew's restaurant every Friday for Becca and Corky's high school peers. "The kids would have loved him," Ray rationalizes. "He would have played terrific music, and then maybe too he would have hooked up to a local radio station by remote, and end up becoming a Howard-Stern-type. He would have worn gaudy outfits, and have this outspoken radio personality that would have really worked with the kids."

Whether or not this idea or others would have ever been developed had Buktenica stayed with *Life*, director Michael Lange (who later employed Ray for "The Wedding Destroyer"/Delta Burke episode of *Lois and Clark: The New Adventures of Superman*) puts to words a general consensus: "It was very sad when Ray left the show."

Many had the same feeling when Mary Page Keller, who played Libby's sister Gina for a short time in the second year, exited the series. She, as with Buktenica, was not extensively employed after a fashion on *LGO*, due to monetary issues. When Patti Lupone returned to the program (after having her baby), it apparently was not cost-effective to retain both she and Keller. "They are very expensive actresses," Michael Braverman explains. "We had a lot of financial constraints. When you're dealing with actors of the caliber and quality that we had on the show, you're talking a lot of money. I would have loved to have everyone continue, but we just didn't have it in the budget. We only had a certain amount of money allocated to us. So we had to shuffle, juggle and do all kinds of things to stay within the budget."

"This was not a show like *Beverly Hills, 90210*," adds Rick Rosenthal, "where everyone knew we were going to be a hit. So not only was there always a little bit of a battle to keep it on the air, but to keep it an ensemble."

Whether it was Mary Page Keller's actual six-episode arc, or Ray Buktenica's unfulfilled Jerry spin-off, there was never a lack of imagination with regards to story ideas for *Life Goes On*. There were even segments envisioned for an implied fifth year, just in case the series was renewed for the 1993-1994 season.

Yet would this really have worked?

"Oh, sure," Chad Hoffman replies. "It could have kept going. The characters were rich enough. The situations were there. Shows with strong characters can run five years, or more; whether the audience wants to stay with it, is another question."

Clearly, considering the passage of time and its undying audience, *Life's* loyal viewers would have stayed with it. For, as Hoffman adds, "it would have been interesting to follow Becca and Corky out into the adult world — to watch what would have happened to Drew and Libby when the kids left home. What it would have been like to have the new child, and at the same time, have adult children. It's kind of like saying, *Does your life get boring after five years?* Maybe some people's lives do. But I think it could have gone on."

If it had, it would have been without Patti Lupone, who had already planned to take leave at the end of the fourth period. She had won the lead stage role in Andrew Lloyd Webber's *Sunset Boulevard*, which was experiencing and causing a major promotional blitz in London. It was not her intent to stay with *Life*, had it been renewed for a fifth interval, which prompted story possibilities with a Libby-less Drew and company.

Michael Braverman had erstwhile penned the first episode of the potential fifth term that never was. Had it come into fruition, the segment would have explored Drew's single fatherhood of young Nick Thacher and, in Bill Smitrovich's eyes, "that would have been just perfect. It would have been like *Bachelor Father* [a 1957-62 series with John Forsythe] all over again."

Alas, it was not meant to be. Braverman, the former ad man, had relayed to Smitrovich the intricacies of how disappointing advertising revenue data translated into denoting *Life's* original network doom.

"In the four years that we were on the air," Smitrovich explains, "we were never in the Top 25. A show never usually gets into a fifth year unless it's a really big hit. Well, we were never a really big hit, *per se*. But we had that loyal wonderful following, and we always came in second to *60 Minutes* for four years in a row. And despite the fact that no other show has ever done that, you can't get advertising revenue based on coming in second. Generally, in the fifth year of a series, production costs go up, salaries go up…everything goes up, consummating on what the fifth year should be. If you get that far. But the revenues couldn't match the amount of increases to demand a fifth year."

Meanwhile, Smitrovich learned that NBC sought to purchase *Life Goes On* for two more years. "But the deal never worked out," he continues. "They would have taken the show and moved it to 8:00 on Sunday, which not only would have been good for the ratings, but it would have allowed us to tackle still other issues, because it was an hour later. But that's all water under the bridge. That is, *no* water under the bridge."

"The numbers the show received were not that bad," says *LGO's* fourth-year story editor Scott Frost, in recalling the ratings for the show's last quarter. "But we were dealing with executives at ABC, who no one will ever accuse of being geniuses…It's a hard business," concludes Frost, who not only penned three of the final year's most compelling episodes ("The Whole Truth," "Incident on Main," "Five to Midnight"), but the ground-startling, short-lived ABC cult-hit, *Twin Peaks*. "Sometimes you don't know what's going to happen from week to week. It's the luck of the draw, and you just scramble, and do the best you can."

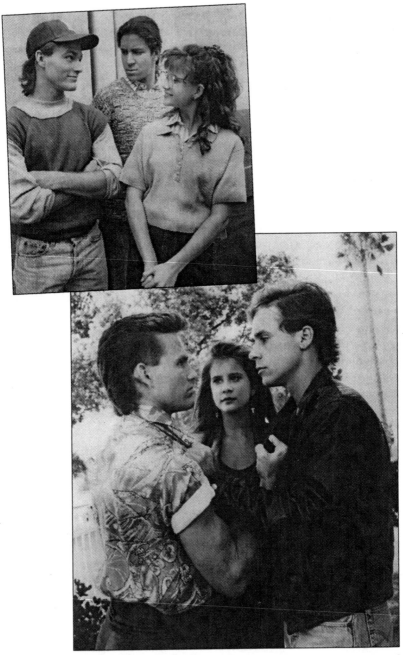

The puppy-love triangle of Tyler-Becca (and Adam Carl as Matt) presented in *Life*'s early years was substantially different from the triple-threat rivalry that was ignited between Tyler and Jesse for Becca's heart in the show's third season. *THE REGAL COLLECTION*

CHAPTER 6

MID-*LIFE* CRISIS

"After four years on the show, you have to let characters
grow and mature. From a practical standpoint, you look at
the arc of a television show from where characters are in
year one, to where they will be down the road and, hopefully, you'll want them to go through changes over time."
— Chad Hoffman, ABC network executive

Those who produced and performed for *Life Goes On* (behind and in
front of the camera) certainly did their best to bring the best to the screen
despite central story, character and actor transitions, throughout the entire
four seasons of the show. Compared to the trials and tribulations of the program's single pilot formation (which seemed, maybe due to time constraints,
to be cut-and-dry minor affairs), later aesthetic alterations would prove to
be more substantial in nature.

The central premise-change from Down's to AIDS, for example, was an
evolution that eventually lead to the departure of Tommy Puett, the death
of Tyler (a familiar character), and the addition of regular appearances by
Chad Lowe's character Jesse This thespian/role shift was quite different,
as opposed to one performer (in the form of Tracey Needham) replacing
another (Monique Lanier) in the same personification (Paige), or one character, like Ray Buktenica's Jerry Berkson, just being deleted all together
(without any replacement whatsoever by a character or an actor).

What was most evident in this mid-series changing of the *Life* guard
was that both Tyler and Jesse were involved with Becca, a leading character. So any handling of their interactions with her had to be cautiously and
gradually executed, with regards to storyline and actual on-screen presentation. The Tyler-Jesse changes were also intrinsically tied to the Corky/
Becca/Jesse passage, and the show's general direction. It was no longer an
upbeat program about a family who happened to have a son who happened
to have Down syndrome. It became a hard-hitting series about a family with
a daughter who happened to have a boyfriend who became infected with
the HIV-virus, which led to AIDS. The show eliminated the more positive

take on the challenges that faced a person born with Down's, and moved toward the more serious implications of dealing with the deadly effects of a person who acquired an incurably fatal disease. Both premises made way for life-affirming dialogue and inspiration but, once Jesse came into Becca's life, there were no more happy endings.

Joy only surfaced after much pain — a development that caused some dissent among certain cast members. David Byrd, for one, who played Hans, Drew's chef at the restaurant, offers his opinion: "My personal feeling is that the AIDS story did not work. I was not thrilled with it, and it bothered me on several levels, one of which allowed Hans fewer and fewer things to do [because the show drifted from the restaurant setting]. I just plain never bought it. It went on too long, and it became repetitive. I felt so sorry for Chad Lowe, because he had to play the same scene over and over again. How many times can you have an attack and die?"

"It did get really *heavy* at the end," adds Tracey Needham, "which I thought was great. AIDS is a very important issue, and it may be more prevalent now in the plots of television shows, but then we were really doing groundbreaking stories, even hiring actors [Richard Frank in "Bedfellows"] who actually had AIDS. And I thought that Kellie and Chad were both brilliant, and that the writers were excellent. For me, personally, however, it was a little frustrating, because I was bored. Paige was out of that storyline."

Writer Marshall Goldberg was also frustrated as to Paige's disarrangement, and Needham's lack of airtime. "Tracey did a great job, and all the writers really liked her," he says, "not only because the actress was pleasant to work with, but because her character was somewhat older than the other Thacher children, making Paige's issues more easily identifiable for the writers. Yet we were always frustrated, because we'd give her great stories, and Tracey would perform them really well. But somehow the audience wouldn't place her at the center of the focus. Yes, of course, we knew the show was really about Becca or Corky, but we would have done more Paige stories had we had been allowed to. But it seemed like the mandate from the network, and from the mail, was for more Becca stories."

Not only was *Life Goes On* missing a lot of Paige toward the end, but also seldom seen were Drew and Libby, portrayed by Bill Smitrovich and Patti Lupone, therefore decentralizing the show's top two billed stars. Fans would watch the show, and wonder, *Where's Mom and Dad?* "I think we all sort of felt that at the end," comments Needham, "even some members of the crew. However important the AIDS storyline was, gone were the family episodes, and the silly, goofy episodes. We all missed doing those."

Still, there were segments in the Becca/Jesse-laden senior year that included Smitrovich and Lupone: "Exposed" and "The Whole Truth," to name a few. In fact, it was in "Truth" — when Libby recounts for the first time a sexual assault in college, after Paige accuses Becca's teacher of attempted date rape — that Lupone had probably more to do than in almost any other segment of the final year. According to fourth season scribe Scott Frost, who authored "Truth," Lupone and Smitrovich's absence in the last year was partially a result of the natural progression of the show, and where it was to be taken, from a dramatic point of view. "It was a fine balance," he says. "I, myself, would work on very specific character stories while, at the same time, the basis for *Life Goes On* was the family, and it was important to involve the family in the whole story."

"It is a shame that Bill and Patti were not utilized as much as they could have been," admits writer Marshall Goldberg. Yet as Goldberg's colleague, Scott Frost, assesses, the change had to do with change, as in money, demographics, and marketability: "I'm not exactly sure of the figures, but let's say the budget of the show was (total) $800,000 per episode ... ABC puts up $650 or so ... Warner Bros. puts up $150. Warner Bros. is turning around and putting that into syndication. ABC wasn't sure about picking it up for the fourth year. At the time, they were making decisions. Their big concern had strictly to do with demographics, and getting the younger audience."

Indeed, the FOX Network had been making inroads with the youthful audience, and ABC was attempting to follow in the same path in appealing to younger viewers. They very clearly stated that they wanted to see more stories with Becca as the centerpiece. "Those were orders from on-high," Frost says. "It wasn't even a creative decision. It was strictly an advertising decision."

Okay. But what about *The Brady Bunch*? We just didn't love the Brady kids; we loved the Brady parents, Mike and Carol (portrayed by Florence Henderson and the late Robert Reed). It was just as much a Mom-and-Pop show, as it was a kid's show. In other words, a family show. Mike and Carol were part of the entire package of Greg, Marcia, Peter, Cindy, etc.

Conversely, on *Life Goes On*, the younger main characters, Corky, Becca, Paige, were who they were mainly because of their parents, Drew and Libby. Libby was the maternal central point of the family; the one who offered unconditional love for her mightily-challenged son and emotionally-strained daughter and stepdaughter. Drew was the proud patriarch who staunchly held his diversely-challenged brood together, through thick or thin. Both were admired and revered by their TV off-spring, while showcasing for the viewers at home model examples of how parents should behave, in the best and worst of times. To lessen their involvement on the show, for any reason, seemed unjustified, particularly at the expense of so talented performers as Bill Smitrovich and Patti Lupone.

So *Life Goes On* stood as one on its own, yet divided. When observed comparatively, the initial dual semesters of this four-semester series may be perceived as "The Corky Years," while the remaining sessions may be dubbed, "The Becca and Jesse Years." From this perspective, *LGO* may almost be screened as two different shows. Or as Rick Rosenthal begins to discuss, the first two years showcased the empowerment of the disadvantaged and the handicapped.

"Corky represented not just how children with Down syndrome get along," Rosenthal says, "but how any underdog finds their way in the world. An underdog who fights hard and valiantly, losing a few but winning some big ones. The show was successful because Chris as Corky was able to transcend being developmentally disabled or just playing a kid with Down syndrome. He became the underdog for all kids; for all people, for that matter. For all people who are prejudiced against, all people who are handicapped, emotionally, as well as physically, all people who are perceived to be losers, when in fact, they are not."

The second *LGO* division of seasons focused on Lowe and Martin, the latter of whom already had Rosenthal in her corner. As previously relayed, he was a stout backer of Martin, and had long been pushing for more Becca stories. Ironically, after Rosenthal left the series, this is the course in which it was ultimately guided. The first two years he kept fighting hard for the show to sail in Kellie's direction, mainly because, according to research, *Life's* target audience was 18-to-34-year-olds. "And my feeling," Rosenthal says, "was that one of the reasons why they were tuning in was because of her."

Subsequently, he was proven correct. As the series slanted more toward Martin, the ratings became stronger and stronger. As the fourth year began, it really was almost completely Kellie and Chad Lowe and, as Rosenthal deciphers, "it was very clear who was holding the show together."

While Becca literally grew up on camera, maturing from a little girl with a big crush on the school jock into a woman coming of age sexually — and dealing with attainment and loss of true love, Jesse was only slightly altered from the third to fourth years. When we first met him, he was full of mystery and depression. Later, as with "Exposed" — when he paints Becca in her birthday suit — we at least had the chance to see his sense of humor. Like Corky was not defined as a character with Down syndrome, but as a young man who happened to have Down syndrome, Jesse became a young man who happened to be HIV-positive, and later, developed AIDS.

Writer Scott Frost pinpoints the face value of Jesse's plight: "The intention was that he was just a kid who was dealing with an illness, and the illness in many respects, was no different from any other potentially fatal disease, except for the fact that it has a stigma that society has placed upon it. He still had the ability to laugh, as much as he did to cry."

Meanwhile, Rick Rosenthal's departure from the series as co-executive producer, before Jesse's arrival, was, in itself, partly due to the program's changing face. "I loved working on the show," he explains, "and I felt that I had a real contribution to make to it, and I believe that I did that. But I also reached a point where, as a director, the canvas became pretty small for me.

So I had to move on."

This exit took place shortly after he directed "Corky's Travels," a second season episode that he considers his best *Life* work. It was a segment that he thought was "really unique and large for that kind of a series. We even had Leon Redbone [the jazz/blues vocalist/musician] sing five original songs for it."

Following Rick Rosenthal's departure, RW Goodwin, also known as Bob Goodwin, was brought in as his replacement. While Rick went off to work in feature films, Bob got his start with motion pictures (with a 1980 film, *Inside Moves*, directed by Richard Donner, and starring John Savage — who appeared in the *LGO* spring-board TV-film *Desperate*, from 1988). From there, he journeyed into television, producing many movies-of-the-week, a Hallmark Hall of Fame, as well as guiding unique TV-films like 1988's *Copacabana*. He made the transition mainly because his children were beginning school, and he could no longer just "pick up the family and take them where I happened to be making some movie."

In the 1980s, and even more so than today, most of series television was produced in Los Angeles, and Goodwin went on to produce two years of *Hooperman* with John Ritter, a year of *Mancuso, FBI* with Robert Loggia, and then *Eddie Dodd* with Treat Williams. He soon learned of the producer opening during the third season of *Life Goes On*. He credits two of the show's directors, Kim Friedman and Larry Shaw, with whom he worked on *Hooperman*, for helping him land the job. As Goodwin explains: "No one actually said this to me, but I think they put in a good word for me to Michael Braverman, and that kind of swayed his decision to hire me."

Once on *Life*, Goodwin (who would later spend five years on *The X-Files*) partnered with executive producer and executive story editor Michael Nankin. "It was like serendipity," describes Goodwin, "because [Nankin] is the most wonderful man that you'll ever want to know in your life…just the greatest guy. There's no one in the world that runs a writing staff better than him. He's so talented, so organized, so conscientious and hard-working, that I never worried about having a script ready to prep, which is rare on a television series. I'd be involved with him on the concept, as much as I could, in terms of potential production conflicts. But for the most part, I never had to worry about a thing. The quality of the work was just so great."

The level of quality work many times matched the amount of various responsibilities involved for an executive producer. As Goodwin details, this position allows its holder to have a hand in everything, beyond penning stories and dialogue. "The executive producer is the one who overviews the actual physical production on a daily basis. You're a sort of creative overseer of transmitting the written word to the visual screen. You choose, hire and supervise the creative team, and help with the casting and finding directors. There's always some casting to do, though on *Life Goes On* there wasn't that much, because a lot of the recurring characters had been previously cast.

"But with directors, there's a lot more involved. You want consistency, from one episode to episode. Directors come and go, and part of my job was to maintain a certain uniformity, without denying each director their own personal style and vision. It's like what I did with *The X-Files*. I helped to create the physical look of the show. I directed several episodes myself, but the ones I didn't direct, I had a heavy hand in designing."

Charting the waters of a show like *The X-Files*, was somewhat different that coordinating the streets and winds of change in Glenbrook from the second-to-third season/Corky-Jesse shift on *LGO*. Yet, those associated with the series say this major *Life* transition merely represented altered points of convergence and growth, which they have referred to as a kind of cinematic maturity.

ABC executive Chad Hoffman, for one, who was there for the pilot and helped to launch the series, left the metamorphic decisions up to Michael Braverman as to which direction the project would take once it became a series. Hoffman, who breakfasted with Braverman at least once or twice a year, usually during the summer (even after he left ABC), always had an emotional interest in *Life*, and remained inquisitive in its development. He had his own ideas of the direction in which *LGO* should go, but allowed Braverman a kind of creative jurisdiction. Or, as Hoffman remembers, "To make it what he wanted it to be."

"After we finished the pilot," Hoffman goes on to explain, "we all agreed that it would not become a Corky's-problem-of-the-week show. While it focused to a certain extent on him and the issues of the family, we felt that story angle would get very stale and very old, very quickly, and wind up becoming somewhat stereotypical. As if to say, *What's wrong with Corky this week? Who's picking on him, now? What 'can't' they do this week because of Corky?* So we tried to make all the characters and their situations as rich as possible. Corky would be part of the storylines, but he would not become the entire focus of the show."

When Hoffman first heard of Braverman's decision to move forward with the AIDS premise, he perceived it as a bold and brave thing to do, "just as we had done with Corky," he says, "to a certain extent, to show someone who might be perceived as having a disability, would then in fact become part of mainstream life, to attempt to deal in a realistic manner with yet another young person's extreme struggle and challenges. I thought that was terrific."

According to Bob Goodwin, the path ahead would be clear-cut. "Michael [Braverman] decided that there needed to be some changes for the third season, and we went from there. The content of what was being written in the third and fourth years became edgier than it had been previously."

Goodwin, who directed the very serious and certainly edgy senior season segment, "Incident on Main Street" — which centered on gay-bashing — admits that there was some "pretty hard-hitting stuff in the latter two years." So serious that, at one point, he, Braverman and Michael Nankin were actually summoned to meet with ABC executives Bob Iger and Ted Harbert, both of whom, Goodwin says, were very concerned about *Life's* general transition and certain "Incident" moments, in particular.

"They were nice guys about it, and cordial, but very alarmed," Goodwin admits. "There were scenes when [the word] 'blood' and 'queer' found their way into the script. Scott Frost wrote a great, wonderfully ambiguous script, in which we find out that this terrible skinhead who beat the crap out of Jesse actually owns a house in a quiet little neighborhood. And he has a little girl who clings to him. He's a human being. We had to assure ABC that these scenes would be done with the same good taste that we had been doing everything else — that they would be thoroughly acceptable for prime-time at 7:00 P.M. on a Sunday night."

In the end, "Incident" evolved into one of Goodwin's proudest moments on the series. He explains: "There's a man named John Leonard who reviews television for *New York* magazine. In those days, Charles Kuralt was doing [the show] *Sunday Morning* on CBS, and Leonard would do the TV segment. So here it was, Sunday morning on CBS — another network — John Leonard came on and showed about seven minutes of clips from 'Incident on Main,' essentially saying, *This is what television should be all about.* It was like Macy's advertising Gimble's. I couldn't believe it."

Certainly, this may have been the response in some viewers' homes when Chad Lowe came aboard as Jesse, introducing the AIDS arc with an episode, "Life After Death," which debuted November 3, 1991. The show's Syndrome/HIV transformation took one of its earliest frightening turns in a scene from this segment when Becca formally begins to lose interest in Tyler, whom she loved for years. Now there's Jesse — friendly and intelligent, but strangely aloof. She innocently kisses him during an after-dinner walk. He rejects her. She wants to know why. The reason is devastating. He's tested HIV-positive. Becca is supportive and swears to keep his secret. Then, Jesse and Tyler get into a fight. Blood spills. Becca blurts out in front of everyone at school, "Get away from him — he's got AIDS!"

Michael Braverman was inspired to introduce the AIDS segments in order to present a more realistic family perspective of the disease. He had interviewed small-focus groups and discovered that many teens thought the ailment could be contracted through casual interaction. He sought to dispel this ignorance, as he did with the scorn aimed at those who are afflicted with Down syndrome. "No one on prime-time television was acknowledging that we were in the middle of an epidemic," he says. "No one was acknowledging that a large number of our audience included adolescents who were sexually educated, but who didn't realize that they could die. I felt that we had the perfect platform to explore this, and I thought we went as far as we could go with Down syndrome. In terms of it being the show's main focus, we played it out, and yet we kept playing it out with Andrea Friedman [who played Amanda, Corky's girlfriend-cum-wife]."

"We did not want to plow the same field over and over again," agrees Michael Nankin, who had taken reins as story editor and supervising producer at the start of the program's third season (and then became co-executive producer with R.W. Goodwin). "We wanted to move on. We extensively explored a certain level of Corky's existence that didn't bear repetition. So it was time to make him more mature. We were presented with an opportunity to do what we had done with Down syndrome. We had given people who had never seen someone with Down's an in-depth vision of what challenges were involved, in a way that no one else had ever done. We thought, *Now we can do the same thing with AIDS.*"

Producer Thania St. John, who had joined *LGO* in the third year (and who later would go on to the new TV adventures of *Superman* in the guise of *Lois and Clark*), had penned the third season's "Life After Death" segment. As she told journalist Brenda Scott Royce, ". . . we knew that at that time in [the] entertainment [industry], AIDS was a very big issue, but no one was doing much about it on TV. There was no series that was dealing with [it], no character with AIDS. We knew we wanted to do an AIDS show, and we talked about it and thought about it. Originally, it was going to be one episode. And then we all sort of realized that we had an opportunity to do something important, especially for the teenaged audience, to show an AIDS story about a heterosexual, because it was spreading wildly among heterosexuals, especially teens. So we thought it was important to tell this story. And we didn't want to just touch on it and say, *Okay…it's touching our lives for an hour, and then it goes away.* We wanted to show someone living with HIV. That people actually live with AIDS, not just die of AIDS. So, all of that went into the decision. When we thought about making it someone that Becca has a relationship with, it really attracted us dramatically. And then we brought in Chad Lowe, and he was incredible."

In early 1991, Chad Lowe, a native of Los Angeles (and brother to movie-heartthrob Rob Lowe), had recently moved to New York City, only to return to the West Coast because, as he says, he was going broke doing theatre in New York. En route back to LA, he had done some work in a couple of odd TV-movies, and a mini-series. "I pretty much intended to go back to New York," he says. "And that was about the time my life changed."

Lowe then received a call from his agent, explaining that the producers of *Life Goes On* were searching for an actor to play a new character, one that would only appear for eight episodes. To Lowe that was ideal because he had no intention at the time of committing to a television series. He also decided that he did not want to read for the part, but that he would simply meet with the show's executives. Subsequently, he found himself in a rather large room, filled with writers and producers.

"They actually didn't even have a script," he recalls, "just mainly a concept. And even though I had no intention of actually reading for them, I did. I automatically felt comfortable, which is hard to do, especially at an audition where there are so many people in the room. I had seen *Life Goes On* only a couple of times, because I don't really watch a lot of TV. I was aware of only the show's theme, but not of any actual episode in particular. I was, however, also aware of the critical acclaim that it had received and was getting, and that it was an exception for television, that they handled all very difficult issues in very tasteful ways. TV does really get a bad rap, deservedly or not, and I have to say that I participated in that kind of sentiment, that TV was garbage, and that there was nothing on it worth watching, nothing on that was worth devoting my time to as an artist."

Yet that all changed for Lowe after his *Life* experience, when he says he went into "suss out their intentions with Jesse," and remained "completely unattached to the audition." Though the show's producers had no formal script for Lowe to peruse, they had written a few pages for him on the spot. He journeyed to a small diner close-by, had breakfast, and worked on the scene for approximately one hour. He returned to meet with the producers and gave the read he said he would not do.

"It was one of the few auditions where, in the middle of the work," he explains, "I had a sense that there was a lot more going on than just the audition process. Seven out of ten times that I've had that feeling, I end up getting pretty far long in the process, if not getting the job. I felt there was more to explore in the character, even in that first meeting. When I got out of there, I was really excited. I left there very emotional, feeling it was meant to be, that it was going to happen. It was one of those rare times when the producers, the writers, the directors and the network got out of it what I got out of it. I was enlightened to the possibilities. And sure enough, I wasn't put through the ringer, or made to wait for two weeks. I actually got the job that same day."

Once he started work as Jesse, Lowe remembers asking himself, *What life-altering, empowering, difficult experience am I placing myself into?* He sensed only that there needed to be some new element to the show, and that people on the crew treated him like somewhat of an enigma. It was like, *Okay, who is the hell is this new guy they're bringing on? What's his story? And why does he have a trailer the size of everyone else? Who does he think he is?* Very few people on the crew were aware that Jesse was HIV-positive. They only knew that there was a new character. In fact, Lowe himself remembers questions he had about the part. He would say to himself, *I don't know who I am either?* He was just there, and he felt that he was going to do something good, but he just didn't know exactly what that was. What he would like to emphasize is, how his entering the show's realm became an "ever-evolving process, on a personal and selfish level." He thought, *What an extraordinary opportunity I was about to embark upon.*

No one on the *LGO* set had any real idea what would follow Jesse's initial appearance. "Life After Death" premiered just as basketball legend Magic Johnson made the tragic announcement that he was HIV-positive. Chad Lowe recalls filming another episode, and someone on the crew yelling out that Johnson was retiring from the Lakers because he had AIDS. "I remember thinking that was such a stupid joke," Lowe says. "I thought to myself, *Is that supposed to be funny?*"

There was even some discussion of having Johnson make a guest appearance on the show. Yet, as Michael Braverman assesses, the concept was abandoned because "it would have broken the reality of what we had. We tossed around several ideas that involved the Lakers traveling to Chicago to play the Bulls, with Magic speaking at a high-school rally. But we subsequently rejected those ideas because they would have broken the reality that we had built and established on the show. We had our own city and all that went along with it, and we didn't want to shatter that. But in terms of publicity-stunting, it would have gone pretty well for our numbers, if Magic had made an appearance."

Yet airing the AIDS story just as Johnson made his dire declaration was never initiated as a manufactured ratings-draw. As Chad Hoffman puts it, "it was just a terrible coincidence."

Indeed. For a television character to appear in an episode of a series that would appear in November, that usually meant the character had to have been created sometime in July and shot in August. The *LGO* AIDS arc had been in development even longer: since late in the show's second year. "The episodes in which Jesse actually got AIDS," Michael Nankin clarifies, "were originally planned for mid-season in the fourth year." Nankin actually wanted them aired sooner because his theory in the story department was to "always use your best ideas first. Never save them for later."

Meanwhile, back at the ranch, Nankin says ABC was just beginning to "get nervous. They were worried that we would lose the audience, mid-season, and never be able to get them back, that it would be too depressing a story-line. There was actually a period of time when they were saying, *Don't do the AIDS story at all.* We had to do a lot of negotiating, and one of the final compromises was that we would be to do the episodes at the end of the season."

In effect, Jesse was introduced as being HIV-positive shortly before mid-season of the third year. He did not get full-blown AIDS until the end of that year. By then, Nankin relays, "the Jesse character just kind of took off. Originally, we had a character named Lester [played by Ryan Bollman] who was to get AIDS. We even thought of doing it with Tyler, but then realized that we needed a completely new character. So we hired Chad for three episodes, in each of which he had only one line, so he would not suddenly appear with the AIDS story. We eased him into it, and never envisioned that the story would expand as much as it did. But in the process, two things happened. First, Chad electrified us with his performance, and we were very happy about his on-screen chemistry with Kellie Martin. Secondly, once we started getting involved with the AIDS community in LA [with regards to research], we realized that we were doing something very important. It felt good, and we just jumped in with both feet."

Affirming Nankin's earlier assessment on the show's growth, and citing the change not only in plots, but with actors, Michael Braverman says: "It is a maturity process. The various actors and characters gained an audience-following of their own. They were no longer just like one-shots. Corky had a very specific following. As Kellie Martin grew and matured, she garnered a larger audience. Her character was able to become involved in more complex stories that could not have wrapped up in 46 minutes. That's what ultimately happened with Tracey [Needham], Bill [Smitrovich] and Patti [Lupone]. The audience became more comfortable when they knew what to expect from these characters."

Tommy Puett, meanwhile, did not expect Tyler Benchfield to die and leave *Life Goes On*, and calls Becca's estrangement from Tyler — and Tyler's demise — "the most untrue-to-life situation that *Life Goes On* dealt with." What would have been more in line with the show's original upbeat theme, Puett explains, was another *Life*.

"In fact," he says, "ABC was thinking of doing a spin-off series in which Becca and Tyler would have gone off to college together with Corky." About the same time, Puett's good friend, Jason Priestly, then-star and once future producer of *Beverly Hills, 90210*, asked, "Hey, Tommy, man…what happened to your show? You guys had such a fantastic set-up for the first couple of seasons. And then it just started to fade."

Apparently, *Beverly's* producer Aaron Spelling had informed Priestly that *Life* was the inspiration for *90210*, which had, in the long-run, ended up becoming what Pruett says the potential Becca/Tyler spin-off would have transmuted into. "It was at least at the core of what we were going to do," Puett recalls, "even though Brenda [Shannen Doherty — who made a pre-*Hills* guest-spot on *Life*] and Brandon [Priestly] were brother and sister on *90210*, while Becca and Tyler would have been boyfriend and girlfriend."

The viewers verily may not have expected Becca to dump the carefree, amiable Tyler, after so many years of fawning over him, hungering for him — leaving him for Jesse, a much more intense, isolated young man with many troubles. This may have been especially difficult for the audience to accept after Tyler ultimately came around and realized how wrong he had been to ignore Becca, how intelligent he became in his realization of her integrity. What may have been perceived as equally odd — and far from *true* to "*Life*" — was having Tyler killed off in the drunk-driving episode, "More Than Friends." It may have seemed rather strange to have Tyler leave the show in this fashion, mostly because Puett's performance as the character was pleasant, and popular with the viewing audience, especially young teenage girls. He was the host of *Casey Kasem's America Top Ten* weekly TV show (which aired for two seasons with him at the helm); there were approximately 100,000 members in his fan club; and he had sold between 100 and 120,000 copies of his first album, even without, as he says, "absolutely no promotion whatsoever." (His record company released the album based solely on his TV-Tyler success.)

Puett was so popular, in fact, that Sears and Roebuck department stores at one point partnered with MJI Broadcasting and The Tommy Puett Fan Club to form the *Sears Sweet 16 Diamond Girl Sweepstakes*. The ad (which appeared in newspapers around the country, as well as upon nearly every Sears counter-top) ran, in part, as follows:

TOMMY PUETT SEARCHES FOR SEARS SWEET 16 DIAMOND GIRL

"For every teenage girl, Sweet 16 is an unforgettable birthday and the perfect occasion to celebrate. In honor of this occasion, Sears has the perfect gift — a chance to win a sparkling Sweet 16 Diamond Pendant and a chance to meet Tommy Puett on the Hollywood set of the hit ABC series *Life Goes On*. Tommy Puett, the sensitive high school heartthrob of *Life Goes On*, and the host of *America's Top 10 Countdown* is waiting for a very lucky young lady to fly to Los Angeles to meet him and have lunch on the set where he will present her with a shimmering 1/2 carat Sweet 16 Diamond Pendant from Sears. Nine 1st Prize winners will also receive 1/2 carat Sweet 16 Diamond Pendants. Twenty-five 2nd Prize winners will receive any one of the following: a Tommy Puett poster, a compact disc, a music video cassette, a T-shirt, a free fan club membership, or a free subscription to *Teen Machine* magazine."

With such notoriety, we have to wonder: Was Puett's *Life* exit really necessary or even warranted? Rick Rosenthal answers the call. "There was a lot of conversation about that," he admits. "We batted it back and forth, and around. Some of it came down to just the pure negotiation of exactly how much we were afforded to pay an actor, and for how many episodes. If this something becomes too expensive, something had to give. Where were we supposed to draw the line? Where did Tommy think the show could have taken him? How much did he think the show was about him? Did we have an obligation to the audience to kind of run that [Becca/Tyler] arc a little longer, because after all, she did spend so much time chasing him? Were we to move on? We had to deal with those kinds of decisions every day."

Interestingly, Chad Lowe, who portrayed Puett's on-screen rival, did not think much of the way in which Tyler's demise was handled in *Confessions*. "I just hate the entire episode in which Tyler dies," he states adamantly. "Corky gets amnesia and the whole thing was contrived. If Tyler was going to die in a car accident because he was intoxicated, then why did we have to place some little kid on a tricycle in the middle of the street, who he had to swerve around in the middle of the night. To me that was cowardly. I know for a fact that it was not, for one, Michael Nankin's idea to do that, but that it may have developed from a note given by the network."

"Though either way," Lowe continues, "it was not one of the show's best moments, and it didn't support any of us very well. It was simply not an honestly-fair way to have the character die. It wasn't fair to the character, and it wasn't fair to the people who followed the show. If you're going to kill-off a character by having him drink while he drives, then do so because he's out of control at the wheel. You don't have to take it any further. People will get the message. I mean, it's real easy to screw with people's hearts. But if an audience gives you their heart, it's a sacred trust that should not be messed with."

"I know some people think it was a cop-out to have Tyler swerve to avoid a kid on a bike," defends writer/producer Toni Graphia, who penned the segment. "But I wasn't writing the episode as a public service announcement for drunk driving. It's obvious that if Tyler hadn't been drinking, his reflexes would have been better and he might not have died trying to avoid the kid. The point of the episode was to shock people — because the audience never expects a main character to die and that's how life is. Sometimes, it's gone in a blink. But like the theme of the show, life goes on. I wanted to display how people go on after an expected death.

"I was interested in exploring how Becca would get on with her life, even with the guilt she felt over Tyler. I wanted to show how Corky refused to go on. It wasn't amnesia; he was in shock and denial. And he retreated into himself because he couldn't deal with it. When he finally does deal, it's because his sister connects with him. I wanted to show how two siblings pull together when they're both hurt beyond words over losing someone they both loved. And the thing with the kid on the bike was just kind of a mystery I built so that there'd be a plot twist on the end. Tyler was a flawed character, but people cared about him and he gets to be somewhat of a hero. The episode is not about drunk driving but about, as the final song by Melissa Etheridge states, *Letting Go*."

As to Jesse's particular conflict with Tyler on-screen, as well as Lowe's real-life interaction with Puett, Chad says: "I don't know Tommy Puett. I only knew him when I would come into work, and say hi. I knew nothing about him as a person. But I do know that Tyler was the personification of everything I hated in most of the guys that I went to high school with. The macho-non-capacity-for-feeling kind-of-brute. Arrogant, cocky. And every time Jesse had to relate to Tyler, it was very easy for me to create conflict, because I [Chad] was extremely unhappy with the way they had Tyler treat Becca."

The *Life* maturity process which Michael Braverman and Michael Nankin envisioned at the beginning of the third year continued as when, in the fourth season, Corky got married — a development of which Chris Burke was not fond. In fact, he was not exactly happy with any of the show's final year segments. "I did not like the fourth season at all," he says. "And I definitely don't think that Corky should have got married. He wasn't ready for it."

Andrea Friedman, who played Corky's girlfriend and later, spouse, agrees. "Corky and Amanda were not prepared for wedlock. Things were moving too fast. They needed more time to develop their relationship."

Truthfully, Corky's nuptials to Amanda did seem like another story development that did not seem to jibe with the realistic flow or consistency that *Life Goes On* came to be known for. Though Corky was four years older than Becca, he still was only graduating high school, and his marriage took place before he even did that.

In defense of this development, Chad Hoffman concludes: "Corky was dealing with all these different kinds of feelings, just like everybody else. He was now at an age where, like so many other people, he was beginning to think about companionship and marriage, which are paramount issues. Ones that he would want to address. Maybe these issues became a little more focused, because of the condition that he was born with. But I thought, as with all good shows, comedy and drama, that we had the chance to see Corky and the other characters in his life, grow, change, and try new things. That's when television series work best."

Corky and Amanda (Andrea Friedman) agree to a trial marriage in order to get to know one another better; and taking care of his little brother Nick helps that process along in "Premarital Syndrome." *THE REGAL COLLECTION*

CHAPTER 7

THE MEANING OF *LIFE*

"The meaning of school is like the meaning of life...Life is belonging."
— Becca, opening fantasy sequence, "La Dolce Becca"

Aside from Tommy Puett's discontent with Tyler's departure, and Chris Burke's discomfort with a few inconsistencies or hurried plot-lines, *Life Goes On* reached for legitimacy from the onset, with its attempt to portray a television family as realistically as possible. Corky's particular problems of adjustment were threads in the total family fabric. They were not unveiled to viewers with too much manufactured uplift, certainly not in the show's final's two years. The series dealt with people who were faced with hard choices, dealing with the outcomes to the best of their abilities. Or as Burke construes, "It was about a family working together facing everyday problems and being happy." Note: Not trying to be happy, but being happy.

According to Tracey Needham, *LGO* "has a very special voice, one that you don't see on television anymore, definitely not in family shows. It was quirky, but it had a lot of strong messages, without being preachy. You could still have a good time watching it."

Troy Evans, who played Artie opposite Tracey's Paige, says the show's beautiful message rests in its title, with a footnote — that we are not merely to endure life's challenges, but to overcome them. "That's why people responded so strongly to it," he believes. "Every family has challenges, and our show said, *When you have a challenge, get together and do the best you can.* That's a message that works every day."

"It was honest," assesses Marshall Goldberg, who was the program's creative consultant in its last season. "Viewers sensed that. It was presented by people who were aiming for a high standard. When someone turned on the television, they knew they would receive the best shot from the actors, directors and writers. The audience appreciated that we weren't just phoning in our jobs. It was all conducted with a kind of a gentle sensibility."

Former ABC executive Chad Hoffman says *LGO* presented a TV series with integrity, a show about a family who had a real enough sense about themselves that most American families have — a family whose parents worked for a living. "People who showed just how a two-fold family can be," he says. "Exciting and fun and yet, at times, difficult and challenging. After they had turned on the set, we wanted viewers to feel that, generally, they had just seen a piece of themselves, in a family situation that was relatable, without the usual television eyes view of family life, where everyone is

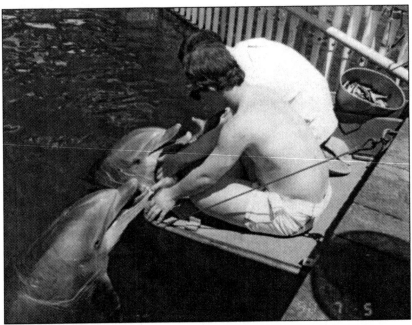

Many of the show's segments had to do with Corky's special bond with all of God's creatures, including wolves and a certain glutton from "Pig O' My Heart"). Here, Chris Burke plays with a few of Corky's and his friends in between filming scenes of "Corky and the Dolphins," the second of the two-part season opener for *LGO's* second season. Dolphins, in particular, have always held a special relationship with those with Down syndrome, in general. *KALEY HUMMEL*

always happy, never having any problems, or just laughing their lives away." At the same time, Hoffman and company did not seek to showcase a program that was depressing and dark, but rather one that possessed legitimate drama, "where the human spirit of its characters could triumph."

From the first episode and onward, Michael Braverman helped to endorse and expand upon the show's unique situation by strictly adhering to and endorsing a very specific set of rules based on character equality, emotional balance, and true-to-life realism. Or, as he says, "To treat Corky like everyone else, to address his weaknesses, as well as his strengths. One of the neat things about the series was how it displayed weakness. None of the Thachers were perfect. Actually, I try to make all my characters imperfect. I prefer those."

"To not have certain people receive special treatment, whatever their situation," Braverman explains. "It doesn't mean they're weak or strong, they're just different. We're all different. That was the whole point of *Life Goes On*. That was the whole point of the Down syndrome storyline and the AIDS arc. It's really that simple."

Further defining Corky and Jesse as those who happen to have Down syndrome and AIDS, Braverman reiterates a verification: "Happens to be or happens to have type-phrasing underscores the entire series. We never defined any one of our characters by a physical trait. There was never any reference to their actual physical description. I always felt that such references would have been very cheap shots at storytelling."

Life Goes On, then, never set out to beat viewers over the head with the idea that Corky or Jesse were dear lads. The portrayal of their characters was of necessity a compromise. It would have been irresponsible to make them either too distressed or too unaffected by their situations.

Though Chad Lowe did not in real life have AIDS, as both Chris Burke and Corky faced the challenge of Down syndrome directly, the actor's portrayal of Jesse was just as honest an appraisal of the character's circumstances as was Burke's of Corky, for two reasons. First, Lowe's manager died of complications of the disease, and second: Rod Garcia, a young man with AIDS, was employed by the producers to make certain the facts of his disease were conveyed correctly.

Dorothy Lyman, who played Jesse's mother, Mary McKenna, remembers Garcia's role as advisor on the show: "He was on the set one day, and I got into quite a long conversation with him. I didn't know who he was at all. He then very proudly told me what he was doing and how the show had really given his life so much meaning. I was quite moved by that. I remember him talking about his father not being very supportive. I can't remember what he said about his mother, but I know he was quite close with his sister. I believe he came from quite a broken home. So he knew how important his influence was to *Life Goes On*, and he was honored by that."

On reviewing such *Life* experiences, Lyman becomes melancholy. "I'm sorry it went off the air," she says. "I thought it had an enormous courage to present the messages that it did."

Lyman's TV son, Chad Lowe, sees *Life's* messages as multi-level, for everyone to grasp, not only for those with a physical or psychological handicap or ailment. "I think everyone feels at times, and sometimes all the time," he says, "different and unique, like an outcast. That's why I think the show worked for everyone, because everyone, on some level, was able to identify with being a victim or an outcast, or not fitting in, not living up to society's perception of what the norm is. I don't know anyone who really feels like they live up to that, completely."

The show's other Chad, network executive Hoffman, recalls an early conversation with Michael Braverman, on trying to target the show's viewers. He wondered, *What audience is this show going to reach? What does it have to say?* "I was almost like on a soapbox," he admits. "But we had a philosophy with every show that we developed at ABC, right or wrong, which permeated everything that we did. Every show had to have a theme and point of view. *Life Goes On* was not so much a show about a family with a son with Down syndrome, but a show about hope, and how a family sticks together, through good times and bad, through the situations they can foresee, and some of the others that they can't. How the main thing is that they love each other, and that they are doing their best, and that they can make it. That may sound overly simplistic, but that's what it was. And I don't think we ever took our eye off the ball, or strayed from that theme, especially in the pilot, but certainly throughout the entire run of the series — how there are no easy answers to what we are given to deal with. But that's life. You just have to confront it, and hopefully, you'll make it through."

Kellie Martin and Chad Lowe's plight as Becca and Jesse came to *Life* — and affected and inspired millions of viewers in the process. *THE REGAL COLLECTION*

CHAPTER 8

WRITE TO *LIFE*

"We felt what we were doing was magical, and when we received letters from families saying how the show changed their lives, those feelings were confirmed."
— Rick Rosenthal

Life Goes On has affected thousands of viewers, in positive, actual ways.

Co-executive producer Rick Rosenthal recalls countless stories of adults and/or children in the midst of challenge (sometimes, beyond Down's or AIDS), who were comforted by watching Corky, Jesse and company. Sometimes, an audience member was psychologically or emotionally eased, and profoundly altered by the series. According to Rosenthal, *LGO* allowed such individuals to perceive themselves and others more gracefully and offered them something with which to bond.

One first season segment, "Thacher and Henderson," in which Drew takes part in an annual football game with his former high-school team, received a strong fan response; not particularly earth-shattering, but precisely a demonstration of the power of the program's influence. "I've had more women tell me," Rosenthal explains, "that they never understood what football was all about and its appeal, until they saw that episode. Then, suddenly, they got it."

Fourth-year story editor Scott Frost also remembers receiving written responses to the series, these resulting from the airing of two episodes he authored: "The Whole Truth," which had to do with Paige's attempted date rape by Becca's English school teacher (played by Leigh J. McCloskey); and the previously discussed "Incident on Main," in which Jesse is severely beaten by a gang of gay-bashing neo-Nazi youths. Frost says the show received *tons* of letters about the episode which was expected, "because we knew there were those who unfortunately experienced similar dealings with skin-heads."

Yet, it was one "Truth" epistle in particular that got under Scott's skin. It was a short note with a heavy message from a woman in the big state of Texas. "She thanked us for doing the episode," he recalls. "Because of watching it, her 16-year-old daughter was able to communicate, when she was only twelve, that she had been molested by a babysitter."

Frost believes this reply was particularly amazing, mostly due to a subplot involving Libby breaking a long, painful silence, dating back to a disturbing event: In college years, she herself was sexually assaulted, and actually raped by a coed. In one concluding, revealing sequence, she carefully

Paige is flattered by the attentions of Becca's English poetry teacher (played by Leigh J. McCloskey), until their date goes unsettling awry in "The Whole Truth," a *Life* episode that ultimately spoke to viewers in many surprisingly ways. *THE REGAL COLLECTION*

utters this startling disclosure: "Silence is much worse than fear. Silence becomes your companion. Your ally. It's difficult to let go of it." It was upon hearing this statement, Frost appraises, that a young child was able to say, *I've been hurt.* "It was quite gratifying to know that we were part of her healing process," he says.

Michael Lange, who, in echoing Rick Rosenthal's comments, calls the eye-opening viewer response from the young girl, a result of powerful television, directed "Truth." It was so mighty an influence that Lange believed upon hearing it he should have quit directing while he was ahead. "How often can you be a part of an experience like that?" he asks. "You can't top that. That's the height of the art."

What's more, Lange remembers countless letters from parents who were initially ashamed of their children with Down's. "Their perception changed because of *Life Goes On*," he says. "The show widened their awareness."

Further still, as if a child's mental, physical and emotional healing as a result of viewing *Life Goes On* isn't enough, casting director Dee Dee Bradley recalls an additional experience that takes the simple event of watching a TV show even further:

"We once had a receptionist who for some reason was not giving me my mail. She was fired, and we hired a new receptionist who did bring me mail. Not only the recent mail, but the mail from the months that had gone by of unreceived mail. And in the huge packet were all these letters from a man in Arizona, telling me that he had a son in his twenties who had Down's, and that it would be the most wonderful thing in the world if his son could be on the show. There was letter after letter after letter. I felt so bad that I hadn't answered them. I couldn't possibly have answered every letter, but this one affected me so much. So I called, finally, after getting these letters late, and spoke to his wife, who said her husband had just died. It just tore me apart. She said, *Dee Dee, it meant so much to him to see his son on Life Goes On.* Then I told Michael Braverman what had happened, and he said, *Let's get his son on Life Goes On!* So we brought him out to LA, and he ended up having a small part on the show, which was his father's dream."

Certain fan letters were penned by soon-to-be parents relaying the results of amniocentesis tests that uncovered a child with Down's. These typed testaments explained how such births would never have taken place had it not been for *Life*.

"That's a very powerful position to be in," Rosenthal says of his involvement with a television show that produces such an emphatic response from its audience. "That's why we were always so increasingly careful not to portray Corky as Superman, which is what I think we did in some of the first episodes."

Rosenthal refers to episodes, pre-"Break a Leg, Mom," from the first season. With "Leg," Rosenthal believes Corky's journey became more realistic and thus, believable. Here he's experiencing learning difficulties in school, and agrees to additional tutoring (if Libby returns to the stage in a community theatre musical). "This was a very honest appraisal of the circumstances," assesses Rosenthal.

Bradley, too, remembers more letters from people all over the world, professing how positive an influence *LGO* played in their lives. One piece of potent correspondence came from an expectant mother. She learned that she would have a child with Down's, and then decided not to have an abortion because of the series. "There are so many more children alive today because of the show," Bradley says. "Their parents decided not to have an abortion because they knew their child would have Down's. Because of Corky, they knew their children could function in the world."

In fact, a fourth-season *Life* seg, "Choices," deals directly with abortion (which also received its share of pro and con mail). Here, Paige becomes pregnant with Michael's child, and he decides against having the baby. As a result, she is presented with many options, including interrupting the birth and becoming romantically involved with Artie who, though he is opposed to abortion, professes his undying love for her during her turmoil, and promises to stand by her no matter which choice she makes.

Troy Evans, who played Artie, says this episode is less about abortion, and more about loyalty, true companionship, and the ultimate test of friendship. Paige comes to him for help, and says, *I know you don't believe in this, but I need you to help me.* And he did. "He helped her as a friend, without judgment," Evans assesses. "He just knew that whatever would happen, he would be there for her. He knew that what she needed most was a friend. As far as I'm concerned, this is everyone's highest calling."

Therefore, the issue here may not be not whether or not Paige or Artie are presented as pro-choice but, again, just how strong and life-altering an effect a television program may have on a viewer. Without *Life Goes On*, there would not have been the major strides made in social acceptance of those with disabilities; or in the fight against prejudices of all kinds. Not only that, but the unaffected spirit and joy embodied by Chris Burke, or as Chad Lowe will later define as "the miracle of who Chris Burke is," is a substantial gap to fill.

As Burke himself relays, "I always wanted to be an actor. I always wanted to help the handicapped. Now I'm doing both." His performance as Corky proved likable, popular, and nothing short of monumental and inspiring. From the get-go he's been an incredibly positive force in the media, representing the challenged of any community with unstoppable confidence. As he said in one early interview, "I don't have Down syndrome. I have *Up* syndrome."

Burke has become a spokesperson for The National Down Syndrome Congress and Ronald McDonald charities. He's received numerous awards from various organizations, and a Golden Globe nomination for Best Supporting Actor in a Drama Series. He remains a frequent guest on television and radio talk shows, including *Victory and Valor: A Special Olympic's All-Star Celebration* and, as mentioned, was seen as a semi-regular on TV's *Touched by an Angel.* He's also been featured in anti-drug commercials, and was named one of the Top Ten Faces of *Faces International* magazine. "I'd like to be the role model to teach other people who have Down syndrome to be actors and actresses," he once told *The Los Angeles Times,* "and not try to be a big shot."

Dee Dee Bradley remembers a response to Burke, which she experienced first hand, during production of the first season *LGO* episode, "Brothers." Here, the Special Olympics parlayed heavily into the plot, and Michael Braverman made it a point to employ several of those with Down syndrome — "Just about everyone who auditioned," Bradley says. "If we didn't use them in a speaking part, we would use them as extras. They worshiped Chris Burke. They had a role model. All they wanted to do was to meet Corky. That's all that mattered to them. And Michael was so caring, just a pleasure to work for him. He deeply cared about every single person connected with the show, the actors and the crew. He inspired so many lives."

For Bradley, casting for *Life Goes On* was "the most emotionally rewarding experience" of her life and career. "I loved working on that show," she says. "It meant so much to me, and to so many people in so many ways. I don't think we'll ever know how much it truly affected people, for generations to come."

Mostly every member of the *LGO* cast, crew, and executive and creative team has experienced the show's positive effect upon the audience — everyone from former ABC executive Chad Hoffman to Bill Smitrovich, Tracey Needham, and Chad Lowe. And again, though Lowe does not have AIDS in reality (as Chris Burke has Down's), his *Life* impact on viewers who know the pangs of being HIV-positive or having AIDS, or knowing someone who is affected by either, has been monumental. People have shared with him, and continue to share with him, so many specific instances that Lowe says, it's overwhelming, truly overwhelming. Whether they come up to me on the street, or I receive letters, or I know people, personally, who share their feelings, it just continues to happen."

As when, one time, Lowe was dining in New York with his then-girlfriend (now former-wife) Oscar-winning actress Hilary Swank (*Boys Don't Cry,* 1999). As he recalls: "We were having a huge argument. We were not talking to each other, actually, just eating. We argued walking from the theatre where we had seen a play to this little diner. We were both tired, grumpy and hungry, and being petty. And some man who was obviously very sick, came up to me and told me that he had AIDS and that he thanked me from the bottom of his heart for what I was doing on the show and what the show was doing, and how it helped enlighten and educate his parents…to develop a relationship with them. It encouraged them to help him. It helped them to understand him and what he was going through. He was so thankful. I was floored."

Lowe is touched by such responses, but also perplexed. "I can't take the credit," he admits. "I appreciate it. My heart and sympathy go out to him, along with my prayers and to all the people who have shared with me what the show has meant. But somehow I always end up feeling like I'm not worthy. There's so many pieces that make something good, and to single out one piece, and to accept all the accolades, all the attention, all the credit, is hard to take."

In contrast, Kellie Martin, who played the now-famous murdered-intern Lucy on TV's equally inspiring drama, *ER*, actually pines for such a response as part of her goal of performing, in general. "I always hope that whoever watches any show I'm on or any character I'm playing, that they learn something…that it touches them in some way. That was inevitable with *Life Goes On*. I hope whoever watches the show takes something with them, that they have a better understanding of compassion. As long as the viewer takes something with them, I think we're [those behind and in front of the camera] doing our job."

Martin's TV sister Tracey Needham gets recognized as Paige from *Life* more than anything else she has done professionally (including a role on the hit CBS adventure series, *JAG*). On more than one occasion the response received has been exhilarating. As she recalls, "I was shooting on location, and I met a woman who had a baby with Down's. She explained how the show had made such a difference in her life; how it made her feel hopeful for her child. That she and her family could have a somewhat regular life, and that how, in general, it changed the way she viewed those with Down syndrome."

For Chad Hoffman, the former Vice-President of Dramatic Television at ABC, *LGO* helped to change the way he views his personal day-to-day experiences. Today, Hoffman teaches at Boston University, where he remains as a consultant to some entertainment companies. But he took his family away from the Hollywood scene and he's in the midst of his own life going on, at a more regular pace, in a more regular fashion. Yet, he's still not far from the positive effect of *Life Goes On*, as when he took his children to camp at Cape Cod, a few years back.

"I was wearing a *Life Goes On* T-shirt," he says. "And some of the other camp kids asked if I had anything to do with that show. I then explained my involvement. And they said, *Oh, I loved that show. Why did they take it off the air?* It's nice to hear that, because when you're in Hollywood, you don't always hear that kind of response. You're really not aware of the impact of the things you do, or of how much it's appreciated. And I think many people in Hollywood had no sense of what the show meant. But the people at home did and still do."

"Some of the best things that ever happened to me, happened because of *Life Goes On*," adds Bill Smitrovich. For one, having viewers of the show approach him with praise; those who have identified with Drew's experience as a father of a child with Down's. "To play a character that is so close to the true experience of what it means to be human. And then to have the people who actually personify or embody that character on a day-to-day basis, to have them come up to you and say thank you. Or it's as when I played a cop [on *Crime Story*]; people came up to me and said, *You know you look like a real cop*. Or like doing *Ghosts of Mississippi* and talking about Margaret Evers and being part of that movie. It was very important to me, and every member of that cast, the director and everyone who worked on the film. Especially the Evers family."

"People that lay it down every day," Smitrovich says, "whether they be parents of challenged children, fireman, policeman, or people that are real everyday heroes, come up to you and say, *You really got it! You don't know how much what you've done has meant to me*. Well, every actor should have that experience. There's no greater gratification for an actor. Because that's what the best of us try to strive for…is truth. Truth with a purpose. It's a very important part of what we do."

As to *Life*, and its overall importance, Smitrovich adds: "Down syndrome is still a mystery. No one knows why there is that extra chromosome. No one knows which mate it comes from, why it comes. Down syndrome children have a myriad of physical maladies when they're born. It ranges anywhere from enlarged hearts to cleft pallets, to enlarged tongues to severe eyesight challenges. Those with Down's and their troubles are quite real, and yet I think that they offer the rest of us a great gift. If we could only look at them in an objective way, and see the intangibles that they bring to us. I mean, when you go to a Special Olympics [SO] event, you can't help walking out of there feeling better. It's like going to church."

Surely, the SO event is very near and dear to Bill's heart, and not only does he encourage everyone to contribute to the Special Olympics in their area, but his involvement with the physically and mentally challenged certainly reaches beyond just playing Drew on TV.

Smitrovich plays host for the annual *Life Goes On Golf Tournament*, benefiting the Down Syndrome Association of Los Angeles, which consists of parents. He also served as a member on the Board of the International Special Olympics in Connecticut. Unfortunately, however, he was filming *Nick of Time* in 1990 and he was unable to make that event. "But I was honored to be on the board," he says.

Expanding upon a point previously made by Dee Dee Bradley, and speaking for everyone associated with *Life Goes On*, Bill Smitrovich asserts: "I don't think people really understand just how much the show has crossed all lines of culture, ethnicity, religion, and race. With Corky, everyone has a hero. If you're feeling low, all you have to do is look at Corky and say, *How inspirational.* You look at Corky, and then you look at yourself and ask, *What color am I? Really? Black? White? Red? Pink? Green? Does it matter?* No, man. It doesn't. Because we're all part of something much bigger than ourselves. We're all part of the One."

Writer Toni Graphia, author of such heralded fourth year segments as "Last Wish" and "PMS," the latter of which featured real-life couples being interviewed on screen (*a la When Harry Met Sally* ...), concludes on the positive response *LGO* received, written and otherwise:

"We received a lot of letters, especially for "PMS," which I think is one of the most important episodes we ever did. Even though Chris Burke really has Down syndrome, and he impressed people who watched the show, I believe part of them still saw him as an actor and probably thought some of what we did was make-believe. They didn't know for sure if it was real until they saw the featured couples in "PMS." I received many letters that said, *Gee, I kind of always thought this was TV, until I saw that episode.* It was more like a documentary and it made people see that what we were writing about was real. In fact, we shot a little interview segment with Corky and Amanda and then debated as to whether to include it because it was crossing the line. They were the actors, characters, and everyone else in the interviews were authentic. Then we said, *Wait a minute. Who is more authentic than Chris and Andrea* (actress Friedman)? And we closed the show with their segment."

Overall, Graphia discovered, "Everywhere I went, people knew the show. Even in the most unexpected places. I remember I'd go to Pep Boys to have my tires changed and this huge, macho mechanic would see my *Life Goes On* jacket in the car and say, *I love that show. It made me cry last night.* I figured if we could make the guy at Pep Boys cry, we were doing something right."

The Thachers donned Hawaiian garb for the second-season premiere episode, "Honeymoon from Hell," which is one of LGO's most comic-laden episodes. *THE REGAL COLLECTION*

CHAPTER 9

LIFE AND THE WORLD LAUGHS WITH IT

"I'm a mother...I'm *never* alone."
— Libby

One of *LGO's* most appealing aspects is its poised, tasteful mix of humor, while in the midst of serious issues. As in real life, the series clearly conveys that both joy and sorrow have their place in a well-balanced world. Fine examples of this occur in several episodes.

From the first season: "Ordinary Heroes," when questions by Drew's friend (played by Louis Giambalvo) regarding his unborn child with Down's is countered with Corky's genial wit; and "Pig O' My Heart," when Corky's hide-away pet ends up turning a profit for Drew's restaurant. From semester two: "La Dolce Becca," in which Becca flirts with disaster while Maxie nearly drinks herself to death (as both bow to peer pressure); and "Thanks a Bunch, Dr. Lamaze," in which tension increases between Libby and Drew during baby-breathing sessions (resulting in her temporarily partnering with Jerry in class).

Though presented with edgier tones, merriment-oriented concepts would periodically return in the third and fourth years. "We actually thought about some of these ideas in the first and second season," Michael Braverman confesses. One of these was Michael Nankin's trimester outing, "Invasion of the Thacher Snatchers," in which Corky is obsessed with a sci-fi film on TV, thinking his family has turned into aliens. Braverman, who still has the space helmets adorned by the cast as the fictional Venusians in Corky's fantasy sequences, calls this "another Michael Nankin special."

When Nankin was hired near the end of season one, "Snatchers" was one of the initial ideas that he brought to the fold. "We didn't get around to it for two years, because it didn't fall into the mix," Braverman elucidates. "We just couldn't get it going. We did that with a lot of stories. We would have them in the bag early on, sometimes before we were able to even read through them."

Segments like "Dueling Divas" showed up in the third year, allowing

Patti Lupone the chance to portray the double role of Libby and Gabriella, her outrageous (comparatively speaking) cousin from Sicily. Also that year came "Struck by Lightning," in which the Thachers are jolted by a thunderstorm into acting strange. Episodes such as these filled a niche, with Braverman and company thinking along the lines of, *We want to entertain you.* "We felt that at least once or twice a year we should do something really silly," he says. "There was a real need to do a variety. To really shake up our viewers. I don't know if the audience cared for it or not, but I think people want to tune into a certain kind of show every week."

Sometimes the fun journeyed beyond the scripts and into casting. As with the fourth-season opener, "Bec to the Future," which was directed by Michael Nankin and penned by Toni Graphia and Thania S. John. The story featured an adult Becca, played by Kellie-Martin-lookalike, Pamela (*Dynasty*) Bellwood, reflecting on her past. "It was Michael Nankin's choice to go with an actress who resembled Kellie, as he predicted she would look like in fifteen years," Braverman sustains. "Pamela was absolutely excellent. Wonderful. That's how we decided to kick off the season. To confuse the audience from the start. Prior to the season beginning, we would have major discussions, literally for weeks, looking for ways to thrust ahead for the upcoming year. 'Bec to the Future' was a perfect example of that, and we thought it was fun to project what we felt Becca's appearance would someday be."

More fourth-season antics appeared in "Confessions," in which Paige gets locked in a bakery freezer with Michael (Lance Guest), when shopping for a wedding cake for her intended nuptials to Kenny (Steve Eckholtd). Tracey Needham also found it amusing that Paige, in this same episode, would, as she says, "even consider marrying Artie." In "Udder Madness," the show once again takes to the animals, as Becca enters a homecoming queen contest at school and somehow ends up atop a cow. In "Exposed," Jesse paints a nude portrait of Becca that is later purchased by her bookstore boss, Harris Cassidy (Martin Milner). Drew, Jesse and Corky then don black clothing and make a not-so-careful attempt to steal the painting back, *a la The Pink Panther* (inspired by a *Panther* film festival at Corky's theatre).

Bill Smitrovich credits "Exposed" director Michael Lange (who has guided the TV versions of *Buffy the Vampire Slayer* and *Honey, I Shrunk the Kids*) for the segments' choice symmetry of drama and comedy: "Michael was a lot of fun to work with. He did a lot of the really good episodes. He understood how humor belonged with the pathos, side by side."

Some of Lange's other episodes include "Isn't It Romantic," "Toast," "Choices" and "Armageddon," the latter during which Drew and Libby intensely argue throughout, after their roles as family breadwinner and homemaker are reversed. Many of the tense moments between them are quite comical: Libby gets hiccups because she's angry, forcing her to ask at one point, "How come men don't know how to suffer...[hiccup]...silently?" Her can't-break-it-habit coincides with Drew's nasal grunting, which makes for more laughs, climaxing when Corky somehow maneuvers his parents into the theatre at which he works to screen the monster movie, *Lost Plateau* (a play on words of *Lost World*). One fantasy scene here, in fact, features two dinosaurs in battle, symbolically representing the Thacher husband/wife

The featured lead guest star from the first-season segment, "Pig O' My Heart." *KALEY HUMMEL*

duo (when Corky has nightmares about the battling dinos speaking with Drew's and Libby's voices).

While Lange says that bits like the hiccup/grunt angle were "something we sort of came up with at the end of the day. [*She had something, and he had something*]," Bill Smitrovich viewed the entire episode as an opportunity to explore artistic challenges and serious issues, via comedy: "... two of the things that the show did best," he reconfirms. "It's like that old joke, about the guy who finds a lamp. He rubs it and a genie pops out, and says, *I'll grant you one wish.* The guys say, *Well, um...I want to do what no man has ever done or could ever think of doing.* The genie says, *Poof...you're a housewife.*"

In contrast, there were certain lost opportunities for Smitrovich during production of the second year's "A Thacher Thanksgiving." "They cut a big, long funny speech of mine," the actor recalls. "It would have been hilarious had they left it in. But they wanted Drew to be more serious, and I played it sort of tongue and cheek."

For many moments during "Thanksgiving," on and off screen, there would have been little other choice but to, if not hold the tongue, certainly rework it. Bill and the entire cast had to assume Pilgrim wardrobe and certain language colloquialisms, due to a lengthy back-in-time fantasy sequence. "There were times during filming that it was so funny," he relays, "because there were so many weird things to say in that old English dialect. We would all laugh. We couldn't stop laughing, actually."

He remembers a similar incident while making "Pig O' My Heart," from the first season: "Drew had the pig in his restaurant, and it must have taken us more than twenty takes where I just could not say this one line. I had to stand there [in a master shot], and I couldn't stop laughing. I never had a laughing jag as bad as that. People were standing around me, going, *But would you please stop it already.* I'm like, *I can't. I'm sorry. I'm trying. But I can't.*

This, in turn, sounds like what Ray Buktenica experienced on the set of the second semester's "Isn't It Romantic" (one of Michael Lange's fun outings), in which Cupid (played by a very young Ben Savage of *Boy Meets World*) goes a little wild with many of the characters. "We were laughing and laughing and laughing when we made this episode," Ray says. "And I mean belly laughs."

Rick Rosenthal reveals some details behind "Romantic," referring to a scene between Ray, and Mary Page Keller as Gina, Libby's sister: "At one moment, he actually gets the nerve to ask out Gina. But he couldn't seem to get the full question out, and stammers along the way, repeating *I was wondering... I was wondering... I was wondering.* That was my idea, and everyone thought I was crazy. But I said, *I guarantee you that Ray Buktenica can pull it off.* Michael Lange understood what I wanted to do. Mary Page got it, and she sort of encouraged me and said, *I think you're right. Let's go for it.* From my perspective, it was a chance to do some physical comedy. It was risky, but that was half the fun. And we laughed a lot while filming it."

Another of the "Romantic" scenes that triggered smirks off-screen also involved Buktenica's Jerry. This time, he was paired with Tommy Puett's Tyler. Suddenly, after years of Becca pining after him, Tyler now has a thing for her, but it may be too late. His love may be unrequited, and his ego has a real problem with that. Meanwhile, Jerry, further pangs over Gina, with his confidence growing increasingly shaky. Bruised egos collide when Tyler and Jerry butt heads on the Thacher front lawn, and have this brief, but telling, Robert De Nero-esque conversation, as if to say, "You talking to *me?*"

Jerry: What are *you* looking at?
Tyler: What am *I* looking at? What are *you* looking at?

That may have actually been kind of an *improv,* Buktenica explains about the style of acting he summoned to perform the scene with Puett. Mostly because he went off-camera, muttering. "And whenever you hear me muttering," he says, "I'm usually stumped as to what I'm supposed to do in a scene. But then I'm told, *Yeah...okay use it.*"

"Some of the extremely broad comedy that we did on the show," he goes on to say, "began with the writing. When I do a part, I live the lines, though I try to bring to the script my own little nuances. That's basically what I do."

Other times, Ray was encouraged to partake in certain physical bits that were written into the script, that he wasn't all that crazy about. As in one episode, when Libby cuts off Jerry's tie. Or when Jerry staples a note to his tie by accident, or bangs his head against the Plexiglas window in his office. "I don't even know if I ever saw those scenes on the air," Buktenica wonders, "or if I just remember doing them." Either way, Ray would say to the powers that be, *You know, please don't make me do stuff this far out. This is really stretching it. I mean, come on!*

Always a trooper, however, Ray says, "You just kind of whip through those very, very broad things. You can essentially do anything [as an actor] if you're given enough time to work out the logistics of the bit. Like tripping through a doorway or throwing your hat across a room and have it meet the hat rack or something of that nature. You can do those things, but you obviously have to make sure they work on cue. And to do that, of course, you have to practice a couple of times. That's why we have rehearsals."

When push came to shove, or trip, as it were, Ray admits, he was somewhat attracted to the physical comedy. In fact, when he first read certain comic bits in the scripts, he would drool. "That's one of the great things about *Life Goes On*," he says. "It really gave me so many opportunities to go to the edge."

Juxtaposed to drama, Buktenica believes it's more arduous to perform comedy. "As some actor once said on his deathbed," he explains, "*Dying is easy, comedy is hard.* Though comedy and drama are very close in many ways. Presenting it in such a way that the person who's going to get a kick out of it, however, is a very difficult thing to do, unless you're born with it or study well. If you're born with it, okay. But comedy can be very difficult because it's so risky. When you're doing drama, you're doing drama. You don't have the opportunity to have egg on your face, like you do when you do comedy."

One of the secrets in doing comedy, for Ray, at least, is to act as though one is always speaking the truth, and not telling a joke. "If you're telling a joke," he says, "and nobody laughs, you feel horrible. You're there with egg on your face, and it's disgusting. If you're telling the truth, and no one laughs, it really doesn't matter, because you weren't reaching for a joke, or asking the audience to laugh. That's what it comes down to. You ask people to laugh and it gets tedious. I get caught up in it myself, sometimes, too. But basically, you evolve into an on-camera flexible persona, one that will adhere to the demands of whatever you happen to be working on."

"Basically," he deciphers, "you are who you are. Hopefully, when you choose a script, it will jump out at you, and you'll say, *Well, I don't really need to do a lot of work on this. Because I see something there, and I'm comfortable with what it is. I identify somehow with this character, and I can justify these lines.* And sometimes I'll pick up a script, and won't have a clue as to who the character is."

David *Hans* Byrd, whom Jerry called Hanzee, labels Buktenica "a won-derfully-gifted physical-comedic actor," and targets Ray's philosophy as on the money, by applauding his very techniques. "If I could have used any of his material, I would have stolen it."

LGO actors utilized additional theatrical styles in contrasting the show's tears with laughter. Bill Smitrovich, for one, found himself wanting to find the humor in even the darkest of situations. "That's what American people do," he says. "For the most part, that's how a lot of people survive."

An actor would be hard put to find grimmer situations than those that Smitrovich discovered while appearing on TV's *Millennium*, the surreal detective drama from the late 1990s, created by *X-Files* mind-bending mogul, Chris Carter. "One of the things that I was very happy about in the pilot for that show," he explains, "was that my character [an investigator] had a little humor. There were even times when he had a sardonic wit. That, to me, was personifying a real policeman's life, dealing in homicide everyday. What else would he do but try to deal with the situation with humor? The same thing holds true for people who are challenged with their lives. You don't want to make something funny that isn't funny. But what you try to do is find the humor in the situation."

Certainly, Bill Smitrovich's staple sense of humor found its way into the exercycle scene in the opening credits of *Life* when Drew wakes up in the morning, attempts to work out on the machine, and then turns away in dis-gust as if to say, *No way...not this morning.* Much in the same way Mary Richard's reluctantly throws the meat in her basket, despite its high cost (knowing she has to eat), when grocery shopping during the opening credit sequence of *The Mary Tyler Moore Show.*

"That was scripted," Smitrovich says of the Drew-cycle sequence. "That wasn't my idea. That was probably Michael Braverman's idea. He's a very funny guy. He has a great sense about him as to what is humanly funny. His humor is not set kick-'em-through-the-field-goal humor. His is more of an innate, ingrown, organic humor. But you'll notice that I wore a shirt during the last two seasons of the show."

"I was in better shape when I put the shirt on, damn it," he muses. "They did a lot of weight jokes on Drew. It wasn't fair. But when we first did it, it was my choice to leave my shirt off. I said, *Oh, come on! What guys sleeps with his shirt on when getting out of bed?"*

Smitrovich's sense of humor in talking about the seriousness of his then-possible extended two-year employment in keeping with the previously-stated understanding of the importance of balancing the happy with the sad, on screen and off. The actor recalls filming on the show's last day: "I looked at some note cards that I had printed up with the *Life Goes On* logo on it, and my name below it. I had a stack of those things. Anyway, I asked myself, *What am I supposed to do with these now?* So I just scratched over the *On*, and scribbled in *Off*, and said, *Yeah…well now they can call it 'Life Goes* Off.'"

Heavy on the Make-Up: A fantasy sequence in which Kellie Martin and Tommy Puett are near-unrecognizable is played for laughs in the third season episode, "Armageddon." Here, Becca (Martin) thinks about living a middle-aged life with Tyler (Puett), challenged by marital issues. *THE REGAL COLLECTION*

CHAPTER 10

STARS OF INTELLIGENT *LIFE*

"I realize how fortunate I am to have had the opportunity
to play Jesse on a show that's as classy and well-done as
Life Goes On."
— Chad Lowe

The reasons are many as to why *Life Goes On* was and remains popular:
The stories. The high attention given to detail, in front of and behind the
scenes. The premise and character developments with which it proceeded,
allowing it to sometimes be viewed almost as two separate series (i.e., the
Corky-Becca/Jesse transition).

The main evidence, however, for its original and continued success rests
with the casting of topnotch actors. The central *Life* characters — Drew,
Libby, Corky, Becca, Paige, Jesse and Tyler — were interpreted by a group
of high-caliber theatrical professionals who strictly adhered to specific
guidelines established by the show's producers, writers and directors. They
remained concordant throughout the program's four seasons, and explicated
their characters with dedication and regulation, frequently drawing lessons
from real life, and applying them to their craft.

For starters, there's Bill Smitrovich, the versatile actor who portrayed
LGO's father figure, Drew Thacher. He was born William S. Zmitrowics on
May 16, 1947, in Bridgeport, Connecticut, the son of Stanley William, a
tool and dye maker (who, despite asthma, kept the family going), and wife
Anna (Wojna). In playing Drew, Corky's sometimes crusty but caring dad,
Bill turned to memories of his own hard-working pop. As he told *TV Guide*
in 1989, "I went to 13 or 14 schools — parochial schools — till the fifth
grade. I was expelled. It was a very proud moment for my dad."

Smitrovich remembered a timid young boy in one of his early classes
who suffered from ringworm. The child was forced to shave his head and
wear a knit cap, which, at one point, compelled an insensitive teacher to
demand for the student to remove his hat. When the young boy declined,
the instructor abruptly removed it, which resulted in the baring of his hair-
less, contaminated scalp. Smitrovich snatched the small hat, returned it to

his young pal's head, and shouted a few choice words to the supposed professional school official. A heartbeat later, Bill found himself waiting for his father in the principal's office with the Mother Superior.

"I thought I'd never see the light of day for the next year," he said.

Yet his dad listened attentively, and asked, "Well, son, do you want to be here?"

Bill Smitrovich was near-perfect Thacher clan Dad named Drew. *BILL SMITROVICH*

That gentle, diplomatic paternal manner of dealing with such uncomfortable situations made a mark on how Bill would conduct himself as a father in real life, as well as on *Life Goes On*. As the actor told talk show host Sally Jesse Raphael in 1990: "I can say that I base [Drew] on my father. More so than I base it on anything that I would know. I don't have a second marriage. I don't have a child [who] has Down syndrome [though he would go on to have one who would be challenged]. But I think that Drew Thacher wants to be a better father than his father was, which is something my father wanted to do. I think that Drew Thacher has the values, the work ethic, and the discipline that my father had."

In present reflection, Smitrovich details one minor regret with his Drew interpretation. "I don't think I would have been as emotional," he says. "I let my emotions get away from me from time to time in playing Drew. I didn't mind that he could be the kind of a guy who could get emotional, but I might have gone into that well a few too many times. I'm not one to think that men shouldn't cry, but I'm more than ten years older now and have two children. Knowing what I know now, I've learned through my experience that it's okay for men to cry. After you have a child who is physically or mentally challenged, you have to journey to other parts of yourself, stronger, deeper parts of yourself, if you don't want it to destroy you. When I was playing Drew I always felt obligated to represent the character properly."

While admitting the responsibility of playing a Down's child's dad wore him out from time to time, Bill also calls being Corky's father the "greatest job in the world," one from which he received "enormous gratification." He's also quick to claim his affection for Chris Burke. "I love that kid," he says, "and I wouldn't for a second give up any of the emotion that transpired between us on the show, for some kind of artistic merit." Bill credits Burke's parents in allowing him additional insight on portraying Drew, calling them "tremendous people." "Frank, in particular," he says of Burke's father, "was a great inspiration. He and Marion have been such a help to me, professionally and personally as time went on."

Down to earth, and with an honest demeanor, Smitrovich once more turns to discussing his own paternal upbringing: "I'm a junior, and I kept my name because my dad died when I was only 17. I loved him very much, and I thought that my name was more important than having people pronounce my name [correctly], to make it easy for them to say it, or make it seem like a Hollywood name."

Bill always sought to have the merit of his work make people remember his name, rather than having them recall only his name, and then wonder, *Now which character was he? What did he do? I know that name, but what was he in?* "If people know my name, they know my work," he figures. "If people can say my name, and come up to me and ask, *Aren't you Bill Smitrovich* or *Smitr-oh-vich*, or however they want to say it, that's fine with me. It doesn't make any difference, because I'm floored, either way. I love it. And I don't love it because, *Hey, they recognize me.* I love it because of the fact that I've reached them. They know my name, and my dad's name lives on. He lives on. I can't tell you how proud my few remaining relatives are, from the Smitrovich side of the family. These are coal miners from Pennsylvania, people who didn't have in-door plumbing until the '50s, and now people all over the country know their name."

Smitrovich's strong work-ethic background certainly contributed to his unaffected poise, which bled into Drew. "I'm probably more blue-color than any other color," he explains. "I worked my way through college. I hustled my way across country after my dad died, bowling and shooting pool, came back and so many things happened to me in college in such serendipitous, incredibly coincidental ways."

In some of those ways, Bill believes he may have been destined to play Drew, as he attained a minor in Special Education at college. His first role, his epiphany, he explains, in terms of what changed his life and career, was playing Lenny in *Of Mice and Men* — a challenged character with a challenged life. Soon following, he tutored children with Down's in Special Ed classes for two months, while attending college. "I lived across the street from the Kennedy Center facility," he recalls, "and watched those kids get on the bus in 1966." He was also employed in a work-study program that involved, not only kids with Down's, but cerebral palsy. Later, he was performing on the New York stage, right around the time auditions were held for *Life Goes On.*

Through it all, too, Smitrovich lost three agents to AIDS, in succession. "I miss those guys," he says, as his voice begins to crack. His last agent to succumb to the disease, David Liebhart, was responsible for bringing Bill to *Life Goes On.* "So, I don't know," he wonders, "maybe it was all meant to be."

It was not only his talent, virtue and possibly fate that drew Bill to Drew, but also the actor's personal sense of whimsy. One of his favorite quotes of the last twenty years has been, *All art aspires to music.* "When you're talking about acting," he explains, "you're dealing with rhythms, beats, and tempo. In college, I had my own way of doing things. I didn't fall into line so much with the orthodox manner in which they taught acting. I tend to use whatever works, whether it be [techniques from] Chekhov, Benedeto, Misnor, Stanoslavsky, Strassburg. I just try to make the thing work."

Many of Bill's *LGO* colleagues attest to just how well the actor made it work for them. Dorothy Lyman, who played Jesse's mother, sees Bill as a dedicated, amiable actor for whom she has immense respect. *Hello...I admire your work,* she remembers him saying upon their first meeting. We're *so happy to have you here.* "He was just immensely open with me right from the beginning," she clarifies. "He made me feel so immediately welcome. I liked him, and we talked about a lot of things. He was in the midst of just starting his family. He had small children. And I have three kids. That's always an area where you can talk with someone."

Chris Burke and Kellie Martin agree with Lyman when it comes to Smitrovich's sociability, leaning once more toward paternal instincts, in defining the actor and his skills. "Bill was someone for me to look up to," Burke says. "He helped me quite a bit. He was actually like my second father." "Bill is very similar to my dad," Martin adds, "in the sense that he's very caring, kind, and loving."

Simple, yet substantial traits he brought to the Thacher's patriarch. "He was outstanding as Drew," Rick Rosenthal appraises of Bill's theatrical talents. "Very real. He possesses many of the same gifts that Gene Hackman has; in the sense that he's a really wonderful *Everyman*, and he's also quite appealing."

Smitrovich got along well with everyone on the *Life* set, including David Byrd, who played irascible Hans, the cook, at Drew's Glenbrook Grill. The two would frequently rehearse lines between scenes, particularly if they were extensive, as while shooting "A Thacher Thanksgiving," from the second season. In Byrd's eye, Bill was mindful to what became the first dramatic scene to include Hans, who makes a startling revelation as to how he made it through World War II — how he never experienced the simple luxury of enjoying a meal with silverware until he was twenty-three years old. "That just broke my heart," Byrd says. "And Bill was very attentive to what I needed to do to prepare for that scene, in terms of privacy and what not. So much so, that we ended up shooting the scene in just two takes."

"When you came on the show, it was as if you were walking into his home," Troy *Artie* Evans assess, on working with Smitrovich. "That meant a lot to me. I've probably done more than 200 guest shots and, frequently, you show up for work, and the other actors don't know your name. They don't know who you are, and they don't want to know who you are. They don't care. If you have a scene with them, they may or may not rehearse it with you. But that's not they way it was with Bill."

Smitrovich's pleasant demeanor is without question unique to the acting world. There he was, receiving top billing, the star of a main television network program, and lacking in affectation. The actor makes a modest attempt to explain his humility: "When you work a lot, everyone's working around you, trying to please you, getting you this, that and the other thing, asking questions like, *Are you happy? Is everything okay? Can we get you anything else?* After a while, it becomes like feeding a rat until it explodes with cheese. It's like a never-ending thing. But then it does end, and you return to reality. I always try to keep that in perspective. I never wanted a publicist because I think they are basically made for people who need one. Though I actually tried it for a few months and hated it. It wasn't for me."

Many thespians retain publicists, including Glenn Close, with whom

Bill appeared in *Air Force One* in 1997. He asked her why. *Well*, she said, *when I was [on the Broadway stage] in 'Barnum' with Jim Dale, I was working my ass off in eight shows a week. I was just as important as he was to the show, and I wasn't getting any credit or any attention. So I hired a publicist.*

Yet, Bill did not understand that. He never had a desire to spend $2,000 or $5,000 a month for someone to call him and tell him how wonderful he

The legendary Patti Lupone portrayed the extraordinary working-mom Libby Thacher. *THE REGAL COLLECTION*

was, or to book him on all the right talk shows. He always thought publicists were for those performers who received so much attention, that they needed someone to guard the gate. "But I never had that," he says. "I never had the media coming at me in such a flurry that I couldn't handle it. I've just got other things to spend my money on."

Still, Bill admits, that if an actor, or any public figure, seeks to retain a publicist, or more personal attention, then he suggests that such individuals nurture their decision with discretion.

Sage advice from a gentle professional.

Next in line for star billing on *Life Goes On* is the multi-faceted Patti Lupone, whom many from the show claim was just as easy to work with as Bill Smitrovich. David Byrd, in fact, calls performing with Lupone "a very positive experience." Though he only appeared with Patti a few times, he found her to be "very responsive to my needs as an actor."

Social similarities aside, *LGO's* co-executive producer Bob Goodwin says Patti and Bill employ two completely different styles of acting — a dynamic that proved intriguing on screen. "Bill is a very thoughtful actor who's had a lot of training," Goodwin explains. "He comes out of the New York stage, and works with a technique called 'effective memory' [similar to method acting: interpreting a character via the actor attempting to place themselves, mentally, in a similar situation]. He developed the ability to focus on certain emotions, to call them up on cue. Patti, on the other hand, is simply a very strong personality who sets her sights on an emotion, and then just goes from there. She doesn't think about it. She just does it."

Goodwin once lunched with Lupone at The Mayflower in New York, shortly after she replaced actress Zoe Caldwell (who received the Tony) in the stage version of *Master Class*, about Maria Callas teaching a master class in music at Julliard. As Goodwin perceived it, stepping into that role would be a rather daunting challenge. When he met with Lupone, she was opening in the show within a month, getting fitted for wigs, and she did not appear the least bit nervous. *Naw*, she told Goodwin with a casual tone, *the only thing I'm concerned about is if the wig fits*. Either way, as Goodwin points out, Lupone "opened to rave reviews, and was a huge hit in the play."

The seat of Lupone's talent, however, could hardly be defined as relaxed, but rather intense. Her good friend and former *Life* co-star Kellie Martin helped define Patti's theatrical sense during an interview with *The New York Times* in 1994. She compared working with Lupone to Tyne Daly on the short-lived 1993-1994 CBS series, *Christy*. "They are both strong women but very different," Martin intoned. "Tyne is more motherly, but she throws curve balls at you, and she brings a real no-nonsense approach to [*Christy*], which is good because it could get sort of corny. Patti is in control of her emotions at all times."

Martin still keeps in touch with Lupone, whom she admiringly calls amazing. "Patti taught me so much," Kellie beams today. "She's a free-spirit. Gutsy and talented. I remember the first time I heard her voice when she sang 'The Wind Beneath My Wings' [in 'Break a Leg, Mom,' from *LGO's* first year]. It just blew me away. I was just a little thirteen-year-old girl from Los Angeles. I didn't know who Patti Lupone was. It's not like I was from New York, and I was familiar with Broadway. That wasn't the case. Patti essentially introduced the theatre to me. She would take me to see plays all the time. She instilled that love of the stage in me. I was really shocked when she told me she played Fantine in the London version of *Les Miserable*. At the time, that was the only stage play I had ever seen."

Approximately one year later, Lupone invited Martin to not only view a live performance of renowned Kenneth Branaugh and Emma Thompson in *A Midsummer Night's Dream*, but to meet the Shakespearean-trained duo, backstage, after the performance. "It's because of Patti and phenomenal experiences like that," Martin says, "that I enjoy going to theatre so much now."

One of Lupone's own remarkable moments was giving birth to her first child, Joshua Luke Johnson, with husband/cameraman Matt Johnson (whom she met while filming *LBJ: The Early Years* in 1987). "Everyone was shocked when we found that out," Martin reveals. "No one really knew if that was what she would have wanted, to be a mom. But she surprised us all. She became a terrific mother."

As Libby Thacher on *Life*, Lupone was also pretty terrific, and will most likely go down in small-screen history as the first major TV mom of the 1990s, a media matriarch who imparts compassion, honesty, stamina, guts and humor, in ways that not even the iconic Mrs. Brady or Mrs. Partridge ever could.

Like Kellie Martin, Chris Burke, another of Lupone's TV-children, enjoyed working with the Broadway diva when she sang "The Wind Beneath My Wings." Burke says he relished performing with her in every episode, because the actress would always make him laugh. "She has such a great sense of humor. She reminds me of Lucy Ricardo [Lucille Ball's classic on-screen persona from *I Love Lucy*]." At the same time, he adds, "She has her own sense of humor, and that made it easy to work with her."

From the writers' standpoint, "Patti was a joy to work with," says scribe Toni Graphia. "I think coming from her theatre background, she had a great respect for writing. Other actors would come whining into your office and want to change lines. Or worse, they'd jut improvise on the set and you'd watch dailies and freak out. But not with Patti. She stuck to the script. And when you watched her dailies, you realized her talent because she was able to put her own spin on something, without changing the dialogue. She could add a pause or a look or do something that you didn't even know was in those words, but she'd find it. That's the mark of a great actress."

A merry Lupone mood came into play on screen when, in the opening sequence for *LGO's* fourth-season segment "Armageddon," her Libby character ends up falling on her behind, while entering the Thacher home, via her return from work. Michael Lange directed the episode (one of which offered a happy balance to the show's dramatic edge], and says Lupone was "into physical comedy. She loved it."

According to Lange, "Patti is one of a kind. She's the greatest. She loved any chance to do something that was over the top. That was sort of a constant struggle with her throughout the series, where she should be with this top that she was never supposed to go over. That's why we all had so much fun with 'Armageddon,' because even though the underline theme [Drew and Libby argue] was played seriously, it was done in a very wacky way [comparing battling dinosaurs to Corky's parents]."

As to working with Lupone, in general, Lange says the actress is "a very volatile human being, who I personally adore." "If you are strong, inside," he goes on explain, "she's great to work with. If you are not strong, you are going to die. She's a very hard person. She's not particularly sentimental. She basically calls it the way she sees it, and she's so talented."

It was partially due to Lupone's staunch talents that Ray *Jerry* Buktenica considered working on *Life*. "I had an appointment to read for this new series," he recalls, "and the only thing I knew was that Patti Lupone was in it. I was very happy to hear that. I figured the show had to have something going for it, if she was involved. I knew it certainly wasn't going to be some fluffy, inconsequential turkey."

Had Lupone indeed envisioned *LGO* as such, she certainly would not have jumped at the chance to perform on it, leaving in its wake — if only for a brief time — her beloved association with live theatre. As she told *The Los Angeles Times* in 1997, she was most comfortable with stage-performing. "There is nothing like standing center stage in a darkened theatre," she said, "opening my mouth and letting it out."

As told by Rick Rosenthal, Patti is a spectacularly talented musical performer, whose singing on *Life Goes On* was "astounding." Yet her ability to listen and more subtle emotions "allowed us to peek inside of her soul." He goes on to classify Lupone's work on the show as "larger-than-life Libby outbursts of energy," calling her theatrics "a wonderful part of her spirit."

Still, like others who directed Lupone on *Life*, Rosenthal would frequently suggest a less-is-more style of acting. "There was a fine line between trying to keep her reined-in and allowing her the flamboyance that defines her, and makes her so appealing," he says. While Rosenthal believes Lupone had more fun playing Libby as bigger, displaying flashes of brilliance, he thinks that she never quite trusted how powerful, strong and gifted she was in her simplicity.

"Patti would always keep that in reserve," he details. "But when she allowed us to see that side of her talent — a style of acting that I just happen to prefer — and when we were on the same wavelength, I thought she was extraordinary." Overall, Rosenthal calls Lupone's Libby interpretation "an authentic mom who tried to hold the family together."

Certainly, Corky was affected by Libby's actions. But there would have been no Corky without Chris Burke.

The extraordinary Chris Burke played the extraordinary Corky Thacher.
CHRIS BURKE

Born on August 26, 1965, in New York City, Burke may never have played Corky had he not had faith in himself. His determination to succeed was rewarded. While appearing on *Life*, he wrote (with Joebeth McDaniel) a book on his life, *A Special Kind of Hero*. He's recorded children's tapes, *Lollipops and Love Songs*, and *Singer with the Band*, with good friends Joe and John DeMasi. Produced by Emmy Award-winning entertainer Fred Miller, the latter album is a compilation of fun and uplifting music for the entire family (and includes a rendition of "Ob La Di, Ob, La Da," the famous Beatles song which was employed as the *LGO* theme.)

Before *Life Goes On* he attended the Kennedy Study Center in New York, Cardinal Cushing Training School in Hanover, Massachusetts, and graduated from Don Guannell School, which is located in Springfield, Pennsylvania. Chris has also worked for the Board of Education in New York City as an elevator operator and as a teacher's aid to handicapped children. He enjoys all kinds of music, especially country music, and owns an impressive collection of CDs, tapes and records. He also enjoys swimming and watching television.

Chris Burke confirms, "I loved working on so much on *Life Goes On*, because I was happy that Corky was courageous." The actor goes on to refer to the first season segment, "Corky for President," in which the Thacher's middle child runs for a position on his high school's student council. He's ridiculed by his less-than-enlightened peer opponents and voters. Their behavior could almost be considered and accepted as regular, if not normal fodder for the allegedly more fully-healthy politicians on all levels of the ballot, in school or in the government. It's simply made more poignant on *LGO* by the fact that Corky has Down's.

Yet, Burke says, "It didn't really matter for Corky to win, just as long as he was in the race. Though he didn't like being made fun of, it took a lot of guts for him to be who he was. And I thought that was cool."

Life's Eric Welch, who played Brian Russo, the school bully and main nemesis for Corky in the early years, found some interesting challenges in working with Burke. "I'm usually pretty good with people with Down syndrome," he admits.

That's why he was somewhat dismayed when, around the third episode, Chris approached him and said, *I like you now, Eric. At first I didn't think you were a nice guy because of Brian Russo. But I know now that you really are a good guy, and that you're my friend.* Welch says this was "such a neat moment for me to see Chris make that realization. It's what made him so great on the show. He didn't see a big difference between the acting and real life. But when he realized that I wasn't Brian Russo, and that I was Eric Welch, it was really kind of a beautiful moment."

Life's Director of Photography Joe Pennella once told journalist Pauline Rogers what his view on Burke was for the September 1992 issue of

International Photographer. "Working with Chris Burke is a wonderful, but challenging experience," he bared. "It's amazing, the things they ask him to do — and what he can do. Each script he gets is a new and different challenge, and he accepts it."

Even Kellie Martin admitted to some initial apprehension in working with the actor. "I just had never met anyone with Down syndrome before," she once told a reporter. "I wondered who would want to watch a show about this week after week. But after we did the pilot, he's so warm and so compassionate, that it became just a family show, it wasn't a show about Chris who has Down syndrome, it became secondary, and you forget that he has Down syndrome. He's just Corky. He's just a guy, and he's warm and he's caring and he's loving. He can't do everything, but he's a really neat person."

Looking back today, Kellie says, "I was very nervous at first to work with Chris. I was even stupid enough to ask on my first day with him, *So is a boy with Down syndrome really playing Corky?* I didn't know anything." Meanwhile, too, she recalls, how Burke was frequently surprising her with his talent. "Some of my best work on the show was with Chris," she says, "because he is so honest in what he does and what he feels. There are no barriers. No walls for Chris Burke. What you see is what you get. He doesn't pretend anything. He speaks his lines with heart."

Off screen, Kellie believes Burke says what he thinks "everything that we all want to say." Like, once, after she opted for a new hairstyle. *Oh,* he told her, somewhat surprised. *You got your haircut. It'll grow back…Won't it?* "It's not like he wants to hurt your feelings," Martin cautions, "because that's the last thing he would ever want to do. He just has such a good heart that usually everything he says is taken well." And she would never change her four years in working with the actor. "He really changed a lot of people's lives," she determines. "He taught me so much about patience and understanding. I can't say enough nice things about Chris. He's one of a kind, and incredible. I just love him."

Tanya *Maxie* Fenmore concurs with Martin on Burke's personality. "It's easy to forget that he has Down syndrome," she says. "He's different from Corky, but he's also different than we are, even though that's hard to distinguish because he's such a wonderful guy. He made going to the set an incredible experience. I remember at one of the wrap parties, he was kind of flirting with all the women. Then I later saw him at a celebrity charity. He threw me on his lap, and said, *It's Maxie.*"

Though such a move may appear even more daring than something Burke's TV alter ego may have attempted, Fenmore thinks Corky was a very well-developed character. Partly, of course, due to the writers, but mostly because of the unselfish charm that Burke brought to the role — a real-life trait that was transferred to the screen- a natural outgrowth of his personality and of what he viewed as a personal responsibility with his position on the show. As he told *Ladies Home Journal* in 1990, "I have a motto. Think of others, then of yourself."

Compassion comes naturally to Chris, who was 24 years old when he started *Life*. Marion Burke and her husband, Frank, a former police captain, brought their son up among three loving siblings and taught him everything they could. Today, he continues to progress than most with Down syndrome: His health is good, and he reads well, as was clearly proven during *Life*. "It's amazing," his mother then told *Ladies Home Journal*. She marveled at her son's ability to work ten-to-fifteen-hour days and memorize up to forty pages of script a week. "Whoever thought that this could happen?"

Marion Burke points to two people who helped make that happen: Kali Hummel, Chris' dialogue coach, and John Lindsmire, a close friend. "These are two very important individuals who contributed to Chris' performance as Corky," Mrs. Burke sustains. She defines Hummel as "marvelous, wonderful, and super," and says the word instructor and her son "got along so well together, and he learned much as a result." Marion says Chris and Lindsmire, whom she calls fantastic, also hit it off well. "These two very special people," she upholds, "helped so much in the course of Chris' four-year relationship with *Life Goes On*."

Certainly another special relationship had been formed between Chris and a fellow *Life* mate: Chad Lowe. When Burke and Lowe appeared on-screen as Corky and Jesse it was like Superman meeting Captain Marvel. Off-screen, the connection was just as dynamic. Lowe explains, with a rude awakening: "I'm not the best in the morning. I have a real hard time in the makeup trailer when someone else is happy around me at 6:00 A.M. I used to walk in that trailer tired, exhausted, knowing that I had a lot of hard work ahead of me. Then I would see Chris there with this huge smile on his face, as though he had twelve hours of sleep with a full meal, knowing that he was just as tired as I was. But his spirits were always so high. It was always such an inspiration to work with him."

For Lowe, working with Burke was always extremely emotional. "I was always very aware of the *miracle of Chris Burke* as a human being," he says, "and the opportunity that he had to portray Corky on television. I was always aware of how extraordinary that was on all levels. Most importantly on the level that he himself was able to deliver with such honesty in such a difficult medium. Acting is not easy. It's the best when it looks easy, but that's usually when it's the hardest work. But I was always just in awe of Chris and his ability. There's a magic about being around him. And when the cameras were rolling, it was very moving, many times to get the chance just to work with him. A couple of times I found myself welled up in the eyes, off camera, just because I was watching Chris, and seeing the goodness of his heart, his soul. There's an innocence about everyone I've met with Down syndrome. And Chris is absolutely no exception. In fact, he's more."

"Chris Burke is a wonderful actor," adds *Life* actor Troy Evans. "I consider him to be a hero. Because acting is hard work. If it was easy, everyone would be an actor. Having done lengthy scenes with him, watching him force his mind to focus, making one hundred times the effort it required from the rest of us to do the same. But he would muster the power to do so, and to do so in good humor — and with generosity. He's terrific. He's not just a guy who had Down syndrome, and that's why he got the job. He is an actor. And he had a purpose in doing the show."

It's been more than a decade since *LGO* debuted, and Ray *Jerry* Buktenica believes people don't raise their eyebrows at those with Down's — due to Chris. Before the series aired, there was talk about how people would not want to watch a show about a kid with Down's. *They won't want to deal with it. It's too disturbing.* Now, Buktenica says the attitude has been altered tremendously, because Burke has since "changed the perception of millions and millions of people all over the world," by simply playing himself. "He's obviously one of the more high-achieving people with Down's that there ever was. That aside, he did it. He did a hundred episodes or so. He was there every day."

Yet what bothers Buktenica from time to time, is when he hears criticisms about Burke's performance, how *he's just a kid with Down syndrome playing a kid with Down syndrome.* "That really raises my hackles," Ray reveals. "If you're a paraplegic and you play a paraplegic, does that make you not an actor? If Harrison Ford got a job as a carpenter, he is not an actor now because he once really was a carpenter? Of course not. Chris was acting on the show...and he got better. He's the kind of [actor] who watches and learns."

Buktenica remembers his initial impression of Chris, and it's worthy of commentary. On Ray's first day on the set, he looked at Burke and said to himself, *Well...what's the story here? Is this history-in-the-making or what?* Then he saw Chris drop a line, become somewhat tense, and walk off the set. Upon Burke's return, he finished playing the scene, after which he did one of those "victory punches to the air," and was real happy with himself.

"I saw him as an actor who dropped a line," Ray assesses. "Not as a person with Down syndrome trying to be actor [who dropped a line]. But as an actor, equal to any one of us on the set. That's the impression he presented. I mean, I drop lines all the time. Everybody drops lines. That's the way it is. That's a built-in part of being an actor. Those are the things that happen to everyone, not just those who happened to be challenged with some disability. So all I have is praise for Chris Burke. He isn't some former football quarterback who moved into acting because he was in the public eye. That's not the case here. That kind of thing can be done, obviously, and it happens all the time. But Chris is an actor first — an actor with obvious limitations, but everyone has limitations. He just happened to be a kid who went after what he wanted, and was fortunate enough to be placed in a position where his dream came true. He was up to the test. He's still doing it. The kid is working more than me. The kid is an actor."

Burke keeps surprising people with his talents. He frequently travels, for one — minus his Mom and Dad — with the Debasi Brothers musical group. Bob Goodwin, *Life Goes On's* co-executive producer, periodically sees Burke and, as he claims, up through *LGO*, Chris had only spent one night without his parents. "He really had a tough time," Goodwin recalls. "But now, the last time I saw him, he just had lunch, upon arriving from New Zealand, and he was leaving that night to go to Dallas."

Bill Smitrovich sums it all up with his favorite way of describing Burke: "When Chris started out, he was a kid with Down syndrome who wanted to be an actor. By the fourth year he was an actor who just happened to have Down syndrome. And if anyone says that they came up with that quote, I'll sue." [It's too late, similar commentary runs rampant throughout this book.]. "But, seriously, he was able to make distinctions and get some separation, and it just took him a little longer, and you never know how much you're gonna get, but whatever it is that he delivers will be his best effort, every time. And it gets better."

In discussing Kellie Martin's theatrical abilities, *LGO* writer Thania St. John was once quite direct and clear with a reporter. "Kellie Martin," she said, "is a very special actor. She has quality about her that not very many others have. She can really take you into places and make you feel things that a lot of actors can't do. She has this idealism, and compassion and energy. And all of those traits combined lent itself to this situation. You can see things through her eyes. When she's listening to someone, you can see what she's thinking and hearing and feeling...She's very intense, very dramatic."

In playing younger sister to Chris Burke's Corky throughout *Life's* four-year span, Martin was essentially raised into adulthood. Upon first interpreting Becca, she portrayed a smart-mouthed, acrimonious, lanky little teenage girl with ruby-rimmed glasses (which the actress still has, along with several other *Life* mementos).

Becca was frequently ashamed of Corky, spat caustic remarks, and was restless with her journey into puberty. (As previously addressed, during the show's first-season opening-credit sequences, she would stare in her bedroom mirror, offer a quick gaze toward her bustless form, and groan, "Come on, where are you guys already?") Later, as Martin matured, so did her interpretation of Becca, who began to emote the joys and serious philosophies of a confident young lady, while attempting to comprehend the pangs of being a high-school student who loved so deeply her boyfriend with AIDS.

"It's funny," she says. "I'm either mature, or very, very immature. So it's like I'm 12 or 40. It's like I love to watch Saturday morning cartoons, and I still sleep with a teddy bear."

Martin's talent, however, was far from fuzzy from the start. Her star appeal was luminous, and did not go unnoticed. An early *Variety* review of the *LGO* pilot said of the actress, "Her acerbic outbursts give the show its only bite," while John Leonard of *New York* magazine named her "a wonderful, bespectacled bundle of internal contradictions, of pubescent seething."

Yet, as Kellie admitted to *The Hollywood Reporter* in 1989, when she was

Kellie Martin played Rebecca Becca Thacher, older sister to Chris Burke's Corky and first love to Chad Lowe's Jesse. *KELLIE MARTIN*

only 14, acting is not all fun and games; balancing work, school and personal time in real life can be a demanding task. And she didn't believe that her life as a young actress was more stressful than being a "regular kid." "I think everybody has to deal with pressure," she said. "If I wasn't on the set and I was in school, I'd have to deal with the pressure of teachers and classes."

As to how she would define Becca now, she says: "Becca changed a lot. She started out as this precocious, insecure, adolescent girl who loved and appreciated her family very much. But at the same time was completely embarrassed by her family. So I think they allowed Becca to change. As I changed, Becca changed. Becca and I are so much alike in so many ways, except that Becca was always a step ahead of me. Like she experienced everything before I did.

"The first season, she was very sassy, and then she started to grow up. I think her relationship with her father was really important. She was daddy's little girl. That was a very outstanding relationship to me. And she, of course, had this big crush on Tyler, and was all ga-ga over him."

Still, upon Jesse's arrival, Becca started to grow up. "Her relationship with him completely changed her life, and her outlook on life," Martin says. "And I think it also put a damper on her. Life became so much more meaningful and so much more precious to her. She just became much more mature and wise. She realized what she had with Jesse, and she knew that it was going to be very transient, and a very short of amount of time that she would have with him. I think she just became much more aware of what she wanted in life." Or, as Becca once said to Jesse at one of their first meetings: "I was a little girl when you met me, and you made me care about what really matters."

As to the initial atmosphere on *Life Goes On*, Martin once she said: "It's a very calm set and they don't put pressure on us. We're not pressured to say our lines perfectly every time and to know the scenes perfectly because in rehearsal we learn the flow. I don't feel that it's a great deal of pressure, except sometimes when I do a big scene. I think I'm harder on myself than anybody. Sometimes it's good pressure and sometimes it gets a little too much."

Rick Rosenthal, one of Kellie's earliest supporters, believed the performer to be "incredibly intuitive for a teenager. She was easy to direct. Such a professional. That compensated for some of the problems that Chris would have with lines. She'll tell me to this day that there were three lines in the course of two years that she felt she never quite gave the right meaning to. But through the early years, I saw her natural talent, and thought she was the show's secret weapon. Ironically, she really came through after I left the series."

"Kellie really is good," adds *Life* fellow cast mate Dorothy Lyman. "For a young woman to be that savvy about acting is really terrifically encouraging to see." Michael Braverman agrees with Rosenthal and Lyman, with one exception: "Kellie was absolutely wonderful on the show," he clarifies. "But there was one thing that she couldn't do...sing. Not a note. Couldn't carry a tune in a wheel barrel," he laughs. (Becca's insecurity about her singing voice was at the center of the second season episode, "Becca and the Band.")

Aside from her lack of vocal talents, in 1993 Martin received the first American Television Award for Best Supporting Actress in a Drama Series, and certainly made her mark as Becca. Though the character was at first overly self-conscious about going to school with her brother, she would always defend him. Though she may have mistreated Tyler near the end of his life, she loved Jesse despite his affliction, and not out of sympathy.

As the actress once revealed to *USA Today*, filming the AIDS episodes were the hardest scenes she had ever performed. "They made me dig down deep," she explained. "I didn't have a lot of life experience to draw from at 17. It wasn't easy, but it was quite a challenge." Doing the scenes taught her that AIDS is "one of the scariest things in life, and how important it is to be there to offer support." And as she once told *Teen Beat* magazine, "Becca is so challenging. All the AIDS storylines are challenging and heavy — it hurts me sometimes because I read the script and I cry, it's so heavy and emotional. But it's good for me. I would rather be challenged, but it is hard, day in day out, to play a character who's plagued with this sort of situation."

Monique Lanier played the first Paige. *THE REGAL COLLECTION*

Tanya Fenmore became a close friend to Martin during *Life's* run, and the two remain pals today. She remembers Martin's melancholy when the series ended: "Kellie had a real adjustment to make because, for her, *Life Goes On* was her family. She used to say that the show was her home away from home. I remember how very difficult it was for her when it was cancelled. She was not used to not going to her *Life Goes On* family."

Being an integral part of *Life* certainly granted Martin a variety of experiences that would have bonded anyone to any family within a four-year period. "It's the only show," she says, "where you could graduate, get married, have a baby [in a fantasy sequence], become a widow, then get married again, and have another child [in the fourth season]."

At the same time, the series influenced many perceptions in her real life. "All of my college essays were written about AIDS and education," she reveals. "I also wrote about Chris Burke, and what I learned from him. So the show certainly taught me a lot, and changed my life completely. My life would be totally different had I not worked on *Life Goes On*. I would be a different person. I'm glad I'm not that person because I like the person I am. *Life Goes On* has a lot to do with that. All the people I met. All the people I worked with. All the scenes I did, and the feelings I felt, which I would not have normally experienced.

"I never had a relationship with someone who has AIDS, like Becca had with Jesse," she continues. "So I may never know what that feels like, or what Becca went through. But I played a character that had a boyfriend who was dying from AIDS for two years, and I probably won't ever feel that, except when I was working on the show. I don't know what it feels like to have a brother with Down syndrome, but I worked with Chris, and played a character that did, for four years. So it changed my life and made me feel things that I would have never felt, and I'm very grateful to the people who hired me, first of all, and allowed me that experience."

Others who were party to *Life's* fictional lineage on screen and who enjoyed the family atmosphere the show encouraged behind the scenes, included Monique Lanier and Tracey Needham, both of whom shared the role of Paige, Becca and Corky's stepsister, via Drew's first marriage.

As established, Monique Lanier was new to television acting when she began *Life*. She was a conservative young woman who was raised a Mormon in Utah. Tanya Fenmore recalls Lanier as a free spirit, like Paige, but even more so. "She and her boyfriend had Japanese love letters," Fenmore says, "and she showed us tattoos." And apparently, Lanier's decision to leave *Life* came out of nowhere. "I heard that she simply did not want to do it anymore," Fenmore reveals. "She chose the life of Salt Lake City, instead of life on Burbank lot."

Had Monique stayed with *Life* — and her career as an actress in Los Angeles — casting director Dee Dee Bradley believes "she would have been a big, big star by now." Bradley, who remains in contact with Monique, had brought the actress back out to L.A. in 1995 to co-star in a TV film with Ann Jillian. The two had not seen one another for a long time, when Bradley began casting for the movie. "Just as when we were casting for Paige," Bradley recalls, "it seemed like we auditioned every young actress in the whole world to play Ann Jillian's daughter." The television motion picture was originally scheduled to shoot in Canada but, by a fluke, it was decided to film it in Utah — Lanier's home state.

Listen, Bradley said to the movie's producer, *this may look like a long shot, and I haven't seen this girl in years, but look up Monique Lanier when you're in Utah.* The producer did so, and he called Bradley, impressed with what he

Tracey Needham played the second Paige. *THE REGAL COLLECTION*

saw. *Dee Dee,* he said, *she's magnificent.* "To quote him exactly, Bradley clarifies, "he said, *She's a f . . .in' star.*"

Consequently, Lanier got to play Ann Jillian's daughter, years after portraying Drew's on *Life.* She moved back to L.A. and renewed her friendship with Bradley. "She actually ended up staying with me for a while and tried to pursue her career," Dee Dee recalls. "The problem was, she had a child who had a severe breathing difficulty, and who couldn't live in Los Angeles because of the bad air-quality. So she only ended up staying in town for six weeks. Today, she's studying to be a nurse, going to college in Utah."

Lanier's story is unique, to say the least. Thousands of young performers journey to Los Angeles and struggle for years to become, if not stars, merely working actors. And Lanier just walked away from the bright lights. Not once, but twice, though for very personal reasons. "Stardom was handed to her many times," Bradley admits. "But she was never able to do it. Then at one point, she finally decided it was what she wanted to do, for the sake of her child. She needed money. But when she seriously tried to pursue it, nothing happened, because she was only out here [L.A.] for a very short time. She had to go back. Her little girl missed her, and that was that. Now she's leading a real non-Hollywood life, and she's very happy about it."

Into Paige's shoes stepped Tracey Needham, who describes Drew's daughter as confused. "She originally started as a hippie of the "90s," Needham says, "and then she just sort of became a lost soul. But she was a sweet character who was always trying to do the right thing." At the same time, Paige would take on these very strong employment positions. "And that was great for me," Needham adds, "because I felt lucky that I had the chance to play a non-traditional woman's role, like being a pipe-fitter. And she dealt with a lot of serious issues [as with attempted date rape in 'The Whole Truth']."

An international model at the age of 17, Needham gained the backbone to interpret such topics, via her independent travels through Europe immediately following high school graduation. "It was good for me," she says of modeling, "because I was very shy. At the same time, it was hard. It's not an easy job. It's a boring job. The people that you work for are not always the nicest, kindest people in the world. It's not really a good job for your self-esteem. So it took me a long time to sort of recover from that. On the flip side, I got to see the world, which was a great education. And when I moved to LA to become an actress, I didn't have to wait tables. I would just go to catalogue work for a week, and I'd be set for a month or two."

Though she never actually waited tables, as did Paige at Drew's restaurant, Needham was a hostess in a restaurant, while attending high school. "And it was a disaster," she says. "I cost the restaurant a lot of money, because I was always knocking things over."

Like so many of the *Life* cast, Needham has evidently retained a down-to-earth personality. She credits this balanced perception to having "a really good family, and a fantastic upbringing." As she goes on to explain: "I got lucky in that department. I just see acting for what it is: a great job. I love what I do. I have a good time." Echoing Bill Smitrovich's previously-related sentiments on star-treatment, Tracey says she enjoys all those with whom she works on a set: "I know that when someone brings me a glass of water, it's not because I'm more special than anyone else who works on the show. It's because they don't want me to leave the set. Or they want me to stay cool, and be comfortable so I'm not sweating during the scene. It usually has nothing to do with who I am as a person. Or what my standing is on the set. I appreciate that glass of water, and I also know that it just becomes a part of the job. But I never see the situation as if I'm some goddess, who needs to be treated in a certain way."

Needham's experience as Paige was of an academic nature. She had performed in a few small roles before *Life Goes On*. But playing Paige was her first big part and, as she says, "The show was certainly an amazing place to get an education. It made such a difference, career-wise, for me because I had such a great foundation in working with people like Patti and Bill. And the writers were brilliant. It was simply a very special, special time in my life."

Producer Rick Rosenthal liked Tracey as Paige, and thinks she had a natural ability to act. "She grew on you," he says, "and added a lot to show. You had more of a sense of [the Paige character], from episode to episode. Tracey became a little bit like a really strong pinch-hitter on a bench, someone you could count on to come in to spruce things up."

In comparing Needham's Paige performance to Monique Lanier's, Rosenthal's colleague Michael Braverman refers back to the maturity process of the show. "Paige matured over the years," he says. "When you have as many talented writers creating episodes as we did, they tend to write more scenes for more accomplished actresses and actors. It's just because they knew that they are going to get what they want. This is very selfish perspective coming from the point of view of a writer, but the fact of the matter is: Tracey was able to bring a lot more to the table than Monique, who was rather new at the game."

"Tracey had a really hard job when she stepped in the role," admits Kellie Martin. "She had to fill Monique's shoes. Everyone was sitting back, looking at her, and watching every move she made. She knew that she had a difficult challenge ahead of her, because people grew to love the Paige character with Monique. But I commend Tracey for her work. By about her fourth or fifth episode, she was able to do more what she wanted to do with the part, and the writers adapted the character more toward who Tracey was. Because she was just kind of filling in Paige's shoes, in the beginning. They could have just said, *Paige moved to Spain or whatever*. And I don't think they ever found out exactly what they wanted to do with Paige. They had her in so many different places."

"They were both wonderful actresses, and certainly two different people," says Bill Smitrovich, of Lanier and Needham. "Monique had other things that she wanted to do. She's a little bit strong-willed. She's got a lot of talent, and she wasn't ready for the experience of being on the show. Or the experience wasn't ready for her. She's a wonderfully, natural talented actress. As is

Tracey, who I think has more range. And I think, too, given the opportunity, she can really display qualities of a very fine actress."

Next in line to the Thacher family in regular appearances on *Life Goes On* was Tommy Puett, who played Tyler Benchfield, Becca's first love. When Puett auditioned for the role, however, his appearance was originally envisioned solely for the pilot. "It was a really small part; only a couple of lines,

Teen sensation Tommy Puett portrayed Tyler Benchfield, Becca's big crush.
TOMMY PUETT

as Tyler was never intended as a series regular. But he rated highly with test audiences, so we ended up adding him as a regular," explains casting director Dee Dee Bradley.

In defining Tyler, Puett says his TV persona embellishes "the boy that you always want your daughter to come home with. He was respectable, and he didn't really have a shady side. As a young parent, I can understand

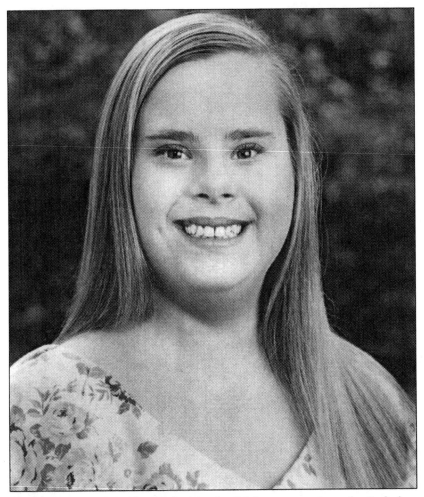

Andrea Friedman joined *LGO's* cast in the third season as Amanda, Corky's girlfriend-turned-wife. *ANDREA FRIEDMAN*

what my mom and dad went through when my sister was 16 years old. She was once dating a guy that we were not too hip on. I can safely say that if someone like Tyler had walked in the door with my sister, my mom and dad would have been like, *Oh, what a nice young man.* He was always like *Hi, Mr.*

and Mrs. Thacher. He didn't have anything to hide.

"He was into school, he struggled with it, but he was into it. He was into sports, and he was always there for everyone, right off the bat. He set everyone aside; all his jock buddies and took Corky under his wing. And then later, we learn that he has a brother who has Down syndrome. And of course that angle allowed him to be more respectable and understanding of Becca's situation with Corky. And I also think that it endeared him to Drew and Libby."

It took little effort for Andrea Friedman to endear herself as Amanda, Corky's girlfriend-turned-wife, on *Life Goes On.* For her ability to understand and express her feelings was in large part responsible for her winning the part, and that charm just carried over on to the screen.

Friedman was invited, along with other young people with Down syndrome, to suggest story ideas for the show to the producers and writers. Her idea was that Corky needed a girlfriend, just like other young men his age. Andrea's concept was selected as part of the show's permanent storyline. She auditioned for the part with a group of other young actresses and was chosen to play the part she suggested. She became a permanent member of the cast for two seasons.

Andrea's greatest challenge was not acting, which came naturally to her. It was learning to drive, which became part of the storyline related to Amanda on *Life Goes On.* It took her two years of practice before she received her license on June 14, 1989. (Her father claims she is now one of the best drivers in Los Angeles.)

On playing Amanda who faced much discrimination on *Life*, Andrea drew from her real-life experiences to perform the character. For example, she was faced with prejudice when she entered University Elementary School at UCLA in 1974. Andrea's younger sister Katherine also attended University Elementary School. As she recalls, "I often had to deflect the cruel remarks and torments that were hurled toward Andrea in the school yard... Andrea would become upset briefly, and then collect herself and continue with her activities; but I still flinch from the memory of many of these incidents."

"She's a great gal," says Bill Smitrovich of Andrea. "She's wonderful. I went to go and see her movie, *Smudge*, and she's very good in that, as well. And there was a moment when she was at the podium at the premiere, and she introduced me in the audience, which I thought was very sweet."

Last, but certainly not least, on the list of regular actors on *Life Goes On* is Chad Lowe who, of course, played Jesse McKenna.

Brother to movie heartthrob Rob Lowe, Chad started working at a very young age, appearing some years before *Life* in his own sitcom, *Spencer* (NBC, 1984-1985), which centered around the adventures of young, libidinous teen in junior high (almost a seemingly early carefree version of McKenna?). Yet when Chad was all of 16, he quit the show after only six episodes, because, he said, "it had lost its responsibility to be tasteful to a young audience."

Shortly before Lowe won the McKenna part, his manager, Tim Woods, died of complications from AIDS. "I remember going to the hospital nurses' station and having them point out his room," the actor told *People*, "and seeing that big orange sticker on the door. It warned against coming in contact

Chad Lowe played Jesse McKenna with Emmy-winning skill. *CHAD LOWE*

with [his] blood. My heart just stopped, and I got a big lump in my throat. I walked in, and he was all smiles. He confronted AIDS. It's such a painful memory — and he was with me from the beginning."

Today, Lowe says, Woods was sick for approximately one year. And when Wood revealed to Lowe that he AIDS, Lowe was angry, frustrated and sad. "I knew he was HIV-positive," the actor says, "but when it had developed into full-blown AIDS, I remember feeling helpless, watching someone that I loved dearly, suffer, and knowing that there was no cure, that his death was eminent, months away or a year. But not much more than that."

With *Life Goes On*, that responsibility increased tremendously. Lowe found himself in the midst of portraying one of the most ineffable characters in the history of television entertainment. In 1993, a reporter asked Lowe what if, like Jesse, he found out he could die prematurely. "I'd be sorry for not having found that special someone," Lowe replied. "I'd be sorry for not having children. But I would also know that I've done everything I've ever dreamed of doing. I know how important my life, or someone like Jesse's life, is."

Lowe went into *Life* with a completely open mind and yet also with a touch of skepticism. He felt the evolution of Jesse was "very complete, very factual, very realistic," so much so, that in his first season on *Life*, he was granted the opportunity to show the pain, the suffering, and the feeling of injustice that one would feel with the diagnosis of being HIV-positive, the helplessness which was with Lowe on a personal level because of his relationship with his manager. "Then to internalize this," he says, "to imagine, *What if this had been me? What if this was me? How angry would I be?* I really don't think there is a way to express the anger, but you do the best you can. And with Jesse, we were given the forum to explore that anger."

At the end of his first year with the show, which was actually *Life's* third semester, Lowe did not know whether or not the series would be renewed. "So I wished and prayed," he says, "that we would be in order to further explore the other sides of Jesse. In reality, there are moments of joy and laughter walking hand-in-hand with pain, sorrow and suffering. And I was hopeful that we be renewed for another year so that we could explore these other facets of Jesse's personality."

That's quite a transition from the person who went in and met with the producers the year before, feeling somewhat anxious about not wanting to commit to a television series for more than eight episodes. Here he was at the end, thinking, "Please, God, there's so much more to say as this character." Lowe now felt an enormous responsibility to not just leave Jesse where we found him at the end of the third season — bidding his mother goodbye to stay with Becca. "There was a lot more educating to do," Lowe reveals, "as well as, of course, entertaining. Because let's face it, entertainment is what it's all about."

"Chad Lowe," concludes Troy Evans, "is as generous a gentleman as you'll ever meet, and a wonderful actor, and charming and fun to be around. And I was extremely glad to work with him. I thought he was miraculously effective in portraying Jesse. I obviously knew that it was fiction, but charisma was astounding. When I would watch him work, or when I saw him in his makeup when Jesse was beaten ["Incident on Main"], my heart would ache. I felt as if he was a member of my family."

As to working with all the central stars of the *Life Goes On* family, actor Charles Frank, who played Jack Benchfield, Tyler's somewhat estranged father, says: "They were all wonderful. Bill is a close friend. Patti has been a friend ever since we did *LBJ* together years ago. Tommy's wonderful. Kellie is one of the best young actresses that I've ever seen. She has an incredible talent at her beck and call. And she should have won that Emmy. She deserved it."

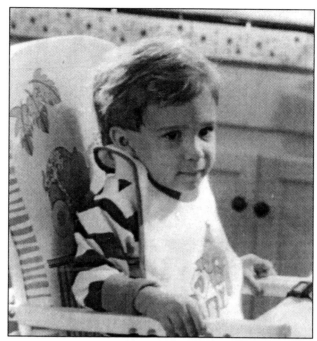

Twins Kevin and Christopher Graves shared the role of baby Nick Thacher.
THE REGAL COLLECTION

Arnold, the dog, played by Bullet, the dog in real life, was an intricate part of Corky's *Life*. *THE REGAL COLLECTION*

Al Ruscio played Libby's Italian-American father, Sal Giordano. *AL RUSCIO*

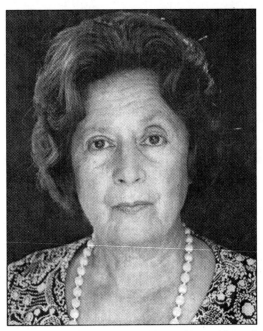

Penny Santon portrayed Libby's strong-willed, old-world mother Teresa Giordano. *PENNY SANTON*

CHAPTER 11

STRONG *LIFE* SUPPORT GROUP

"It was a throwaway. But when he delivered it, it became the funniest line I ever wrote. Not only that, but you could just smell that bread when he said it."
— Michael Nankin, (on Al Ruscio's interpretation of Sal Giordano's line, "My Godfather, your Uncle Vincent … taught me how to make bread.")

A solid cast of supporting and semi-regular performers appeared on *Life Goes On* in the guise of the Thacher's extended family, friends, love interests, work associates and passers-by. Like the show's main characters, these were real people, depicted with credence, by a cast of thespian professionals.

Penny Santon and Al Ruscio played Mr. and Mrs. Giordano, Libby's old-world mother and father; Mary Page Keller was Gina Giordano, Libby's moody sister; Leigh Ann Orsi was Zoe, Gina's precocious ten-year-old-daughter; Dorothy Lyman portrayed Mary McKenna, Jesse's heart-wrenched mother; Tanya Fenmore offered a lively Maxi, Becca's first best friend; Michael Goorjian presented a balanced blend of bluntness and benevolence with Ray Nelson, Jesse's good pal (who ended up falling for Becca).

Other recurring characters included Ray Buktenica's Jerry Berkson, Libby's selfish-turned-generous employer; David Byrd as Hans, the sardonic Swedish cook at Drew's restaurant; Gina Hecht as timid cousin Angela; Barney Martin as Stan Baker, Corky's fatherly manager at the theatre; Martin Milner as Harris Cassidy, Becca's eccentric bookstore boss; a plethora of Paige's beaus variedly played by Steven Eckholtd (Kenny Stollmark, Jr.), Lance Guest (Michael Romanov) and Troy Evans (Artie McDonald); a surplus of Becca and Corky's high-strung, high-school pals brought to earnest by Michelle Matheson (Rona Liberman), Eric Welch (Brian Russo), Kiersten Warren (Goodman), and many more.

Each gave their all, working diligently, in a series that they not only believed in, but enjoyed performing on, sometimes for a modest pay.

While series regulars earn whatever their agents are able to negotiate (anywhere from $5,000 to $50,000 a week, or sometimes, $100,000 to

$600,000 to $1 million — as was the case with *Seinfeld* and *Mad About You*), *LGO's* semi-regulars or guest stars established an industry figure called "top of the show." "Normally," Troy Evans explains, "that's around $3,000 an appearance. When the actor is first hired, that's the top amount of his or her negotiation. They say, *Okay... you're hired as a guest star. You get top of the show.* No one gets over that, unless maybe if it's a Bette Davis or someone of that stature. Then they do what they call 'breaking top of the show.'"

For example, an actress such as Donna Hansen, who initially interpreted Libby's mother in "The Pilot," received a regular top of the show payment of $3,000 for what ultimately became a one-time performance. Penny Santon stepped in Hansen's shoes for future episodes, for the same amount of money.

The Hansen/Santon exchange, in fact, was *Life's* only altered-casting of the same character that transpired besides Monique Lanier and Tracey Needham's turning of the Paige character. When Hansen played Libby's mom, the character was without a name (not even Libby's maiden name was known at the time). "Donna did not seem like a good fit," says Michael Braverman. The actress was simply not right for the part. She appeared too all-American and white-bread. Libby is an Italian character. Her mama obviously needed to be as well. Santon was more suited to playing Libby's forbear. When the veteran stage actress, who's made hundreds of guest TV appearances and commercial shots, joined the series in "Corky's Crush" (from the first season), the character was finally given a name, Teresa Giordano, and a spouse in the guise of Al Ruscio's Sal.

Teresa and Sal were in frequent conflict and, though Libby's mom was now more well defined, Santon did not like at all what they did with the part, or how they treated the character. "They made her quarrel with her husband," she says, "and not be empathetic toward her daughter. I can understand her being hurt and disappointed, yes, but not in the way it was written," she says.

Santon refers specifically to an *I love you scene* with Ruscio (from "Crush"), for which she had in mind a vastly different ending. She wanted to break down in tears of joy. Apparently, there was a note after the line in the script instructing her to do so, operatic-like, but in control, and Santon was prepared to exhibit that. But director Gene Reynolds had a different vision. "He just wanted me to smile," she says. "So the scene was changed at the last minute."

There were, however, instances when the actress and the character saw to eye-to-eye. Santon thought, for example, that many on-screen sequences with Patti Lupone worked well, particularly a charming moment in the kitchen, again from "Crush," when Mrs. Giordano tells Libby about never hearing that "love" phrase from husband Sal. "Those scenes went off so well, so fast," Santon intones. "When a scene is written well like that, and I am given a certain amount of freedom, as to how to interpret it — and when you're working with so wonderful a performer as Patti — there are no obstacles. Everything works perfectly." And with the "Crush"-kitchen scene, there was no need to over-rehearse. "It was written, we filmed it, and it was done," Santon says. "Sometimes it's difficult to capture chemistry, but with Patti that was never a problem, or Kellie or Al [Ruscio], for that matter. With Patti, too, many people thought that physically, there was a great resemblance between she and myself."

"I must be doing something right," she concludes, "because wherever I go, whether I am in small or large groups, people remember me from *Life Goes On.*"

As Penny Santon's partner in *Life*, Al Ruscio presented a flawless portrayal of Libby's father in the image of Sal Giordano. Like Santon and Ann Hansen, Ruscio was in competition with another actor for the role of one of Libby's parents. "My understanding was that they had someone else in mind for the part," he recalls. "I auditioned at Warner Bros. with Penny, and used an Italian accent. It was a scene with Corky, where Sal had to tell him about life, how you have to be strong."

For the audition, Ruscio mimicked the accent of his real-life grandfather, Steven Colletti, whom he believed was quite similar to the Sal character. Yet when director Gene Reynolds heard the inflection, he responded with, *Gee, that was great, Al. But we would like to do it without the accent. Though keep the feeling.* So Al did it Gene's way and, as the actor summarizes, "I was hired, and they went on to write some very wonderful scenes for me."

Some that stand out include sequences from "Corky's Crush," the segment to which Penny Santon referenced earlier. "That was the first episode I did," Al details. For the now famous *I love you* scene between Sal and Teresa, Ruscio remembered that his own grandfather never professed his amour to his "nonna":

"They had ten children, and he was a very poor man. He made his own wine in the basement. Many of my early memories consist of going down in that basement and having a glass of 'vino' with him. Those are special memories. But I never heard him say *I love you* to my grandmother. It was very hard for him. He did things, and he would say, *You'll know how I feel by my actions, not my words.*

"But he never said *I love you*, because that was just a little bit too sentimental for him." Flash forward a few decades, to *LGO* — for "Corky's Crush," when Sal had trouble saying *I love you* to Teresa — Ruscio was able to identify with that. He employed his personal life as motivation for his character's interpretation, once again splicing *LGO's* real-to-reel worlds. [Teresa, however, was unimpressed with Sal's initial profession. First he said, *Ti amo*, which is *I love you* in Italian. But that wasn't enough. She wanted to hear it in English, and Sal finally complied.]

Another special *Life* juncture for Ruscio transpired in "Happy Holidays," a Christmas memory from the fourth year, when Sal dreams about a real Christmas tree. At one point, Ruscio explains, a tree appears in the backyard, and Sal looks up to heaven like it came from God. "That was very touching for me to play" — one of several satisfying *Life* moments for the actor, who says he spent four wonderful years on the series.

Mary Page Keller was Libby's younger sister Gina Giordano in many appearances during the first few seasons of *Life*. MARY PAGE KELLER

Shortly after *LGO*, Al Ruscio portrayed Frank Rossi on the short-lived ABC sitcom *Joe's Life*. Rossi was a father to a character played by Peter Onorato, who was married to another character interpreted by none other than *Life's* very own Mary Page Keller. Consequently, Keller was Ruscio's daughter in one television show, and his daughter-in-law in another.

Keller came to *LGO*, due to a couple of pregnancies; one, behind-the-cameras, with Patti Lupone, and the other, on-screen, with Libby Thacher. Patti and Libby's airtime became limited, a gap needed to be filled, and Keller fit the bill. The result: a theatrical contribution that is hard to forget. As Libby's moody sister Gina, Keller electrified the screen with a substantial amount of charisma, and interpreted a complex character that struggled with many challenges of her own.

Leigh Ann Orsi, here with Chris Burke, played Zoe, daughter to Gina, and niece to Libby. *FRANK AND MARIAN BURKE*

Gina Giordano was a financially-strapped, emotionally-worn single mom. She moved into the Thacher home with daughter Zoe, and it was supposed to be profitable for all of those concerned. But everyone in the home was at a loss. Gina did not get along with Drew, and Becca became jealous of Drew's attention to Zoe. When Grandma and Grandpa Giordano paid visits, the tension increased. Gina also did not see eye-to-eye with her mother, Teresa, who, as previously addressed, had issues with the way Zoe was being raised.

Through it all, Keller's rendition of Gina was consistently inconsistent, and offered a savory blend of biting sarcasm, compassion, credibility and appeal. "I liked Mary Page tremendously," assesses Rick Rosenthal. "She's a talented actress. She's got very interesting looks. She's extremely attractive, and she can hide her looks behind some very interesting body language. Unfortunately," he adds, "she's been relegated to sitcoms [namely, the WB's late *Zoe, Duncan, Jack & Jane*, ironically playing another Zoe's mom], which is too bad because she could go all the way, and become a movie star."

"Mary Page basically just came in and read for the show, was great, and got the part," gleams casting director Dee Dee Bradley. "Same thing with Leigh Ann Orsi. Michael Braverman just loved them both, especially Leigh Ann."

One of the Orsi's most appealing traits, in particular, Bradley says, was her real honest-to-goodness little girl personality. "During her audition," Dee Dee recalls, "she was fidgeting in her chair. Slouching. Playing with

Ray Buktenica was Libby's self-absorbed ad-man boss Jerry Berkson in *Life*'s initial three semesters. *RAY BUKTENICA*

her hair. Doing all the little-girl-things that most child actresses don't do. She was not affected in the least. There wasn't any of that, *Oh-it's-so- nice-to- meet-you* type of conversation. Or *I-look-forward-to-working-with-you* stuff. No. Leigh Ann just came in and she was *a* kid. She really listened when you talked to her. She reacted and acted like a real little girl. She dressed like a little girl, and behaved like a little girl. That's why she got the part. She was very natural, and very real."

The additional group of actors who left early on, but whom the *LGO* producers would have preferred to retain, included Ray Buktenica, who played Jerry Berkson. Rick Rosenthal, for one, "so loved the stuff we did with Jerry." As Rick goes on to say, Jerry was "a wonderful character, and Ray was terrific in the part. He has the ability to be comedic and real at the same time." Referring to an aforementioned Jerry-moment, Rick says, "There's one scene when Libby comes into Jerry's office, and he's got scotch tape on his fingers. Jerry's in trouble, and Ray is completely in the moment. His character was a very funny guy, who retained certain ethnic qualities, though we could never quite decide if he was Jewish or Italian, or what his story was." [It was later decided that he was Jewish.]

Still, as Braverman had believed, the *Life* audience had come to expect certain behaviors from the show's characters, and Jerry was no exception. "Every time we went to the advertising agency," he states, "there were specific expectations about what Ray Buktenica was going to do as Jerry Berkson. The audience was very comfortable with him. They liked seeing him, and what a goof he was. Though we redeemed him several times."

Buktenica also proved himself worthy from the onset, when he auditioned for the Jerry role. "I got the part, and I was very happy to get it," he admits. "I went in there with a lot of energy." Later, when he went to shoot his first episode, Ray had discovered some alterations. "The script had actually changed quite a bit from what I had originally read," he says, "but it still fit what I was doing, in playing the kind of manic-pain-in-the-neck-kind-of-guy that Jerry was." The actor's initial Jerry audition lines concerned his wife, who was later deleted and rarely referred to during the course of the show. "But it really didn't make much difference," he says. "I just went in, and did the best job I could."

Some have speculated that Ray, for inspiration, employed the late actor David White, who also played one of TV's funny, self-absorbed ad men: Larry Tate on the classic sitcom, *Bewitched*. Buktenica, however, is quick to override that correlation. "Actually," he remarks, "I don't make any connection with anything I do, when it comes to interpreting a character. I'm basically out there, scrambling, trying to survive in a medium that places demands on you to simply get a job done, well, and to do it quickly."

Defining Jerry was a complicated experience for Buktenica. "Although the show's writers were writing specifically for a character," he declares, "they were interpreting a character that was not really on-track with anything specific that was going on in my mind about who I was, and what I was doing as Ray. It's like that with any recurring character that an actor plays on television. Each time you get the next script, something else is revealed about the role you're playing."

A prime Jerry example from *Life* rests with "Toast," the episode that

Charles Frank was Tyler's dad in periodic sequences of *Life*. *CHARLES FRANK*

opened the third year, when Libby asked him to be the godfather to little Nicky Thacher. "That's one of my favorites," Buktenica confesses. "It exposed his generosity, and that was never revealed before. I always played him as the penny-pinching-lovable-guy-to-hate. Someone that you enjoyed being bothered by, and having around even though he's high maintenance. Essentially, a guy who's protecting himself."

Another *LGO* semi-regular character was that of Tyler's dad, Jack Benchfield, projected by Charles Frank, who was originally considered for the part of Drew. Yet, as he recalls, "I was too straight-laced looking. I wasn't construction-enough for that character."

Frank came to *Life* after completing a film for Rick Rosenthal and Michael Braverman, both of whom wondered if he would be interested in the Benchfield-dad role (which was somewhat upscale from the Drew character). The actor jumped at the chance. "The show was written and structured so well that they pretty much trusted me to do what I did with character," he says.

"They all knew me, and I was clear on what my motivation was for the character: Mr. Benchfield was closed off from the world on a day-to-day basis. Though he loved Tyler dearly, I felt he was incapable of expressing himself to his children," one of whom included Donnie (played by Michael Rankin), who had Down's.

Frank was later granted the opportunity to explore other sides to the elder Benchfield role, namely the character's reaction to Tyler's death, via drunk driving, and Becca's subsequent intense relationship with Jesse. "That arc of episodes was very telling," Frank explains, ". . . something that kids needed to see. I don't think Tyler was capable of handling the kind of rejection he was experiencing with Becca. So he drank. He didn't have the background or depth to handle rejection, which I viewed as a result of his lack of any kind of strong relationship between him and his parents, particularly his father."

Despite the on-screen gap in communication between the Benchfield men, Frank believes there were several instances between he and Puett that worked well. Principally, one in the Benchfield driveway, with Tyler shooting hoops, during the first-year-episode, "Brothers," in which Tyler attempts to illuminate — and eliminate — his father's ignorance and lack of compassion toward Donnie, who yearns to be involved with the Special Olympics, an aspiration his father forbids. "What Tommy and I would do in rehearsal," Frank reveals, "is to run a scene as much as we could. And we ran that scene a lot, because we knew it was important, and we both really enjoyed playing it."

Frank enjoyed working on *LGO* so much, that he was slated to direct an episode in the fourth season. Though this plan never panned out, he relished any time that he could spend with the cast, especially Chris Burke: "Chris always wanted me to come in and direct the show," he said. "He really liked me. And Michael Rankin [Donnie] was an amazing little guy, as well."

Frank remembers the first morning he arrived on the set of "Brothers," which included a main scene at a gymnasium. A two-shot camera angle with Rankin was to be established, and Frank remembers telling the young actor, "Now, look, you've got to have your head in line with mine so we can

Dorothy Lyman played Jesse's long-suffering mother, Mary. *DOROTHY LYMAN*

get this two-shot right." Rankin made a face and said, "You know something...I missed you all weekend, Charlie."

One of the most dramatic *LGO* moments that Frank was called to interpret, took place in "More Than Friends," the third-season segment in which Tyler shows up drunk at Becca's party. This eventually leads to Tyler's death and a haunting moment between Frank and Tyler in the hospital: a distraught father clinging to his dying son's past, by screening film footage of Tyler's high-school football career. "It was a very difficult scene to play as an actor," Frank admits. "What they teach you as an actor is to always be in touch with whatever is going to happen inside of your body. There are very few parts that come along in this business where you have the opportunity to experience what's going to come flooding up to you as you're going through a scene while you're shooting it. And that was one of those scenes where everything just came flooding up. As if, *Oh holy cow! What's going on here?* And there was nothing you could do, because if you're a trained actor, you should just bring that stuff up or let it go."

Another of the credible supporting personas brought to *Life*, was Mary McKenna, another parent — Jesse's mom, played by Dorothy Lyman, who almost did not get the part. "At first," she explains, "the casting director didn't want to see me, because she just knew my work as a comedian [TV's *Mama's Family*]. But after my manager begged and begged, she finally relented and allowed me to come in and audition. I knew it was a wonderful opportunity for me to perform something dramatic on TV, which I'm not usually given the chance to do. So I worked hard on my audition, reading the speech which Mary gives to the PTA [in the episode, "Life After Death"]. I brought a tear to the producer's eye, and they hired me right on the spot."

Actually, when Lyman filmed the PTA scene, the actors playing the parents burst into applause. "I couldn't for a moment imagine what they were cheering for," she declares. "It was amazing."

Just as remarkable was the stamina that Mary possessed in supporting Jesse. Lyman believed the character grew stronger as the series continued. The actress thought, *It must be horrible to have that happen to a child of yours,* and she believes Mary and Jesse became closer because of his affliction.

For Lyman, performing as Mary McKenna was a joy, with the crew and fellow actors being supportive, which further motivated her. "Everything was fine from my point of view," she says. "They pretty much let me do what I wanted with the part. I would work in one scene per episode, go in, shoot it, and leave. So basically, I was there about half-a-day or so for each of the episodes I did."

One scene, however, stands out above all the rest for Lyman. It's an after-hours moment in the Glenbrook Grill from "The Blues," in which Mary confronts Drew, who hires Jesse as a waiter; and with whom he soon discovers a common love for the blues. "The scene was true," Lyman says, "because it showed another side of Mary, not just this sort of long-suffering, grief-stricken, in shock mother. But someone who was going to try and fight for her son. She displayed that she had some power. It made me think of how people with handicaps must feel — how they live with their disability day-in and day-out. Along comes somebody who knows them for five minutes and comes to all these conclusions that they need this or that. *Well*, they think, *where were you for the rest of our lives?*"

An additional jarring moment for Lyman transpired in "Consenting Adults," when Jesse chose to stay with Becca and not move away with his mom: "Oh, God," the actress stunningly recalls. "I was horrified with that scene, on several levels." First, from Mary's point of view, that Jesse would choose his life with Becca over his mom. And secondly, from Lyman's point of view. She began to worry, "They don't want to pay me for the next season. I guess this role won't be continuing."

The latter did not transpire but, from a dramatic perspective, she believes the sequence introduced an interesting story line with Mary's second husband, who was not at all fond of Jesse, and who was actually afraid of him and AIDS. "That's why Mary and Jesse originally moved to Glenbrook," Lyman explains, "because the father would not let him live there with his other son. And I thought that was an extremely interesting storyline that was never developed. That's why in the closing sequence for ["Consenting Adults"], the car stops, Jesse gets out, leaves and then Mary gets out of the car, because she feels she can't just simply let this go. She gets into an argument with the father, and she can't imagine that, after giving up everything for Jesse to come be with him, that he would opt to be with Becca."

"That is the only thing about the show that struck me as extremely odd," Lyman admits. "I really had to wrestle with that whole situation. We had spent the first four episodes establishing that, here was this woman who had sacrificed a lot for her son, and that she was going to see his struggles through with him to their conclusion. The only justification I came up with for me as an actress, was that Mary's actions were for her son whom she loved unconditionally. I mean, I've heard people say that they have healthy kids, and then suddenly they have a child who is disabled, or has some severe health problems. More times than not, the other children in the family get somewhat neglected, while the misfortunate child gets everything. But I didn't want Mary to have that mentality with Jesse, and I didn't want her to deny him anything, either. Jesse was at an age when boys are supposed to be drawing away from their mothers. He didn't have full-blown AIDS in the beginning, so I remember thinking that I wanted Mary to be the kind of mother who would give her son as normal a life as possible. And when it came down to the wire that included finding the strength to allow him to stay with the girl he loved, even if it meant leaving his mother who sacrificed everything for him."

Other supporting *Life* characters included David Byrd's interpretation of Hans, as well as Cousin Angela, who was played by Gina (pronounced Geena with a hard g) Hecht. For starters, Michael Braverman explains the creation of Angela: "When Drew was going to buy the restaurant. It was just a character that we introduced. But I happened to like Gina also, so every time we needed some legal advice we brought her back. We introduced

David Byrd played Hans, the curmudgeon cook with a heart at the hearth of the Thacher's restaurant. *DAVID BYRD*

her in the funeral [from 'The Return of Uncle Richard']. She brought the nerves and the sniffling and all of that to the character. I had a slightly different character in mind. She always had a handkerchief tucked in the sleeve of her sweater."

"I adore her," says casting Director Dee Dee Bradley of Hecht. "And everyone loves her. She's from the group of people in the industry that we know, and we know who the good actors are, and we use them."

Byrd, meanwhile, explains his Hans attachment: "I had gone into read for a single episode ["Ordinary Heroes"], which is when they changed the storyline from Drew being a construction worker to owning a restaurant. And we assumed that it was going to be a one-shot deal. And I remember sitting in the bathtub reading the script, and thinking, *Boy, he's going to get this restaurant, and that means I'll have a recurring role.* Then I reached the last few pages, and found out that the other brother [there were two who owned the restaurant] wouldn't sell it to Drew because of Corky. Then I thought, *Oh shit, well it's a nice guest-spot, anyway.*"

Ultimately, however, the producers liked what Byrd did with the role and, when Drew finally did take ownership of the Glenbrook Grill, they decided to keep Hans.

As to the character's foreign inflection (which Michael Braverman requested to be heavier), Byrd has a good ear for language and sounds, and particularly enjoys doing a German accent. "I love doing all accents," he explains. "There's a kind of freedom in working with them, something that you don't have that much of when working with your own voice. Any role that you play is the product of the voices that you hear."

There were several moments on *Life Goes On*, of course, when Byrd got to play up more than his talent for vocal sounds, as in "Isn't It Romantic," from the second season. The actor recalls working on the episode, in which Cupid's arrow strikes many of the show's characters: "I drove onto the lot one day, and someone from the wardrobe department said, *Well, you know you're going to be getting married next week.* And I said, *No…no I didn't.* "And they said, *Oh, yeah…didn't you see the script?*"

On that note, Byrd immediately ran to his dressing room and began to peruse the script. The whole relationship with the woman had been quite different. Originally, he had fallen madly in love with her. "The script pretty much followed that storyline until we reached the big dinner that he creates for her," Byrd recalls. "So Hans says, *I'm in love with you and I want to marry you.* She started to pull away, and he's thinking, *What's the matter?* She says, *I can't talk about this and I can't see you anymore,* and then she goes to leave. Hans then grabs her hand and pull her back and, in the process of doing that, he looks at her wrist and notices a concentration camp tattoo on it. She then says, *I can't love someone who's German,* and then she leaves. Then there's a great jump in the story and suddenly we're into a wedding. It became discernible to me that there was no way that we could play this scene. There was no groundwork established for it in anything that I had done as Hans before. It seemed awfully heavy-handed."

Byrd does remembering working on the scene for a day or so, though. "When I received the final script," he recalls, "they cut the whole aspect about her out, and made some excuse that her husband had suddenly died.

Steven Eckholtd and Troy Evans were surprising rivals for Paige's love in the show's final two years. *STEVEN ECKHOLTD/TROY EVANS*

And I thought what did actually make it to the screen, really never rang true. The entire concentration camp angle was an extraordinarily powerful piece, but it became out of context. Though I do think, in retrospect, the audience wanted to know more about where she came from."

Another wrenching scene for Byrd to play transpired in an episode from the first season, when Hans was to perform with an accordion. "I was having a back problem with my disc," the actor recalls, "and I was in a great deal of pain. Unfortunately, there was nothing anyone could have done to alleviate the pain, the way the pressure was on the vertebrae. Not even painkillers would have worked. And suddenly I receive this script where I was supposed to play the accordion, which is a very heavy instrument. So they had to bring me aside and show me how to play. Well, I was just in absolute agony during that whole thing. About every five minutes I was like, *Hey, can we take a break?* Then someone would lift the accordion off me, rest, and then I'd get back into it."

Lighter moments surfaced for Byrd while filming *LGO*, like in "The Uncle Return of Uncle Richard," in which co-executive producer Rick

Rosenthal played the lead guest character, and during which a dueling Hans and Richard were tied up. "I enjoyed playing that scene with him," says Byrd. "I wish he had appeared more often in front of the camera. He was fun to work with, both as an actor and as a director. He's even sillier than I am."

Although Byrd did not get have the opportunity to establish any strong friendships with anyone on the set of *Life Goes On*, he says his entire experience with the show was extremely positive.

A troupe of actors who appeared in other periodic roles like Hans, were Steven Eckholtd (*Grapevine, It's Like...You Know...*), Lance Guest, and Troy Evans, all of whom played love interests opposite to Tracey Needham.

As Kenny Stollmark, Jr., Eckholtd (who would go on to play Ellen DeGeneres' last straight boyfriend in *Ellen*) portrayed a somewhat arrogant, distant boyfriend-turned-fiancé-turned-almost-husband to Paige. Also, for a time, early on, he even expressed prejudice toward Corky. Lance Guest played Michael, a moody-but sensitive man who Paige ended up marrying and then leaving, due to a disagreement of whether or not to have their baby. Troy Evans had first played Artie, Paige's welding supervisor (under Kenny) in several third-season episodes, before he became Paige's business partner, friend, confident and receiver of her unrequited love.

Off-screen, Needham eventually became "good buddies" with Eckholtd (who was a groomsmen at her real-life wedding), she loved working Lance Guest (whom she calls "a real special guy"), and she has worked many times after *Life Goes On* with Evans (once playing his daughter in a pilot). She's glad that Paige left Kenny for Michael, though she felt strange about Paige's budding romance with Artie. "I thought that was a little weird," she relays.

As Michael Nankin explains, "The whole idea of hooking up Paige and Artie romantically was my idea. A lot of people resisted, and the reason was always that Paige was young and beautiful and Artie was older and fatter and uglier. How can that be a valid reason on *Life Goes On*? How can someone be unlovable based on his appearance? It went against the grain of the whole series and I was always very frustrated that I couldn't make it happen. We got very close through. There was a scene considered for 'Bec to the Future' [from the fourth year] where we saw their kids — little mini-versions of Paige and Artie."

According to Troy Evans, the Artie/Paige amour had not crossed anyone's mind when the character was first created. In fact, when he was initially introduced, he was, as Evans puts it, "a really crass, sexist swine, with no socially redeeming values whatsoever. The guy was just a pig. But he did evolve from there. And for whatever reason, the writers and the producers liked the chemistry they saw between Tracey and me, and expanded on that."

Like many of the *Life* cast, Evans also drew from his reality for theatrical inspiration, as he's been living with a younger woman for over a decade that happens to work in a field dominated by men; she's a blacksmith. "I weigh 220 pounds and she weighs about 100 pounds," Evans explains. "She heats steel for a living, and bends it with her hands. We go to a welding supply store, and there are people who still can't quite grasp the concept that I'm not the welder in the family. The flipside is, when people get to know her, they accept her. And it's not as though what she does for a living doesn't matter, but it kind of goes the other way. They treat her very well, and with respect."

That also can be said of how Artie eventually treated Paige, though Evans was disappointed that the relationship did not go as far as he would have liked it to have gone. "Artie was basically a good person," Evans says, "whose prejudices [toward women] were ill-founded, and he finally realized that. He thought, *Well, you know…Paige is not just a quota-chick.* She can do the job. And that's what we pay people for…to do the job. We don't pay them for what they look like, or for what we think they can't do, we pay them for what they can do.'"

In all fairness, Paige also felt some prejudice toward Artie, because she believed, in her heart, that he was too old for her. "There were some producers on the show who wanted Paige and Artie to get married," Evans admits. But like so many other potential storylines for the show, this never developed. And though the actor remained open to any resolution of the Paige/Artie association, given the vast differences between the two characters, he admits an actual romance for them was pretty far-fetched. "Not impossible," he adds, "but there was wide-gap."

Yet we later learned a secret about Artie that further complicated his character and, in event, his relationship with Paige: His affinity for and ability to write haiku poetry. "The moment you see him in the street playing the flute [in the fourth-season seg, 'Choices']," Evans assesses, "you realize there were all sorts of sides to him. So a case certainly could have been made that the two got along, and the fact that he was a far more enlightened person than when the audience first met him, and complex."

All things considered, Evans believes that Artie was deeply in love with Paige. "No question about it," he affirms. "Here was a guy who had been married before to someone who offered him nothing of any interest. It didn't work out, and his whole grasp of what a relationship was, was primitive. Basically, he met someone that he didn't hate, and he lived with her. Then he met Paige, this woman who really caught his imagination. Someone who wasn't afraid to make challenges, and went where others didn't dare go. She had her own ideas, and was tough, and he thought, *Oh, man…if I could just be with her, this would be great.* Then he eventually just comes out and says, *Marry me, Paige.* He knew what he wanted, and he took a shot at it. He didn't get it, but he took a shot."

Though Artie had certain freedoms, he was never motivated to do anything especially unique with his career. That is, until Paige influenced him into establishing his own business, Darlin' Construction Co., taken from Artie's affectionate nickname for Paige, which itself was improvised by Evans one day while filming. After that, he manages to even purchase a home, all due to Paige's inspiration.

The on-screen time between Evans and Tracey Needham was just as motivational. "Our scenes always worked," he says. "We never had to do a scene repeatedly to try and get the chemistry. We went in, popped those scenes off, and the dynamic was always in the first take. We looked forward to doing our scenes, which were snappy, mostly because Artie and Paige were always bickering."

One episode holds particularly stimulating memories for Evans. It's where Artie and Paige are remodeling the house, and in walks a female building inspector who Artie finds attractive. "Paige wasn't exactly interested in Artie, at this time," Evans explains, "but it became obvious that she was capable of feeling jealousy toward someone who was interested in him. And that's human nature at its basic. She thought, *It's not as though I want him, but I just don't want anyone else to have him, either.* Or, *Now that someone else does want him, that just might pique my interest.*"

Someone else, however, always wanted Paige. And though Artie would have given his left arm to be with her, marry her, and even father a child with her — and though she came close to wedding Kenny [Steven Eckholtd] — there was only one man whom she loved enough to marry, and seriously considered having children with: Michael Romanov.

In the previously-mentioned "Choices," Paige actually becomes pregnant with Michael's child. But he decides he doesn't want his wife to keep their baby. Tracey Needham thought his decision was perfect. "It presented an interesting perspective," she says. "Michael was a wonderful, sweet, caring man, who really loved Paige. But he didn't want children. And just because someone doesn't want to bring children into the world, doesn't mean they're evil."

"The frustrating thing for me," Needham adds, "is that I thought this was going to be a storyline that would continue. But, sure enough, it wasn't. It was like, Paige was married, pregnant, she decides to abort the child, can't do it, miscarries, and gets a divorce all in one episode." This lengthy storyline could have been serialized, over an arc of segments. "I think it was supposed to be, originally," Needham reveals, "but then they decided not to."

There were several other *Life* supporting characters beyond Paige's vast selection of suitors. Certainly an important semi-regular character — if only developed near the show's demise — was Ray Nelson, played by Michael Goorjian who was destined to receive a raise had *Life* gone on into a fifth year. Ray was one of Becca's more serious high-school classmates. Early in the show's run, he started out in just one-line appearances, playing a bully to Corky. But later, Ray became infatuated with Becca.

Goorjian explains: "Technically, I just did a guest spot on the show, and they just started to write more and more for the character. Then after the initial guest spot they waited a good five or six episodes before they brought Ray back, so he wasn't too connected to how he used to be, which was not-so-nice. They just didn't want Becca to start hanging out with this guy who had previously been picking on Corky.

Michael Goorjian as Ray Nelson made a play for Becca's affection during the Jesse years. *MICHAEL GOORJIAN*

"It was more interesting and not so black and white to have a character like Ray be involved with Becca than some regular jock guy, like she had with Tyler. With Ray and Jesse, you had moody *artsy* guy verses moody *arts* guy. Ray was pretty smart, though not as good-natured as someone like Tyler, or a nerdy computer guy [like Lester from the show's first season]."

Yet he was wise enough to be voted Valedictorian of Becca's graduating class, so noted in the final episode, "Life Goes On (And On...And On)." "Yeah," Goorjian states, "no one expected that he would win."

Further developments transpired in that last segment, namely the by-then evolved-triangular relationship between Becca, Ray and Jesse. "They left that pretty open-ended in the last episode," Goorjian explains, "which was done in a kind of flashback. No one was really sure if that was real or not. And there were actually two ways to look at it: realistically and as a television plotline. Realistically, I think Ray and Becca's relationship was based on the trouble that was going on between her and Jesse."

Chad Lowe says the Ray Nelson character was brought into the fold specifically to create a triangle between Jesse and Becca. "The producers wanted someone a little more equal to Jesse," Lowe explains, "someone with an appeal that was just as mysterious."

Lowe admits to always liking the Ray role, and Goorjian's interpretation of him, and wanted to make sure the character was in proper alignment with Jesse. "Sometimes Michael and I would be sitting there on the set," Lowe explains, "and we would have to change a line which presented that Jesse and Ray got along. Then it would change to that we didn't get along. I just thought that his character was cool. It was hard for me to have Jesse angry at him. Had we gone another season, Ray would have become very important."

Lowe says this is a testament to the creation of the character and to the execution of Goorjian as an actor. "There was a quirkiness about him," Lowe says, "an off-beat quality and likeability, a sympathy that you felt toward him. He wasn't the obvious, stereotypical Tyler-type. He came in through another door, much in the same way that Jesse did. I liked the relationship he had with Jesse. I always thought it was fun to explore, and I felt that from the get-go — that Jesse and Ray had respect for each other, that they were cut from the same cloth, that Jesse looked at Ray as his younger brother, that he would pass on the legacy of Becca."

As Lowe sees it, the latter happens in real life when someone knows that they are going to die, and given a certain time frame. "You start looking at who you want the people you love to be surrounded by when you're gone," Lowe says. "That's why, after all, we have wills. And so every time Jesse was interacting with Ray, I always felt like he had an eye on Ray as a potential ally and friend for Becca when Jesse died, a source of strength. And there were some episodes where I would have liked that to develop more fully."

Other regular supporting actors on *Life* were more of Becca's friends, including Tanya Fenmore as Maxie; Michelle Matheson as Rona Lieberman, Tyler's arrogant girlfriend and nemesis to Becca; and Eric Welch, who played *bully Brian Russo*.

Out of all these actors, Welch was the oldest, playing the youngest. He recalls his mixed feelings in auditioning for the Russo role: "I was probably around 21 or 22 years old at the time, and the part called for a sixteen-year-old. I was pretty upset with my agent because I thought, *This is getting ridiculous...I'm too old for these kinds of roles.* So when I went in to audition, I didn't really care if I got the part. I was ready to leave the minute that I arrived, then run straight to my agent, and say, *Okay, enough of the sixteen-year-olds. Can we get into the eighteen- and nineteen-year-olds?*"

Yet Welch was wearing his real-life letterman jacket from his own high-school days, and he got called back with other "jock-looking guys" who, he says, "looked really young." During the audition, he retained the attitude of a school bully, and "pretty much stayed in character straight through, creating the Brian Russo laugh right there on the spot."

Such antics were encouraged by director Kim Friedman, who was at the audition, and who was set to direct the show's second episode, "Corky for President." As Welch recalls, Friedman later granted him "free reign" to improve as much as he wanted to in "President," which included coming up with the nickname "the Corkster," for Corky.

Eric Welch as jock Brian Russo was one of Corky's protectors at school in the show's initial two seasons. *ERICK WELCH*

On interpreting Russo, who essentially remained Corky's nemesis — as opposed to changing to a more compassionate character (e.g., Michael Goorjian's Ray Nelson), Welch says: "The scripts were all very real life…very good scripts. We didn't see a big difference in general from reality to the show. I mean, obviously I did because Brian Russo was such a jerk. It's what makes acting so interesting. I could come out of me, and see a different person's point of view."

When playing Russo, Welch did not draw from anyone in particular because, as he says, it was "pretty easy because that jock mentality is interesting. It's almost like people don't do that just because they feel like they want to do it. It's [done] to feel good in a crowd, and that's what Brian Russo was about. Brian wanted to be liked. He made fun of Corky to make him feel more powerful. That's what happens in real life. You didn't see that on TV on a weekly basis until *Life Goes On*… how the family dealt with these situations…it wasn't always sugar sweet, just like real life."

Tanya Fenmore was Becca's best friend Maxie in the show's first two years. *TANYA FENMORE*

Certain Russo moments stick out in Welch's mind. "There was the time," Welch explains, "when he was thrown up against the school walls by a bigger school bully than him from "Corky Rebels." It was kind of interesting to have him being bullied on himself and have Corky get the best of Brian Russo."

"There was also a fun episode in which Russo belches right in the middle of class," the actor recalls, "and we went to a party with Shannen Doherty. I knew she was going to be trouble before she *was* trouble. I mean, I got to hand it to her. She knew she was going to be big, and *I* knew she was going to be trouble."

Here, Becca calls Russo and Doherty's character "two of the most insensitive people on the planet." "Shannen kind of stuck to herself a little bit," Welch recalls. "Me, her and Michelle Matheson [who played Rona] went out to lunch the day that we shot the party, at the restaurant across the street. Ten minutes into the lunch, I knew she'd be trouble.

"There was also one wrap party at which the producers showed bloopers from 'Corky's Crush.' I was trying to remember my lines, and I said, *Shit!* And I didn't realize that Chris had seen me. Then I saw him, and he kind of put his hands over his mouth like, *What did you just say?* or like *I can't believe you just said that.*"

Probably the most popular group of supporting characters on *Life Goes On* included Becca's long list of young schoolmates, including Kiersten Warren, Adam Carl, Seth Green, Michelle Matheson, and Tanya Fenmore.

Adam Carl's Matt was a semi-regular in the first few seasons of *LGO*. ADAM CARL

Michelle Matheson played Rona Lieberman, Becca's early rival for Tyler (Tommy Puett) in *LGO's* first season. MICHELLE MATHESON

Warren showed up in the last season (and also went on to appear as a regular on shows like *Saved by the Bell: The College Years*, as well as a bit role in 1996's blockbuster feature film *Independence Day*. Green became super popular first as Oz, the half-student/half-werewolf on *Buffy the Vampire Slayer*, and then had a feature bit in *Austin Powers: The Spy Who Shagged Me*.

Green, along with Carl, Matheson, and Fenmore, took class in the show's first few seasons, with Fenmore making the most appearances as Maxie, Becca's best friend. She worked closely with Green and Adam Carl. Fenmore's chemistry flowed well with both actors, particularly during the filming of "The Spring Fling," the second season closer. "It was almost hard for the director to keep the energy down," she explains. "Honestly, because I'm kind of an excitable person, and Seth makes me look like I'm on valium. Then Adam is very mature and calm. He kind of balanced everything out. So when we all got together, between every take, more and more chemistry was in the works. The energy just kept on building and building."

Chris Burke is reminded of Tanya's energy. "You're telling me. I really, really love her. She had been on *Family Ties*, and is truly a great actress. I think you will see a lot more of her."

Before we saw any of her on *Life*, she had originally auditioned for the role of Becca, which eventually went to Kellie Martin, when the show was in the pilot stage. "Yeah, we like her, but she's not quite Becca," the actress recalls of a discussion between series creator Michael Braverman and director Rick Rosenthal. "Then they kind of just looked at each other and said, *Maxie!*"

That was fine with Fenmore, who credits Martin with enhancing her performance. "It turned out great because Kellie's so capable, and we worked well together. Physically, I'm more flamboyant, which fit better with the wardrobe they put me in, and the kind of scenes that I had. When you just get into the moment, the feisty side of Maxie is almost like the feisty side of Tanya. The serious side of Tanya is the one that really doesn't show up on the screen."

"Kellie and I are close," she reveals. "We were always joking around on the set. Whenever I see her today we're still always joking around. So whenever we worked together in a serious scene like that, it was hard for us, personally, to focus on the acting, to have built up to the seriousness needed for that scene."

The scene Fenmore is referring to is from "La Dolce Becca," in which Maxie became extremely inebriated, and for which Fenmore offered a *tour de force* of her theatrical ability, though she's modest in motivation for the performance. "That was different because it showed a different part of her," she explains. "With acting, it's kind of difficult to separate the character from the person. I don't know? Where did it come from? Maybe the chicken I had for lunch was spicy that day? I guess I'm probably more Maxie than Maxie is, at least that's what a lot of people say to me."

One of the regrets that Rick Rosenthal has, with regards to Fenmore's portrayal of Maxie, is that "we never did an episode that really examines when your best friend moves away. And I wanted to do that very much. And you know there's a couple things that we just never got to do, and while I was there that might have been fun."

As Fenmore concludes, her stint as Maxie was "a wonderful experience. I was not a regular. I went so school while I was doing it, and I chose not to be contracted regular on it. I wanted to go to school, and I would not have been able to do that had I been a regular. But while I was there, it was by far the best experience I had as an actress working on that show with those wonderful people. And I don't have one negative thing to say about all those people I worked with."

Many more performers appeared periodically in the same role throughout the four seasons of *Life Goes On*, including Gloria Gifford, who played

Glenbrook principle Mrs. Neffer early on, and showed up in the role in the last episode.

"I worked with Gloria in *Halloween II*," Rick Rosenthal recalls, "which is when she hit the screen with me first. She and I came to acting with a coach named Elton Katselas. And in *Halloween* there was a part of a nurse, color-blind, written as a white nurse. I think this works just as well with a black nurse. Gloria is an incredibly powerful actress. Extremely gifted. I think the only thing holding her back from being a superstar is a tendency to be a little heavy, physically. But she's quite attractive. There were times when I thought she almost over-powered that part. Part of it was that she asked to do a little bit of the stock principal. And we might have incorporated a little bit more of her had we had the ability to expand some of those characters."

"I love Gloria," beams casting director Dee Dee Bradley. "She's a terrific actress… And if I remember correctly, Michael Braverman is the one who told me about her. So I brought her in and, since then, I've cast her in many other shows. I used to cast for *Hangin' with Mr. Copper* [on ABC], and she started recurring on that show as one of the teachers. And I bring her in whenever I can because I really like her. She's a great lady, and a wonderful actress. I adore her."

Dennis Ardnt would make two guest appearances on *LGO*. Here, as an abusive coach in the first season segment "Corky Witnesses a Crime," and later, in the second season, as the befuddled bum-driver who misleadingly chorales the Thachers around on a Hawaiian vacation in the second-year segment "Honeymoon from Hell." *THE REGAL COLLECTION*

CHAPTER 12

LIFE IN THE GUEST LANE

"I simply adored working on *Life Goes On*."
— Actress Frances Bay

Several performers made one-time guest appearances on *Life Goes On*. Some, not more than three shots. Others, before becoming stars. Still others made their initial television emergence, via *Life Goes On*.

For example, Elizabeth Berkley, who played it safe on Saturday mornings with *Saved by the Bell*, was prone to bad decisions as part of the wrong crowd in "La Dolce Becca," from *Life's* second season. Yet another *Life* guest star would also find his way into controversy after the show: Kathie Lee Gifford's husband, Frank Gifford, who played himself in the first season segment, "Corky Witnesses a Crime."

Other guest stars include: thespian vet Pat Hingle ("With a Mighty Heart"), Talia Balsam ("Ghost of Grandpa Past," "Arthur"), *Falcon Crest's* Ana-Alicia ("Lighter Than Air"), *Blossom's* David Lascher ("Dueling Divas"), and *Dynasty's* Pamela Bellwood (as an adult Becca in "Bec to the Future").

Several actors who found fame with *Seinfeld* also made semi-regular appearances on *Life*, before, during and after their stints on "the show about nothing." These include Barney Martin who, while playing Morty, Seinfeld's Florida-abiding dad, was also on *LGO*, interpreting Stan Baker, Corky's boss at the movie theatre. Gina Hecht, who also visited the Thachers on *Life* as Libby's cousin Angela, portrayed George's therapist on Seinfeld. Before Reni Santoni appeared as Jerry's hygienically-challenged friend, Poppi, the actor showed up on *LGO's* first season, in "It Ain't All It's Cracked Up to Be." Frances Bay, from whom the on-screen Jerry Seinfeld once thieved a loaf of rye bread, made two poignant *Life* appearances in "Arthur" and "Love Letters." Also seen in "Letters," as well as in "Windows" and "Babes in the Woods," is the *Seinfeld*-skilled Paula Marshall, who once thought Jerry and George were gay.

Richard Frank and Viveca Lindfors probably made two of the most distinguished guest appearances on *Life Goes On*. Frank, in what had to be the performance of his life, made a guest appearance in "Bedfellows," play-ing Jesse's hospital roommate with AIDS. Frank had AIDS in real life, and died shortly after his guest star stint. Lindfors (who has also since passed away) was responsible for the only other acting Emmy granted to the show, beyond Chad Lowe's consistently riveting performance as Jesse. She won Best Actress in A Guest Role for "Save the Last Dance for Me," playing Becca's aging ballet teacher — a woman forced to move into a retirement home.

Dean Cain, the Clark in *Lois & Clark: The New Adventures of Superman*, and a former football star for Princeton, touched down on *Life* as a Hawaiian surfer who upset Corky, but had a thing for Becca in "Corky and the Dolphins."

Memories of Cain and other guest actors are widespread from those who worked in front of and behind the *Life* scenes. Rick Rosenthal, for one, semi-credits himself for the discovery of Cain, in particular. "I wouldn't say that he was my find," Rosenthal reveals, "but that was his first guest-star-ring role on television. And I thought he was just great. I liked working with him."

The then-23-year-old actor was playing a character in his late teens who was flirting with a 15-year-old Becca. "You know, Dean," Rosenthal said, ". . . you've got to be real careful here, because you're in your twenties and Kellie's only in her mid-teens. And though Becca has a crush on your character, we've got to present it in such a way that it doesn't appear too sexual."

"I hear you loud and clear," Cain replied.

Looking back, Rosenthal believes "we did a good job of not wandering into an area that would have made all of us feel uncomfortable."

Meanwhile, casting director Dee Dee Bradley confirms "Dolphins" as Cain's very first substantial acting jobs on TV. "He may have done one or two parts before, but they were very small. But for this, we needed a great-looking, sexy guy who, preferably, looked Hawaiian. Dean auditioned for the part twice. He read for me, and then I brought him to the producers. He had several callbacks because of his lack of experience, and they were a little nervous about that. But he ended up doing a wonderful job and, of course, went on to become Superman."

Dee Dee Bradley recalls additional *Life* guest casting from two of the show's second season episodes. First, Robin Tunney, who played a young prostitute who semi-seduces Corky in "Corky's Travels." Secondly, Donovan Leitch, who captures Becca's heart, as well as Corky's wrath, in "The Banquet Room Renovation."

Tunney would later appear in theatrical films like *The Craft*, released in 1996. "She started on *Life Goes On* with a small role," Bradley states, "but she primarily has a feature career going now, and doing very well." Leitch, meanwhile, appeared in the 1999 NBC-TV blockbuster mini-series, *The*

'60s, which also featured Bill Smitrovich. "He's so wonderful," Bradley says of Leitch. "I needed someone to play Becca's boyfriend. I heard his name, had seen his work, and thought he was great. He came in, read, and was brilliant. He's so talented."

Co-executive producer Rick Rosenthal himself made a one-shot guest appearance as Drew's brother in the first season segment, "The Return of Uncle Richard." He explains the experience: "Playing Uncle Richard was the first time that I had ever done any really big-time acting. I hadn't studied in a long time, and I was pretty sure I could do the part, mostly because of my relationship with Kellie and Chris, that I thought I would feel very authentic as their uncle. There were obviously other better actors, but no one who had the same relationship that I did with them, and I sort of counted on that. And the character was written for me, and then when it came time to do, Michael Braverman wanted the character to be a little broader than I was comfortable with. And he kept encouraging me to be bigger. And finally I said to Kellie in between takes, everyone wants me to be bigger and I feel like, gee, I'm already pretty broad. Just tell me when I get too big. I'm counting on you. You're the only person that I could really trust. So we do a couple of takes, and Richard is telling this shark story, and this and that, and after each take, I hear, *Bigger*. So finally I do a really big take, I look over at Kellie, and she just leans over and whispers *Rick, I think you're there*."

Other guest actors who graduated to thespian prominence after *Life* include Shannen Doherty, Lisa Kudrow and James Cromwell, the latter of whom appeared as Drew's estranged best friend in a touching segment from the first season, "Thacher and Henderson." Cromwell, Oscar-nominated for his performance in the 1994 theatrical film *Babe*, is probably best known to TV fans as Archie's best friend on *All in the Family*.

As Chris Burke explains, "I really didn't like 'Thacher and Henderson,' mostly because Drew fought with his friend," whom Cromwell portrayed. "It was very depressing to watch. But I liked James Cromwell, who was in *Little House on the Prairie*, which is one of my favorite TV shows. And he's always been one of my favorite actors. So it was fun for me to work with him on *Life Goes On*."

Burke also enjoyed performing with Shannen Doherty on "Corky's Crush," which, like "Thacher and Henderson," was broadcast in the first year. Doherty, best known for her role as Brenda on *Beverly Hills: 90210*, first tricked Corky into believing that she was his girlfriend. "She was great," Burke says. Doherty, in fact, was billed on the show as "with Shannen Doherty," giving rise to the assumption that her character may have become a regular. Yet Michael Braverman says this was not the case. "She was always seen as just a one-shot."

The blonde and bubbly Lisa Kudrow, who is certainly no foreign entity to the press since the debut of *Friends* in the fall of 1994, appeared as a brunette in *LGO's* second season. The episode: "Becca and the Band." The character: Stella, a not-so bright office assistant who appeared at Drew's restaurant.

As Dee Dee Bradley recalls, "Lisa was involved in a scene set at the diner. But she was not a waitress. She was eating with Jerry and had taken Libby's place at this firm. Jerry was trying to convince Libby to come back to work. It was a very small part. One of those little two-line parts, and they wanted someone hysterically funny to do it. And she just came in and blew everyone away. She was really funny."

"At that time," Bradley continues, "the only thing I knew her from was a play she did at the Tiffany Theatre, called *The Ladies Room*. And she was very funny in that, and that was really all I knew about her. And then, when she did our show, everybody said, *She's gonna be somebody*. She was just one of those people who we all felt had a future, and we were right."

Apparently, the same buzz surrounded Greg Kinnear, who was a brief guest in the first-year episode, "Break a Leg, Mom." Kinnear, Oscar-nominated for Best Supporting Actor in 1998 for *As Good As It Gets*, acted on *LGO*, even before his gig as the original host of E!'s *Talk Soup*. As Bradley recalls: "At the time, my assistant and I, Carolyne, were looking for a good-looking guy for two lines. Now, if you're in the world of casting, that's very hard to find. Someone who's a terrific actor, who can do two lines, and who is very handsome. My assistant said, *I have a friend who's an actor, and would you please see him*. I see anyone my assistants recommend. So I brought him in. He read for me. I thought he was pretty good, we brought him to the producers, and he got the part. About a year or two later came *Talk Soup*, and now he's a big star. But this was when Paige opens the door and there's this good-looking guy standing there. I remember him being very cute and very personable."

Bradley also remembers casting Pat Hingle in a character-role — usually co-defined with a supporting part, and not as a lead. Instead, for example, the character-role would be the leading man's best friend or the leading man's relative: Drew's dad. "When it comes time to casting those kinds of roles," Bradley explains, "you want someone with some weight to them, with some name value, and I usually do a list, and the producers pick who they would like, and then we run it by the network. So he was just someone on one of my lists who we made an offer to. I didn't have any personal contact with Pat Hingle at all." Of Hingle, who played Drew's father in "With a Mighty Heart," Bill Smitrovich adds, "My father would have loved that Pat Hingle played Drew's father."

Bill remembers working with another guest character-actor on *Life*: Dennis Arndt, who played a crooked high-school football coach in the first-year segment, "Corky Witnesses a Crime," and later, the somewhat disheveled, taxi-driver/tour guide who gives the Thachers some bad advice (in more ways than one) in the second-season opener, "Honeymoon From Hell." As Smitrovich sees it, Arndt is a "wonderful, wonderful actor," whose less-than-attractive on-screen *Life* characterization only proved his extensive theatrical range. "Dennis is my pal," Bill goes on to say. "A great guy...Vietnam vet...super father...grandfather...sailor...debonair...and all-about-cat-about-town."

Frances Bay (from whom Jerry Seinfeld stole a loaf of bread in the classic episode of his series, "The Rye") two made poignant guest-appearances in the *LGO* episodes: "Arthur" (from the second season) and "Love Letters" (in the fourth year). FRANCES BAY

Chris Burke's Corky is fascinated with the independence of guest-star Ryan Bollman's Arthur in the second-season episode of the same name. THE REGAL COLLECTION

Arndt's roles on *LGO*, meanwhile, were quite different from the other. "The second time he appeared on the show," Dee Dee Bradley explains, "he wasn't recognizable to most people even if they were huge fans of the show and watched every episode. They didn't really know that was the same guy who played the coach the year before. And that's because Dennis is one of those terrific chameleon kind of actors who can play so many different types of characters. He changes with each role. You could give him ten parts, and you wouldn't be able to tell them apart. Because he's just that kind of an actor."

Many *Life* guest actors showed up on the series in two different roles. Frances Bay first appeared in the *Life* segment, "Arthur," from the second season, as the over-protective mother (who dies) of an adult man with

Down's. Later, in the fourth year, she appeared in "Love Letters," portraying a woman whose soldier husband professed his deep love from afar while in battle during World War II. Also, Whip Hubley first appeared as Paige's veterinarian boyfriend in "Thacher and Henderson," and "Pets, Guys & Videotape," then later showed up as Becca's gym-teacher in "Head Over Heels."

Such was not a usual practice for the show. But Bradley explains at least why such a development transpired, specifically, with Bay: "John Levy [who now casts for *ER*] cast the show for the last year, when Frances was cast in 'Love Letters.' He was probably unaware that I had cast her in 'Arthur.'"

Would Bradley ever cast a guest actor who has already appeared on one show in a different guest part on the same series? "It depends," she replies. "It really depends on so many factors. If a role stands out as much as Frances' did in 'Arthur.' It was such an amazing role. So I don't know if I would have brought her back. It would really have to depend on what the other role was. But normally, if an actor does something that stands out that much and is that important to the show, I probably wouldn't bring them back, only because I think it'd be distracting and disturbing to the audience in dual parts. If it's a small part, then I have no problem with it. But with a big part, I probably would not have done it."

Many *LGO* episodes, in fact, featured those with Down syndrome. "It's not easy to make a television show or a film," states Bill Smitrovich, "but then to have to do scenes where you have so many who are challenged, and they all have different diets with specific needs, and to try and make the scenes work, it takes a great amount of patience and persistence and desire. It was always a challenge, but always worthwhile, as with the Special Olympics episode ['Arthur'], which is one of my personal favorites, and I think one of the best we ever did."

Also, Smitrovich would like to corroborate a previous statement made by Chris Burke's mom, regarding her son's acting coach Kali Hummel. "She was just as important as any actor on the show," Bill affirms. "More than she'll ever let you know. I can't stress enough how valuable she became. As Chris' coach, friend, my off-camera stand-in for Chris on many, many occasions. I did a lot of scenes with no one there, for a while. I would have these incredible emotional scenes while looking at a lighting stand called a century stand, as an eye-line. Chris would become fatigued, and doing the scenes would take a lot out of him. And so when they would turn the camera around and get his POV [point of view], he would be gone.

"Then Kali came on board and she became Corky for me on several occasions. And she would do the lines as would Chris in the same tempo, feeling, and it would provide me with an opportunity not to be distracted by Chris' desire and struggle in trying to remember the lines again and again and again. She's a great person, and she helped Chris tremendously."

Some of the more interesting guest stars on the show were not physically human, but certainly possessed human traits. Just as special a bond had been established between Corky and regular non-human characters like Arnold, the semi-wonder dog. Corky's near spiritual connection that was generally explored with Arnold was then expanded to include a wolf in "Call of the Wild," a pig ("Pig of My Heart"), and some dolphins ("Corky and the Dolphins").

Michael Braverman confirms the research conducted on those with Down's, and their relationships with gentle creatures, specifically the dolphins. "I don't know how accurate it is," he says, "but we always felt that Corky had some communication with animals. So we wrote that in."

"This episode was about nature," Chris Burke adds, "and all about saving the animals. I had a great time with each of the animal shows that we did. They were all a great experience. The dolphin story was based on a true story. There are a lot of children with Down syndrome who learned how to ride a dolphin."

As Michael Braverman told entertainment historian Brenda Scott Royce (author of TV literary companions to *Hogan's Heroes* and *Party of Five*) for *Television Chronicles*: "I have always been and still am a great believer in casting even the smallest role with the most appropriate and best actor you can get for the role. We don't throw anything away."

Chris Burke with Life creator Michael Braverman (left) and director/ producer Rick Rosenthal, who briefly transformed his talents into an on-screen appearance as Uncle Richard in "The Return of Uncle Richard" (from the first season). *KALEY HUMMEL*

CHAPTER 13

LIFE PRESERVERS

"I've spent my career searching for another experience like
Life Goes On. It's like trying to reproduce first love."
— Michael Nankin

The writer's function is significant to the structure and content of any television series, and *Life Goes On* was no exception. Many worthy scribes brought intelligence, drama, compassion, comedy, sensitivity and consistency to the *LGO* scripts.

The list of lofty *Life* wordsmiths runs the gamut in the TV industry. Beside series creator Michael Braverman (whose series, *Hope Island*, premiered on PAX-TV in the fall of 1999), several segments were penned by Toni Graphia (*Dr. Quinn, Medicine Woman*), Charles Pratt, Jr. (*Melrose Place*), Thania St. John (*Lois and Clark*), and Scott Frost (*Twin Peaks*). Also on the hit list: Paul Wolff, Jule Selbo, Star Frohman, Liz Coe (*Twice in a Lifetime, Early Edition*), Brad Markowitz, EF Wallengren, Marshall Goldberg and Michael Nankin, the latter of whom functioned in mostly every executive position behind the *LGO* cameras, serving as co-executive producer, producer, director and writer.

The backstory as to how Michael Nankin — the man behind the "Snatchers" (when Corky is convinced his family has been replaced by alien pod-people) — became involved with *Life Goes On* bears witness to the development of how a television show's writing/production team is initially mined and gathered. His prolific *Life* association began by penning the first season segment, "Thacher and Henderson." Shortly thereafter he ended up supervising the story department. Halfway through the third season, he was overviewing the entire series. Here's how it all began:

Back in 1988, Nankin had written a movie, *Ruskies*, which was directed by future *Life* associate Rick Rosenthal. A few years following the film's release, Rosenthal was assisting Michael Braverman with the staffing of *LGO*. He contacted Nankin and said, "Why don't you come on over and write an episode of *Life Goes On?*"

"Oh, no," Nankin politely declined. "I don't understand anything about television. I wouldn't know how to do it. No, thank you." He also admits to a slight case of arrogance in first rejecting Rosenthal's proposal. "I was a feature writer," he clarifies.

Rosenthal remained persistent in his pursuit. When he and Braverman screened the *Life* pilot for a select group of writers, they invited Nankin, who was ultimately "blown away" by what he saw. "Not only by what made it to the screen," he says, "but also by the people involved with the show in

Writer/Director Michael Nankin, an integral part of *Life's* creative core, has an off-camera chat with Chris Burke. *PETER LOVINO/MICHAEL NANKIN*

every aspect. I had never met Michael [Braverman] before, but I walked away feeling that these were people who I really wanted to work with. You can't look into Michael's eyes and not be enchanted by the gentle, generous soul looking back at you."

Nankin was then set to pitch a few story ideas, but each was shot down. The result was an "I told you so" conversation with Rosenthal. "I told you I'm not cut out for this sort of thing," the novice TV man relayed.

A few weeks later, Rick called him a second time, and said, "Okay, we have a story. We'll give it to you and we'll see what you do with it." Nankin agreed, and went on to develop an idea for an episode that eventually became "Thacher and Henderson." The number one guideline: Stay within the budget. Categorized as a bottle show, "Henderson" was shot on one location, in a neighborhood park. The basic idea centered around Drew's annual reunion of his former high-school football team. From there, Nankin fleshed out a story and dialogue, and Rosenthal and Braverman were sold.

Though, as Nankin now admits, "What I didn't tell anyone at the time is that I know absolutely nothing about football. So of course they give me the football show. I just nodded a lot in the story meetings and then rushed to the phone to call friends. Give me ten football terms so I can fool 'em."

When it came down to writing the "Henderson" script, Nankin began by asking himself, "Now how does this show work?" He sought to meet the program's high standards, and would settle for nothing less. He wanted certain to match the quality of the show's previous episodes. "I struggled for about a week to try and change my writing style," he said. "I was used to writing feature films and, basically, I was skirmishing to write a 50-page movie for *Life Goes On*."

The skirmishing paid off. Braverman and Rosenthal not only read Nankin's script, they were so impressed that they made the new-to-TV writer the show's story editor. And Nankin grew from there.

Yet before that transpired, other developments began to transpire with "Thacher and Henderson." Because this segment was initially conceived as an inexpensive bottle show, Rick Rosenthal explains, "We figured it was just one location, that little park [on the backlot at Warner Bros.] which we controlled. But we were lax to consider a few things. First of all, we shot it in the winter, and daylight left us early. So we had short days. We had a lot of actors, approximately 34. Normally, when you do a bottle episode, it's with your show regulars and, if you have some overtime, it's no big deal. Here, we had an hour of overtime, but with a tremendous amount of actors. So we began to think, *Geeze, you know we really have to keep track*."

In the middle of that track, Rosenthal came down with chicken pox [a plotline which was drafted into "Chicken Pox" in the second season] and, he adds, "we also had an actress in Monique, who was pregnant."

No doubt about it: it pays to be cost-effective when producing a television show, especially for a series that's teetering in the eyes of watchful ratings-oriented network executives. When a program is a hit, and bringing in revenue for its network, via commercial advertising, the network will be more prone to generosity with an expanding budget.

Those at *Life* were not as fortunate. The budget was approximately 1.2 million per episode, and though that was hefty for its time (1989-1993) and place (on network television, as opposed to cable or first-run syndication), compared to a show like *Star Trek: Voyager* (a syndicated show), that figure is relatively inexpensive.

"The network pays a license fee of around $950,000," explains Michael Nankin, "and the studio makes up the difference with the amount of revenue that they receive from the amount of foreign sales. So they were deficits in financing the show. They were breaking even. They were always complaining that we were spending too much money. We felt we could have put the same show on the air for about six or seven hundred thousand dollars. That's about all the money that really ended up on the screen. The studio is a very expensive place to produce something. We had a huge overhead. All of the facilities were top dollar. Today, studios go out to a fairly unpopulated part of a city, and rent a warehouse and build sets. That saves a lot of money."

Yet the studio would never let *LGO* off the lot. "We would discuss a season, as a whole," Nankin reveals, "and where we wanted to take the storylines. Everything was deliberated in general terms, sort of thrashing around concepts. We threw in as many ideas as possible. We'd sit down and lock in five or six scripts. Everyone would get their first script assignment, and we would concentrate on those. Then, we had five or six writers at various times, depending on whether I was writing or not. We would go on rotation, in sort of a batting order. "

"Somewhere around the middle of that process," he continues, "we would begin to think about the next six. We didn't lock-in each round until sort of the last minute. Things would change and we wanted to have an idea of where things were going. We didn't want to get too locked in. The general story ideas would start with the group. The individual ideas for the episodes would come from someone who would say, *This is a script that I really want to do*. Or in talking about the story arcs, someone would come out of the group and say, *Oh, let me do that one.*

"The best stories would start with an emotion. 'Let's do a story about real sacrifice … let's do *Dark Night of the Soul*.' Those seeds would always blossom. Whenever we'd start with the camping episode or the prom episode, I always knew we were doomed."

"Every story always went back to the theme of the show," Nankin continues. "The central core, the touchstone of *Life Goes On* was unconditional love. That started with Michael Braverman and the pilot episode and was an integral part of every story. This is why we could vary the look, the directorial style, the storytelling, the structure so successfully — because that was all window dressing. Every episode has the same spine. The same heart. Unconditional love. This is why half the show could be about Down's and the other half about AIDS — the heart of the show was unchanged.

"Everyone worked differently. Some writers wanted to work on a story as a group, other writers would run out of the room and say, *Okay…I'll come back later*. We all worked very closely together. People were constantly walking into each other's offices. There was a lot of group input in a very non-structured way.

"This wasn't a normal writing staff in any sense of the word. This was a love affair. We all had lunch together every day. With all we spent on restaurants, we actually considered hiring a staff chef to save money. We all really liked each other. This was my first TV job — I didn't know how rare this camaraderie was. The spirit of the show infused everything. It was an enchantment. How often do a group of people get to work from the heart?"

Essentially, the season began in June, Nankin says, "and we didn't go on the air until the fall. So we began ahead of the game. We got lucky very quickly. We staffed up early with writers. We usually started to shoot the week after July 4. At that point, we had a couple of scripts that were ready to go, and we started to film. By the time we premiered in September, there were usually five or six episodes done and in the can, ready to screen, which is a lead that disappeared quickly. By about New Year's Day, we were finishing episodes days ahead of airdate. We had an eight-day shooting schedule, with an episode airing every seven days."

"It usually takes seven days to shoot a one-hour script," Nankin goes on to say, "but we took a little longer because of Chris and then, mainly because, when the show shifted focus to Becca and Jesse, we could only work with Kellie Martin at certain times, because she was only 16 years old. By California law, we only had her in front of the camera for about six hours a day, and we had twelve-hour days. But it worked out, because we ended up shooting eight short days, instead of seven long days, and we had more to work with. We had a higher ratio of Becca-time. These were Monday-through-Friday days."

"When ABC was pushing for more Becca stories," Nankin continues, "we went to the studio and asked for an eight-day schedule. It was pretty standard operating procedure. Once you're in series production, you're sort of working on every stage of development, simultaneously. You know a script will go into prep, the director will come on, at which time the cast is gathered, and there's some rewriting. While that's taking place, another episode is shooting, while another one or two are being posted. So the crew is shooting five days a week. As soon as the director yells 'Print!' on the last shot of an episode, another episode begins. We put down the old script, picked up the new one, and moved on to the first scene."

"For me," Nankin decides, "it was a great job. They were very full days, production meetings, screening dailies, dubbing session. It was very exciting."

Writer/producer Toni Graphia details these "full days," and concludes: "We had the best writing staff in town. I haven't been on one as good since. Everyone got along and there wasn't the insanity that can happen when you've got such job pressure. We'd all go to lunch together every day. We usually went to this place called Hampton's because they had the best desserts and we were all choc-o-holics. We'd talk about story ideas during lunch and then we'd always order this monster dessert called Chocolate Morte, which means 'chocolate death.' That's when we'd come up with some of our craziest ideas, like Ernie Wallengren's scene where Becca rides a cow into the school. Or Chuck Pratt's 'Dueling Divas,' with two Patti Lupones! Or Michael and Paige locked in the cake freezer. All the wacky ideas were inspired during our daily sugar rush.

"We didn't need to take network ideas because we had five or six writers constantly coming up with ideas they were burning to do. At the start of each season, we'd put up these cards on the board with ideas. *Paige gets pregnant. Corky and Amanda elope. Becca goes camping.* Loads of ideas. Eventually, they'd all get done. The only one left over that we never got to was *Corky joins the Marines.* That was on the board the whole time I was there and after two seasons, no one ever tackled it. I guess if we had another good year, Corky might have had a stint in the military. I'd still like to see that one."

On working with Michael Nankin and other writers on the show, *Life* creator and executive producer Michael Braverman tried to hire writers who thought the way he did. "It was that simple," he says. "I went over every single script. There wasn't a script in that show that I did not go through. Sometimes I thought that we needed something to juice it up. These are very difficult judgments as I look at them in perspective. At the time, they seemed very much easier."

"Many times," he adds, "I would have *A, B* and *C* stories. The reason for that is that it was very difficult for Chris in the first two years to maintain an episode. He just did not have the capability all that time, though he certainly grew into the role and matured and we were able to do a lot more with him. But from the pilot on, I decided it was best to have an *A* and *B* story and possibly a *C* story. Mostly, just to keep movement in 46 minutes."

Writer/Producer Toni Graphia says working with Braverman was "terrific," and alludes to the producer's infamous rubber stamps: "Unlike some show runners, Michael never took our first drafts away and rewrote them, although he did give notes. Michael Nankin gave him this set of rubber stamps, with all his favorite notes on them, so he could just stamp our pages – which he did. He had little codes like, NWJ, which meant 'No Way Jose.' It meant that he didn't buy the scene or the line for some reason. Or TFS, which was 'Tuna Fish Sandwich,' which meant that he was bored and thinking about his lunch. As the creator, he was always insightful and able to add that special touch that took the material from good to great."

There were many avenues that lead to the script development for the show. One episode, "Last Stand at Glenbrook," from the second season, has an interesting genesis.

Rick Rosenthal was sitting in a restaurant reading a script for *Life Goes On.* His waitress leaned over and asked if everything was okay. Thinking she meant his meal, Rosenthal stockly replied with a "Yes…it's fine. Thanks."

"No, no," she returned, "I mean with the script?"

He countered with, "Excuse me?"

"Well, you know," the server went on to reveal, "I'm a writer, and I've got to tell you that *Life Goes On* is the only series that I would be interested in writing for. Do you guys ever read *spec-scripts* [scripts penned on speculation, without any money, upfront]?"

"We do," Rosenthal returned. "But I don't want to encourage you. We're pretty much committed. Though I'll give you one good piece of advice: If you're serious about writing a spec-script, don't write it without investigating the episodes that we've done and the episodes we're planning to do. You could very well write a wonderful spec-script, but it could cover a story that we've already done."

The waitress was still interested. "So what do I do?" she asked.

"Well," Rosenthal responded, "if you're serious about this, call me at my office tomorrow. I'll set up a time for you to come out. We keep a show Bible and you can read the synopsis. Then we'll bring you up to date and, if you want, you can run by the story that you're interested in writing."

Later, she did just that. Impressed, Rosenthal not only thought she should write the script on spec, but invited her to become his assistant while doing so. "My assistant is leaving," he told her. "And I think you'd be perfect for the job."

Stating that "It sure beat waitressing," the woman proceeded to sign on with Rick about one week later. "So she came to work for me," Rosenthal says today, "and during that period of time, she wrote that spec-script. And I had a hunch that a script that we were supposed to start prepping for would not be ready in time to shoot. So I encouraged her to finish hers, so that we would have it in our hands in case the other script wasn't ready. Sure enough, as it turned out, the other script did not come in as scheduled, and we had a hole in the schedule."

At that point, Rosenthal approached his *LGO* colleagues. "You know," he started, "I've got this script that needs some work. But I think it's pretty good."

The episode turned out to be "Last Stand in Glenbrook."

The woman? An undergrad from the University of Santa Cruz, who majored in Film and Communications, and had also worked for Vid Marcus, the Director of Acquisitions. "She was a very, very bright lady," Rosenthal states.

Indeed. That woman, Marti Noxon, since became a producer for one of television's most realistic horror shows: *Buffy the Vampire Slayer*.

Another writer brought into the fold on *Life Goes On* was feature film scribe Marshall Goldberg, who was credited as creative consultant in the fourth year.

Like Rick Rosenthal and Michael Braverman had initially invited Michael Nankin to screen *Life's* first episode, Braverman and Nankin had now requested Goldberg to do the same in what would become the program's swan season. After Goldberg viewed "The Pilot" ("and loved it"), he interviewed with Braverman and Nankin, and was hired. He still had some feature work to complete, however, and ordinarily, when he would be offered a writing job, for the big or small screen, he retained additional responsibilities as a producer or supervising producer, beyond the categories of the term, writer.

"For professional purposes," Goldberg explains, "my agent did not want me to take a credit that was lower down on the ladder than I had been known for. So there is this position in the industry called a creative consultant, which is considered at the same level as a producer. But I still ended up just being one of a bunch of writers in the room, and I didn't have any more responsibility than anyone else. But I liked the show, I really wanted to write for it, and I was allowed to continue writing for features, and that was good."

Goldberg was also attracted to the series, because he perceived the versatile Michael Nankin to be "a very talented director, in addition to being a very talented writer. He began to view the episodes as little movies, rather than one out of 22 along a continuum. On a lot of series, they make it a major point to have the same rhythm, the same style, the same look from episode to episode, and Michael Nankin, as well as Michael Braverman, didn't think that was necessary. They actually encouraged the writers to write differently from episode to episode. They wanted each director to create a different look from episode to episode. It was all intended in the spirit of creative freedom, which you rarely find in this business. Nankin would actually say 'and then the movie ends,' rather than 'and the episode ends,' which is what is usually said in early roundtable discussions, before an episode of any TV series begins to actually shoot."

Once hired, Goldberg had written three segments – "Love Letters," "Happy Holidays," and "Bedfellows" — while he participated in the discussion of most others.

"Letters" involved Becca's mysterious discovery of love notes from the 1940s, while Drew tries to make his life with Libby more romantic, all in the midst of Corky and Amanda's shocking decision to elope. The letters from the past were employed as backdrop for the Thacher situations of the present. "It was all very intricate," Goldberg explains, with particular reference to Corky and Amanda getting hitched. "The idea, here, was kind of fun...that these two kids have the idea to get married. And you think along the way — when they're getting the blood tests, applying for the license, and going to the justice of the peace — that someone's going to say, *Wait a minute! You kids can't do this!* And you keep expecting someone to stop them. But no one ever does, and they end up really getting married."

By "Happy Holidays," Corky and Amanda are a few months into their wedlock and, as Goldberg assessed while penning the segment, "Okay — now where are they going to spend Christmas?" And this, he says, was essentially the springboard for "the whole issue of family craziness around holidays. It doesn't even have to be Christmas. Whenever there's a holiday, families get together, and it's all nuts. There's usually too much anger when there should be only love." And Goldberg believes what made "Happy" an important episode, was that Corky and Amanda were experiencing what everyone experiences; that it aligned them with what's "real."

"In some ways," he goes on to say, "it's a little bit exasperating for Corky and Amanda, because their parents use the argument that they never experienced their kids sleeping away from them. Corky had always been with Drew and Libby on Christmas morning, and Amanda had always been with her parents on Christmas morning. But now someone was going to have to budge, and give that up. So the episode was really about the family and in-laws having to make accommodations, which is true whether you're talking about Down syndrome or not. The idea was to universalize the experience. Every child has an overly-protective, loving parent at times."

Goldberg's final segment, "Bedfellows," was one of the four excruciating painful episodes in which Jesse experiences the wrenching physical, emotional and psychological agony of full-blown AIDS. In the midst of this, Becca is accepted at a prestigious university, and she becomes torn between love and college. Yet it was this segment's seemingly endless display of turmoil that helps Goldberg define it as a "very human" episode. "I was really pleased with it," he concludes.

Also brought aboard for the fourth year of *Life* was writer Scott Frost, who was hired as a story editor, as opposed to Marshall Goldberg, who was listed as the show's creative consultant. Frost explains the difference: "In terms of actually doing work, there's nothing. Titles in Hollywood don't really mean a lot outside of how it may affect your salary. Every series is different, and that's not across the board. Often what your title is or isn't, is a reflection of what you were doing before, or what you were being paid to do before. And not so much what your responsibilities on the show are. But, again, it varies. For *Life Goes On* we all basically did the same thing, which was being responsible for our own scripts, and we were expected to be there to make sure it was produced, and then in post-production, completed correctly."

"It was generally encouraged that you be on the set, which was rare for a writer," Frost goes on to explain, "and as good as a position as you could want in television work, whether you're a story editor or a creative consultant. I had previously worked on *Twin Peaks* — which was the TV event of the decade — but even that didn't allow for the kind of involvement a writer on *Life Goes On* was allowed."

Frost had never seen an episode of *Life* before he arrived on the series. "It was all kind of new to me," he says, ". . . the characters and all." Though he eventually began to review videotape from a number of previous segments from each season, he came to the series in a very "fresh way, without any preconceived ideas about who the characters might be."

Frost was directly responsible for the literary merit of three episodes: "The Whole Truth," in which Becca's teacher attempts to date rape Paige; "Incident on Main," the skinhead episode, in which the writer tried to include more of the family, "but a lot got cut out"; and "Five to Midnight," the most emotionally explosive and jarring of the three episodes, which just so happened to be directed by Michael Nankin.

Frost details how he and Nankin envisioned the segment. "We were trying to figure out a way to tell the story of Jesse coming down with full-blown AIDS. We very much wanted to do it in a non-traditional way, from a dramatic standpoint. We both remembered a film that was made years ago that debuted at Cannes, and actually ended up as an episode of *The Twilight Zone* ['Incident at Owl Creek Bridge']. So we sort of borrowed that idea, and worked it into 'Five to Midnight.'"

The *Twilight*-"Owl" incident showcased a man having his life flash before him, while he is in the process of being hanged to death, from the moment the rope drops. "We applied that to the stoppage of Jesse's heart," Frost says, "when he went into cardiac arrest, and played out much of the episode through that moment. It was essentially internal dialogue that was taking place, but you didn't know that until the fourth act. Although we gave hints throughout the first three."

From an objective standpoint, Frost admits the viewer's true perception of "Five to Midnight" may only be fully appreciated in retrospect. As if to say, *Oh...so that's why it was like that? Now I get it.* "We wanted to play it very straight," he says, "without Jesse's imaginings giving the appearance of fantasy."

"The great thing about the show, from a writer's standpoint," Frost says, "is that it was like entering college from high school, and finally being able to take the courses that you want to take. I had the chance to write about issues that I actually cared about. I was very proud of the work we did, how my episodes turned out, and the response they received. All the writers generated their own ideas, which is great, because you either rise or fall on the strength of your concept or script, as opposed to what you're allowed to do, or instructed to do, creatively on other television shows. With *Life Goes On*, you took the credit or the blame, depending on how it went."

Two other writers who hold prominence in the *Life* realm are Thania St. John and Toni Graphia, both of whom worked on the WB show *Roswell*. Graphia wrote 10 episodes of *Life*, more than any other writer. Michael Nankin was second, with nine, and St. John is listed as third, with eight. Michael Braverman, Charles Pratt, Brad Markowitz and Ernie Wallengren each had six.

Graphia, for one, recalls how she came to write for *Life*. "The first show I wrote for was the award-winning Vietnam drama, *China Beach*, so when I got the call to interview for *Life Goes On*, I was skeptical. I thought it was a kid's show. After all, it was on Sunday nights and it was about a family. And there were no cops, lawyers or courtrooms. I wanted to write about edgier, meatier things. I took the interview as a courtesy, but had no intention of working there. I met with Michael Braverman and Michael Nankin, who were polite and low key. I kept sidestepping and they didn't pressure me. The meeting ended with me coyly saying, *I'll think about it.* They said *no problem.* But then on the way out, they slipped me a packet of cassette tapes to take home. 'Why don't you watch these and give us a call?' they said. But I never thought I'd see them again. A few days later, I popped in a tape.

"It was Michael Nankin's 'The Visitor.' Before the end credits rolled, I called their office and begged to be on the show! To this day, it's one of my favorite episodes. I thought it was like a little movie. Michael Nankin is one of the most talented guys I know. I knew I could learn a lot from him. We really clicked and he directed several of my episodes, including 'The Blues,' which I think is my best work ever. That's the thing. When you work with great people, they make you look even better."

Graphia also clicked very well with Thania St. John. "She and I wrote a couple of scripts together," Graphia explains. "We had this method. We'd sit and pitch the ideas for stories and scenes to each other until one of us made the other cry. Then we knew we had to write that. It was a battle of who could make who cry first. For example, that's how we came up with the scene in 'PMS' where Libby gives the family ring to Corky to propose to Amanda. We're just a couple of saps. Well, I'm more sappy. And wordy."

"I usually can't stand for anyone to edit me," Graphia continues. "But Thania was an exception. There was this scene where the school principal was giving a speech to Becca and the returning seniors after summer session. I wrote this passionate, page-long speech about how your senior year is the most important year of your life, *yada, yada, yada.* It was like something JFK could have delivered. Thania took a red pen and crossed the whole thing out and wrote, 'Welcome Seniors.' I was furious. *How dare she cut my speech!* But she was right. We needed to conserve space for the more intimate, emotional scenes with Becca and Jesse. After that we became great pals."

So much so, that Graphia was named Godmother to Thania's twins, during their time on *Life.* Graphia recalls the incidents leading up to this special delivery. "Thania was pregnant with twins during one season and insisted on working right up until her due date. At one point, there was some medical concern and she was hospitalized as a precaution. She didn't want to stop writing, so I was there with her in the hospital room. She was lying in bed with a laptop perched on her belly, and with twins coming it was a huge belly. The computer kept sliding off, but she wanted to finish the episode ('PMS'), so we just kept going.

"A nurse came into the room and told her she shouldn't be working and I got into a fight with the nurse because I wouldn't take the computer away. The nurse was glaring at me and making these motions and I soon understood why. Minutes later the doctor came in and said, *They're coming out.* We said, *Who?* and she said, *The babies.* We were both in shock.

"Orderlies entered, tossed her on a gurney and wheeled her to the delivery room. She handed the laptop to me and I followed her all the way down the hall as they were wheeling her. She said, *We've got to finish this scene!* And she was calling out dialogue all the way until the delivery doors swung closed. *Becca says this … and then Corky says that …* I'm sure the doctors thought we were crazy. I was just standing there with my mouth hanging open and minutes later, after the delivery, when they wheeled these tiny babies out, I took one look at them and fainted. Later, she asked me to be a Godmother."

One of Graphia's favorite scenes that she wrote for *Life* was from the episode called "Choices," when Paige has to explain to Corky that she might have an abortion. As Graphia details, "She never uses the word, but she tells Corky she might not be having the baby. He wants to know how that happens. *The baby is never born*, she says. *Where the does the baby go?* he asks.

"It's really powerful and hard to watch because, essentially, that could have happened with Corky. His mother could have chosen not to have him. And many people do, and that's their right. But it makes for great drama because you are hitting on some pretty heavy duty stuff. No one expected such hard issues on this 7:00 family show, but we kept surprising them and sometimes surprising ourselves."

Writer Marti Noxon, who would later find fame as one of the show-runners for *Buffy, the Vampire Slayer*, commenced her career on *LGO* as an assistant to producer/director Rick Rosenthal. She then went on to pen the episode "Last Stand in Glenbrook." *MARTI NOXON*

Director Rick Rosenthal (with sunglasses) melds minds with Bill Smitrovich as Chris Burke (far left) and the *LGO* crew stand by. *KALEY HUMMEL*

CHAPTER 14
LIFE, CAMERA, ACTION

"A script is filled with words and, sometimes, these words are descriptive. On *Life Goes On,* more often than not, the script did not go into great detail about the visuals. Some TV shows do. Some have scripts that are very much blueprints of previous episodes. Most shows, in fact, are strictly formatted, in terms of how they are presented on screen. But not *Life Goes On.* Every episode was unique."
— director Michael Lange

It's difficult to describe how a director visualizes a television script, simply because each cinema supervisor is as different as each series or, as in the case of *Life Goes On,* as different as each episode. Just as he skillfully and diplomatically conducted the writing staff, it was *Life* creator and executive producer Michael Braverman who encouraged the show's various directors to tailor the look each week to the given episode at hand. As a result, each director employed his or her own style in interpreting a writer's script, just as each actor utilized their personalized technique in interpreting a character's words.

LGO director Michael Lange, for one, applied specific methods that permitted his ideas to surface after they "oiled around" inside of him emotionally — a process he employs to this day. More times than not, the first readthrough Lange does of a script is done so to reach a certain goal. This transpires, he says, "when you start envisioning how you want to film it. Basically, my job as a director is to illustrate the theme of the story with visuals, and to enhance it in a subtle way, with optics, yet allowing the words to become more powerful."

When working, Lange employs as a guideline a favorite expression, *It's not radio with pictures.* With such a literary steer, he receives an "emotional take" on the script, and starts thinking, *How do I want this to be shot?* From there, certain technical choices begin to ameliorate the aesthetic decisions. With his navigation of *LGO's* third-year episode, "Armageddon," for example, Lange sought to create a sense of claustrophobia. So he filmed the episode with long-length, 75mm film. This was especially challenging, because while he was readying "Armageddon" (with regards to casting, location selection, billing estimates, etc.), he was shooting "Toast," the third-season opener (in which Corky accidentally torches Drew's restaurant).

Another director was slated to guide "Armageddon," but Michael Braverman thought Lange was best suited for the job because, as Lange recalls, the segment was a "sort of an out-there episode." Braverman approached him on Day 2 of shooting "Toast," which was quite a difficult episode all its own. There were extensive emotional scenes (i.e., Drew and Corky in the charred Glenbrook Grill), and a good amount of special effects and night filming, which was unusual for the show. "Logistically," Lange reveals, "it was more of a challenge. The episode was not easy to film to begin with." "Toast," he goes on to say, was a "couple of steps beyond" what *LGO* was tackling at the time, as it was the first episode of the junior year that initiated the premise changeover from Corky/Becca to Becca/Jesse stories.

Yet, Lange's double-duty on *Life* should not be viewed as jarring, but rather, par for the course when directing a one-hour show. "The process," he says, "usually moves on simultaneously. At any given moment, one episode is in pre-production, while another is in production. There's also usually one in post-production."

Another of Lange's *Life* segments was "Sweet 16," which is also from the show's third year, but somewhat different than either "Toast" or "Armageddon," such that it included additional scenes of broad comedy. Consequently, it was shot with mostly wide-angle lenses, in glistening tones. "The lighting was very bright," he says. "We did everything possible to lighten it up in every way, whereas with an episode like 'Toast,' a moody piece, the lighting was sketchy and dark."

Rick Rosenthal once labeled another of Lange's *LGO* segments, "Isn't It Romantic?," from the second season, as one of the best episodes he ever directed — for *Life* and television, in general. But Lange differed. If Rosenthal had such-labeled Lange's fourth-year episode, "Bedfellows," with Richard Frank — an actor with AIDS, playing a patient with AIDS who befriends Jesse in the hospital — than he would have agreed. "It was a peak experience for me doing 'Bedfellows,'" Lange says. "In fact, I was devastated for having worked on it. It was very emotional. The issue was extremely deep. I was basically a basket case for about three weeks after I finished it."

He refers specifically to a rooftop scene in which Franks' character challenges Lowe's Jesse to a high-rise race, while both were connected to their IV's. Beyond that, "Bedfellows" was primarily shot inside a hospital setting and closed-quarters. According to Lange, these kinds of episodes are difficult to film, "because you want to keep it visually interesting, and yet you're significantly limited, because you're all in one location. On the other hand, it's so challenging that it gets to be exciting when things actually work out like you want. You have to keep the camera doing interesting things. On top of that, the actors, for the most part, were bedridden."

As Lange looks at it, filming "Bedfellows" was an "exhilarating experience." The script, by Marshall Goldberg, he says, "was just fantastic. Though the performances transcended the material, because of what Richard, and, of course, Chad, had brought to it on the set. I still get misty when I think of it. It was such an important subject." For Lange, the "beauty" of "Bedfellows" rests with the innate humanity of having a dying actor's talent and dignity in his last performance, coupled with a strong character. This is essentially why Lange would have agreed with Rick Rosenthal had he called "Bedfellows" his definitive episodic TV sample.

From a technical standpoint, placing *Life Goes On* on the air every week was no easy task. Sometimes, the schedule did not always go as planned, especially during the first few weeks of lensing the series. While shooting "The Babysitter," from year one, Rick Rosenthal remembers hanging off the side of a cliff in Griffith Park, California while attempting to capture on film Chris Burke climbing up a cord. "It was late at night," he recalls, "and I'm tied in next to Kali Hummel, Burke's dialogue coach] and the cameraman. We're all strapped to the same rope, trying to help Chris to get the shot. Meanwhile, the clock is ticking and ticking, and we all got pretty silly."

The absurdity later distended as a result of Corky's line, *I'm back*, which Chris repeatedly and mistakenly recited prior to his character's exit from one scene. "No, no, Chris," Rosenthal directed. "You have to go away first, before you can say, *I'm back*. You can't say *I'm back* if you've never left." A key grip also apparently had it in for Rosenthal, who relays how he was habitually pummeled with falling equipment: "I got hit by several lights. Wherever I'd go, suddenly some lights would fall over me. I didn't think he was trying to get rid of me, but it was very amusing." After that, Rosenthal says, everyone involved with the episode at some point "got the giggles."

Seriously, though, directors were held in high-regard on the *LGO* set, particularly Rick Rosenthal, who also served as the show's co-executive producer for the first few years. He and the other *LGO* directors, as was evident with Michael Lange's previous commentary, had a strong mutual respect for one another.

The director's working relationship with the actor also must run smooth if the actor's performance is to shine. On *Life Goes On*, it was definitely an atmosphere of mutual regard when it came to retaining a professional rapport between the director and the actor. According to Tanya *Maxie* Fenmore, Rick Rosenthal in particular is very much a director who takes input from the actor, and respects the way they would like to do a scene. "He was always there to offer the actors encouragement," she says. Such technical-to-talent support contributed to the quality of each episode. Suggestions from the cast were frequently adhered to by those behind the scenes, even when it came to dialogue.

Fenmore can't recall the specifics, but remembers working on rewrites throughout the one or two weeks that it would take to film an episode. The producers would approach the younger actors for "language checks," and wonder, *How would you say this? How would a teenager say this? What is the teen lingo?*

Suffice it to say, what the show's onscreen talent had to say as characters, and how they said it as actors, was equally important to those behind the camera, as it was to the performers. It was a fine mix. The lines of communication remained open to healthy and productive discussion between any combination of *LGO* producer, director, writer and thespian.

No matter how well written a script, how clear a director's overall view of an episode scene, or how strong an actor's emotion for a scene; none of it would hold any water, if not for the one vital, synergistic, proverbial thread to tie it all together: the ritual of rehearsal.

In shooting his TV classic, *The Honeymooners*, small-screen icon Jackie Gleason did not believe in rehearsal. That probably was due to a combination of reasons. Firstly, it was his show. He allocated his money to finance most of it, and he more than likely attempted to keep time to a minimum. Secondly, *The Honeymooners* was shot like a stage play. Gleason may have received a theatrical high from performing live, and was probably willing to wing it if something should have gone awry. Thirdly, it was the 1950s, and the medium of television was still in the process of defining itself. Those in power would wonder: *Do we really* need *to rehearse? Is TV the same as the stage? What is the difference in the time it takes to make a TV show, as opposed to a motion picture for theatrical release?*

Fortunately, by late 1989, when *Life Goes On* went into production, such wrinkles were ironed out. As *LGO* actor Ray Buktenica has noted elsewhere in this book, rehearsal for the show was a significant element in achieving an optimum performance level. It assisted in laying the groundwork before the cameras rolled — it helped to get it right when the directors yelped *Action!*

Since *Life* was an expensive one-hour television program, rehearsal was mandatory (if not lengthy). Those in front of and behind the cameras were not about to sacrifice their creative integrity or the quality of a dramatic moment in the name of time or money. Granted, how long it took or how much it cost to film an episode was always an issue, but if more time (i.e., money) was required for the polish of a scene, than more time was sanctioned. If that meant more rehearsal, than more rehearsal it was.

Dorothy Lyman, who portrayed Jesse's mom on *Life*, has also established herself as a director for the stage and television [i.e., *The Nanny*]. With the advantage of a double perspective, she outlines the contemporary mutation of general preparation for the TV actor: "You get yourself in costume and makeup and then they call you to the set to block it [matching the actors' lines with movement]. You work for a few minutes with the director figuring out the moves, and then basically you shoot it. It's not like a rehearsal for stage play. You generally work on your own. Occasionally, you run lines in the make-up trailer, between actors, but you kind of don't want to work those emotional things too much. You kind of want to let the impact hit you, when you shoot. You want the emotion to be fresh. I find that if I work a scene too much, I get hardened to the impact that they are to have."

When the actual filming commenced on a scene from *Life,* a variety of camera techniques were employed (as with other contemporary TV shows — and films, for that matter). First, a camera is placed in the distance, with what is called a master shot. Then the camera is moved closer, for general coverage, followed by close-ups of the individual actors. In the end, the best shots, chosen by the director, are spliced together with the editor, resulting in what is hopefully considered the best emotional, aesthetic, and visual results.

For close-ups, the camera will be solely focused on one actor, even though he or she may be performing with another thespian; a technique that contributes rehearsal time for the off-screen actor. "You can basically rehearse while the camera is on the other person," says Lyman.

Though the actress did not see a great deal of the production team, she recalled everyone on the set as "extremely supportive and wonderful to work with, especially the crew...It's a grueling schedule to try and do an hour show. And hardest on the crew, really, because they are the ones who are there day in and day out, from sunset to sunrise. The actors just kind of come in, do their parts, and go home."

At times, working the bugs out of *Life* technical problems became very hard work, as with "Love Letters," from the fourth season. It was a time period piece where many of the actors were playing double parts. As Michael Braverman explains, "The episode was nicely done. George D. [Fenady] directed that. We shot it in a very particular way. You'll notice the [cinematic] tones when we went back in time. We used twice the amount of light to give it a really misty kind of look. It was not, however, an expensive episode to produce, because it was all done on the lot. The costuming was exceptional for that show."

As to the lake used in the scene? "We filled that ourselves," relays Braverman. "Our only major expense was actually filling the lake in the back lot. We even built all those houses around it. We went off the lot, once, when we went to Frances Bay's house." (Bay portrayed an elderly version of the young woman, played by Kellie Martin in the present, who composed the love letters to her war-torn lover.)

Several regular, more recognizable visuals were presented on a weekly basis on *Life Goes On*. As Michael Nankin explains, "We were required to supply two different opening credit sequences to the network. A long version, one minute in length, and a short version, which was thirty-seconds. The thirty-second version was used by the affiliates if they wanted to squeeze in an extra commercial. We prepared an *Arnold gets fed* version, but neglected to prepare a short version of that. Well, we really did, but no one ever saw it, because the affiliates always used the short credit sequence." Suffice it to say, the *Arnold gets fed* opening was employed in the very last episode.

Another part of the opening credit sequence was of the early-teen Becca peering down toward her chest, and blurting out, "Where are you guys?" "First of all," Kellie Martin says with a smile, "it was hard enough to film that scene, much less see it every week for two years. That was awful. I'm not a singer, and I don't even pretend to be a singer. And I had to sing in the opening credits and they turned me up, because when we were recording it, I was in the background, singing very softly. But somehow they turned up the volume on me. So every week I had to hear my horrible voice. Then I had to say, *Well, come on…where are you guys?* And I had this zit on my head. It was not the most flattering credit sequence. But I think it shows that Becca is a normal teenager with major problems."

As Martin told *The Hollywood Reporter* in 1989, "I've actually learned more doing this show than in my seven years of acting — about supporting other actors. The director, Rick [Rosenthal] has taught me so much about camera angles and looping and editing and the aspects of making a TV show or a film that someday it'll be very easy to break into other aspects of the business. So if I don't want to be an actress all my life, I'll always have something else to do."

Fellow actor Michael Goorjian would agree. Goorjian, who came on to the show in its fourth season, now works behind the scenes, directing independent films. His time on *Life* offered some back-of-the-camera inspiration. "I had a great deal of respect for the writers on the show," he says. "It wasn't so *artsy* that a lot of people wouldn't watch it. But at least they did create interesting stuff. It wasn't just the writers, but Joe Pennella [the Director of Photography], who made a great contribution to the series. He really is very talented, and when you watch some of the later episodes of the show, you'll see some pretty extreme techniques. They found many different ways of telling a story visually, as opposed to your standard master shot or general coverage."

As the Director of Photography for *Life Goes On*, it was indeed Joe Pennella's job to create the visual mood of the show. Pennella held the same position on the Fox Network hit, *Party of Five* (where he worked with Goorjian and former *LGO* script supervisor Theresa Eubanks).

On *Life*, Pennella would not simply try to create a different look from season to season, but in keeping with the show's centrally consistent creative integrity, from episode to episode. "There were more humorous episodes that could have been lit a little brighter," he says, "as opposed to the more serious segments which needed a darker look or tone. At the same time, within the framework of the humorous episodes, there would be changes from episode to episode, just as with the more serious episodes."

To start the process, Pennella would receive a script and ask himself, *Okay...how should this particular episode look?* He would then consult with the director at hand, inquire as to what he or she was attempting to present visually, and would try to meet that criteria. Pennella would also attempt to uncover an episode's visceral appearance. He would ask himself, *What's the emotionality of this episode?* "Obviously," he explains, "when we were dealing with the Becca/Jesse arc, we were dealing with a very dark story. But even if you look at some of the episodes from the first few years, there were some dark moments presented there, as well. The necessary visual tone became obvious once we read the script."

Pennella's *Life* work, then, was to summarize the storyline, literally, on film, exploring both the light and dark side of *Life Goes On*. What he finds particularly interesting is how the show mirrored the change in mainstream moods from the late 1980s to the early 1990s.

"The episodes of the first two years reflected a less cynical time in the world," he believes. "They were somewhat brighter in mood. As the 1990s approached, certainly a more cynical time, the show reflected those changes with the more serious Becca/Jesse arc, with an edgier tone, which I then expanded upon, visually. I don't know if that was ever formally planned that way, but that's certainly how things turned out."

For this New York native who began his career in public television and learned by experimenting in the TV commercial arena, each episode of *LGO* offered a new and different challenge. As he told *International Photographer* magazine in 1992, "I remember the first time I walked on the set with Rick Rosenthal. I saw the chalk lines where the walls were going to go for the practical set they were constructing on the sound stage. *This entry hall is tiny*, I said. *It's exactly the same size as the one we used to shoot the pilot*, he told me. *It worked in the pilot, we'll make it work for the series.* That was true, except for the fact that they had twice the amount of time to shoot the pilot as we do with our eight-day-per-episode shooting schedule.

"I guess the first year we set out to prove that we could do this show in a practical location, without green beds and movable walls. And hopefully, we could create a more interesting look. Lighting wasn't that much of a problem. I like to work off the floor and through windows, anyway. I was familiar with that style of shooting through doing commercials in a lot of practical locations. Now, however, we're beginning to pull a few more walls and have green beds placed around the sets. We all want a quality look on this show. A look that fits the content of the script. That sometimes means I will shoot one scene where the story calls for soft light and a lot of diffusion, but the next scene might need hard light and no diffusion."

Overall, Pennella became very involved in the emotional content of the *LGO* scripts. It was hard not to, he said, because he and his colleagues were dealing with family issues…with social issues. "A Down's youth and a young man diagnosed as HIV-positive," he explained, "living day to day with the fear that each one will be his last…It has to be portrayed authentically."

Although many of the *LGO* segments stand out as cinematically different and innovative, the crew found themselves working extra hard on the stories that wrapped themselves around Chad Lowe's Jesse. "It's an important story and it has to be told the right way," Pennella said. He remembered going out on the location scout for the first episode where Jesse tells Becca he's HIV-positive — where she finds him standing by the tracks, and he screams into the train as it goes by. The director wanted to shoot this scene at night, downtown at the railroad tracks. With the amount of area he wanted to light, Pennella knew he would require a specific type of illumination made possible only by a certain kind of technique.

Shortly after, he took a closer look, and realized that the Musco effect would not do the job. As Pennella recalled, the director "wanted to shoot wide, to see at least half a mile of track, the 6th Street Bridge, and the city beyond. The Musco wasn't tall enough because we were actually in a gully, and he wanted to start on a crane, really low under the overpass." A shot, ironically, that was never used. But, still, Pennella had to be prepared.

He started with a smaller lens (20mm) and moved into a larger one (100mm, which had what is called a 5-to-1 zoom). He then attained a 150-foot condor and utilized two 18k HMI lights to display the train. And that was just to backlight it, and lead the train in. After that, he actually had a series of 12k lights working down the tracks to lead the train in on a half-mile stretch, on the reverse angle. He ended up employing the Musco anyway. "It was so far back," he explained, "it looked like it was an industrial kind of light in the distance, to illuminate the railroad yard."

The shot was further complicated because they were shooting with two cameras, close and wide. But as Pennella recalled, "That was simply to save a little time because we had Kellie in the scene, and because of the child labor laws, we could only have her for a certain amount of time…Fortunately, I've had the scripts that allow such a diversity of cinematic approaches and solutions."

Pennella is quick to credit ABC with "allowing us to push the envelope on the type of stories" presented on *LGO*, and the way they were told. As he then told reporter Pauline Rogers for *International Photographer*, "Michael Braverman and Warner Bros. have never said no to anything I've asked for in the way of equipment or crew. It's so amazing, in the days of tight budgets, and streamline cost cutting, that an episodic television show uses [particular lights and cranes], and whatever production tools that we needed to make the shot."

Additionally, like so many of the cast and crew, Pennella found working with Chris Burke to be an exhilarating, life-affirming experience. "It's amazing the things that they ask him to do," he said at the time, "and what he can do. When we were in Hawaii last year [1990-1991] we had him swimming with dolphins, hanging onto their fins. Each script he gets is a new and different challenge, and he accepts it. What we have to remember is that, even though he is high functioning, he does have Down's. When we have a Chris script we know we are going to need extra time. He's a hard worker, but he will often stop a scene when he gets to a word that he can't say, or a thought that will take a little more time to formulate."

One of Pennella's favorite episodes, from a technical standpoint, is "Corky's Travels," when Corky comes of age, with Leon Redbone playing a spirit who guides Corky on an adventurous journey through Chicago. As Pennella told Pauline Rogers, "Rick Rosenthal directed this one. His background is in features, and he approached the entire [episode] in that manner. Many shots were designed as moving masters from a crane. And, in the rain…two minute continuous takes. Fortunately, we were on the back lot of Warner Bros., so we could put lights everywhere and anywhere."

"Travels," Pennella went on to say, "probably has some of the best lit and designed masters I've ever done. It was a cinematographer's dream. The shots had a certain ballet to them. When you add rain and night lightning, neon, smoke, manhole covers with steam, long lenses, it became a mosaic. Every shot looked like a painting. We did very little coverage, so the shots had to stand on their own."

For Rosenthal and Pennella, the crane became an intricate part in telling several *Life* stories, one of which was an early episode about the delicate tale of Becca and Drew's daddy/daughter bonding. As Pennella detailed in *International Photographer*, "We had a wonderful scene where Kellie and Bill are at a father/daughter dance. We wanted to keep the emotional flow smooth and constant. That meant to me, using [something called] a *Louam* crane. It turned out to be a three-minute continuous shot where we started out high and wide, viewing a whole gymnasium. We swooped down over a number of tables and dollied through the crowd, then zoomed in with a 10mm, finding Bill and Kellie.

"We had to carefully choreograph everything when he or she delivered their particular piece of dialogue. Eventually we came down to the floor and we saw that Kellie was standing on Bill's feet, the way she did when she was a little girl. If I didn't have a great crew in key grip Ted Shinneman, gaffer Bobby DePerna, and operator Bruce Pasternack, we couldn't get these impossible feature shots in an eight-day television schedule."

Pasternack's ability to implement Pennella's vision with almost impossible shots came in handy several times over the years, as once later, when Jesse tells Becca about the girl that gave him the HIV-virus. It was set at a carnival, at night. Director Kim Friedman started at the back of the carnival and walked them all the way through the carnival to the front gate.

Composer Craig Safan (along with William Olvis, not pictured) was responsible for the hauntingly-beautiful sounds of *LGO's* solid and versatile score. *CRAIG SAFAN*

Kaley Hummel was Chris Burke's acting coach and friend throughout the four-year *Life* span. *KALEY HUMMEL*

As Pennella revealed, "We got there and started to rehearse the scene. It looked beautiful through the lens, right out of a commercial. The foreground lights were out of focus; the background had layers and depth. But there was something wrong. I turned to Kim and told her I felt the lens was not telling the story. It was too detached. It was giving the audience a totally different point of view. We should be tracking the actors on a steadicam. It was nine at night. There wasn't a steadicam in sight. Fortunately, I had Bruce. I turned to him and said, *Guess what? Put a 29mm lens on the camera.* He handheld it through the three-minute shot. It changed the whole approach.

"And it changed the lighting as well. That meant larger instruments from further back. We also ended up…hiding them behind poles, actually placing them in the shot in certain places, with colored gels. And, because they were out of focus, it just added to the total mosaic. It took us about forty-five minutes to light the shot, but the shot and scene worked like gangbusters."

It's obvious that Joe Pennella had a great time facing all of the unknowns on *LGO*. If any show is a training ground for moving into feature films, *Life* was. "Television is a broad-stroke medium," he recalled, somewhat melancholy. "You don't really have the time to create the nuances you have on the big screen. Basically, you have to create the look and the images as quickly as possibly, so that they fit the overall story."

On *Life Goes On*, he said, they were "fortunate enough to have has much of the best of both worlds as we can. The writers came up with a variety of stories. We have a wonderful cast to bring them to life. And, just as important, the network lets you tell these stories, and Warner Bros. has given us the time and money and equipment and crew to put them on film."

Becca meets her future self (played by Pamela Bellwood of *Dynasty* fame) in the fourth-season segment, "Bec to the Future." *THE REGAL COLLECTION*

CHAPTER 15

LIFE IS BUT A DREAM

"One of the joys for me in working on the show, is that for the first few years, we opened mostly every episode with a fantasy sequence. There was a lot of intricate photography to present, and it usually involved a large cast of extras. To me that was always one of the glories of the show because it set a tone that allowed you to get involved with the story, in the heavier portions of the story."
— Actor David Byrd, who played Hans.

The visual mood and tone for *Life Goes On* was a cinematic style that blended nicely with the show's benchmark fantasy and/or flashback sequences. Several additional means of fanciful dressing were utilized to attain the end-result.

For example, with "A Thacher Thanksgiving," from the second year, an arc of imaginative scenes involved Libby, Drew, Corky, et al, as pilgrims in the 1600s. For many of these moments, Joe Pennella applied a technique called pre-flashing the negative of film, which he was inspired to utilize by recalling Vilmos Zsigmond's similar work on *McCabe & Mrs. Miller*, the 1971 feature movie starring Warren Beatty and Julie Christie.

"I called Technicolor and asked them to pre-flash the Pilgrim sequences," Pennella explains. "Next step was contacting Frederick's of Hollywood, where I found golden sheer linens and shot everything through them. The dailies were beautiful and emotional, and the result, I thought, was quite elegant and believable."

Our friend Joe Pennella, for one, was frequently on the lookout for ways to make *LGO* stories appear more intense and, thus, more believable. According to Pennella, the writers took a bit of a dramatic license, from a story point of view, with episodes such as "The Room," from the third season. The episode explores what life would have been like for the Thachers in different time periods, when they discover another room in their house. Through different artifacts found in the new chamber, the show recreated eras from the 1940s, '50s, and '60s.

A "Rosie the Riveter" sequence was planned for the '40s piece, but was later dropped due to time and budget. As Pennella then recalled to journalist Pauline Rogers, "Although costuming really went all out and brought in some wonderful colors in poodle skirts and other clothing from the '50s, we've decided to shoot those sequences in black and white. This was when television was first coming in, and the shows were in black and white."

Even though television in the 1950s was rather bright and flat, Pennella decided to create more of a '40s *film noir* look. Consequently, the scenes were filmed on a Double X black-and-white stock, and printed on 5302 black-and-white print stock. Fortunately, because the *Life* production team married the entire show on videotape, Pennella was able to shoot and print on three different stocks, and splice it seamlessly.

For the 1960s scenes of "The Room," Pennella and director Lange sought a different look. The obvious way, Pennella said, "Was to go for a grainy, contrasty look, almost like a Pennebaker documentary of the '60s." Thus, he had the opportunity to experiment with what is known as a 96 and 94 film stock, both for which he said didn't look very interesting at all. After several more tests, however, he found what he was looking for. He pushed 96 three stops and underexposed one stop. "I was there," he said. "I reached nirvana."

The resulting footage for the 1960s scenes from "The Room" had a total desaturated, warm, grainy look, with no contrast (and printed on 5384 color stock film). "It looked like old footage or an old photograph," Pennella said. "It was very muted, soft and golden, and there was very little color separation left. For me, it worked."

The remainder segments of "The Room" were set in present time (and printed on a regular 5380 color stock). And, certainly, when the episode was finally put together, it had a unique and interesting look — one that Pennella had "a lot of fun creating."

What about the mythology behind the fantasy on *Life Goes On*? Former ABC executive Chad Hoffman offers an answer. "When we did the pilot, Michael Braverman had wanted to insert a series of fantasy sequences, for the most part from Corky's point of view. The reason he wanted to do it, from when we talked about it, was that he wanted the average viewer to get some sense of what the world might look like from inside Corky's head. Not as a person with a disability, but as a young person with the fears and anxieties we all had as young people. And then just sort of saying, yeah, but what is it like for a guy like Corky? To prove that Corky has the same fears as everyone else. That he was no different from others, in that respect."

Hoffman, however, did not want the *Life* fantasies to become cumbersome. "I remember looking at one of the fantasies from the pilot and thinking that it went on a little long to make its point. We [ABC] had been using fantasy sequences in *thirtysomething* and other shows, and we learned by experience that sometimes a little less is more. I thought we should be careful with using them so that they almost don't become predicable. And then Michael [Braverman] did not disappoint, and became very clever as to how he used them."

"It was a way to present adult themes about family life for viewers of all ages to enjoy," Braverman says of the fantasy techniques. When he was creating the pilot, he thought, "In order to make this interesting, we were dealing with a young man with Down syndrome. He is basically is mentally challenged, but his fears are the same as ours."

Yet, Braverman felt he had to find a way to make those fears filmatically interesting. And the best way to do that, he believed, was to give the show an element of limitlessness, which the fantasy sequences lent themselves to. He also knew what he did not want to achieve: An NBC show called *Our House*, which was broadcast in the 1988-1989 season, was the antithesis of what he sought for *Life Goes On*, when it came to cinematic execution. "That was a very conventional family show, which was shot in a very conventional way," he says. "And I knew early, when doing the pilot, that I did not want to do that with *Life Goes On*. I certainly was not starting with a conventional family, so I knew that I couldn't shoot it in a conventional way."

Consequently, Braverman searched for a theatrical device that would assist him with his unique vision for a unique show, and the show's fantasy sequences were born. "The fantasies to me," concludes Braverman, "added a lot to the mix. It was very unconventional for a family show."

Braverman employed his 9-year-old daughter as a litmus test for one episode, "Ghost of Grandpa Past," from the second season. Here, Drew experienced a mid-life crisis and sought out the advice of his dead grandfather.

"I was hoping it would help children understand what their fathers go through," Braverman relays. "Fathers are like ciphers in a traditional family, and this was a way to give children some insight."

The bottom line?

As Michael Nankin explains, "Michael Braverman created the idea, and Rick Rosenthal picked up the ball. The first season, it was part of the grammar of the show. It was a nice bit of flavoring in the stew that we all lashed on to. Rick pushed it, I believe more than anyone in the first season. When I came on the show, I thought, *Man, I love that kind of stuff.* I thought it was great."

As with "The Visitor" (also from the second year), a pregnant Libby's sleep was disturbed by the presence of a little boy who represented the life she carried within.

"This was one of the first times that we did a whole fantasy show," Nankin says, "where it just wasn't one sequence. I remember having to explain that to a lot of people. A lot of people were worried about that. We shot it at Union Station in Los Angeles, the old train station here in LA. That was my first directing effort."

Adds Michael Braverman: "With scenes like Libby talking to her unborn son, this was not only one of the best fantasy episodes Braverman says the show ever gave birth to, but one of the best episodes we ever did, without question. It was the perfect combination of reality and fantasy. And it had so much heart in it. I think it epitomized our show."

One of the more prevalent comedic fantasy sequences on the show transpired in the first season, with "Becca's First Love," with the brain mush, and

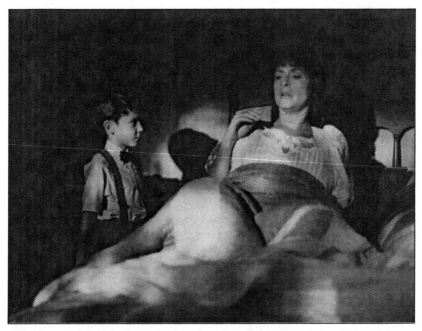

The fantasy element of *Life* is played with poignancy in "The Visitor," from the show's second year. Here, an expectant Libby (Patti Lupone), concerned about the possibility of having another child with Down syndrome, is awakened by a little boy (Bradley M. Pierce), who apparently no one else is able to see. In event, the young child represents the life she carries within.
THE REGAL COLLECTION

Becca being in a cryogenic tube. Of being in the tube, Kellie Martin says, "That was one of the scariest experiences I ever had. I didn't want to do that, because it was like being in a coffin. I fought them on that. I said, I don't want to do this. I don't want to do this. But they talked me into it, and they only put me into it for like a minute at a time, because it really frightened me.

"The mush brain was fun. It was like...okay there's oatmeal in my hair. And being the nun was great. It was like the really first episode where I got to do everything. I had the chance to play every kind of person. The diary was so real for me. I am a fanatic myself keeping a diary. I love keeping a diary. It was a very personal episode, because of the kissing and all."

Sometimes, due to the consistent dialogue of the characters, and lack of mystical special effects, the fantasy sequences were not recognized as fantasy sequences until the scene ended. In other words, even the fantasy sequences on *LGO* were realistic, which was in keeping with the show's general theme. As with the following dream sequence placed as a teaser for "Proms and Prams," the second year's closing episode:

FADE IN:
INT. BERKSON & BERKSON — OUTER OFFICE
NIGHT (DAY ONE)

At an elegant cocktail party, DREW is dressed in a suit and tie and LIBBY wears her most fashionable maternity dress. A prominent sign reads, "WISHING YOU A GOOD MATERNITY LEAVE." Libby looks around, pleased by the warmth around her.

Libby: Was nice of Jerry to throw a party.

Drew: Wouldn't have been nicer had he shown up.

Libby: Not for us. (*smiles*) I wanna try the stuffed mushrooms.

Libby heads for the refreshments.

CAMERA FOLLOWS.
ANGLE — REFRESHMENTS

Man #1 leans towards Libby, who serves herself.

Man #1: Slaton in Personnel says you're having twins. That true?

Libby shakes her head. He smiles, staring at her belly.

Man #1: Triplets?

Libby laughs politely, then moves away smack into the out-stretched palm of Man #2, who feels her belly.

Man #2: I've wanted to do that for eight months.

Libby: Wait another eight months before doing it again.

He smiles. Offended, Libby moves on.

CAMERA FOLLOWS.
ANGLE — BAR

Libby addresses a nice-looking bartender.

Libby: Some seltzer, please.

Woman: When's your due date?

Libby: May…

Before Libby can fully answer, the Woman continues.

Woman: A Taurus or a Gemini?

Libby: Probably a Taurus.

Woman: Pity. They're stubborn, temperamental, and lazy.

Libby: We'll try to love it anyway.

Libby walks towards Drew with her food and drink.

Man #2: Watching what you eat or just leaving that to everyone else?

Libby: Drew, let's go home.

Libby crosses by Drew, who is eating and talking.

Woman: You know, they say you never completely get your figure back.

Libby: Are you coming, Drew?

Woman: Even if you exercise and have your mouth wired shut.

Man #1: Did I tell you about my wife's labor? Thirty-two hours. And that was just the first stage.

Libby: I've got to get out of here.

Man #1: Lucky for us, she likes pain.

Libby: I can't take any more of this!

Woman: Yeah. You look like you're just about to pop.

About to explode, Libby tires to control her anger. But she cannot contain herself…literally. She inflates, becoming bigger and bigger until she actually POPS.

INT. THACHER HOUSE — MASTER BEDROOM NIGHT

Libby screams, bolting upright in bed. Drew sits up.

Drew: What's wrong?!

Libby: Nothing…Nothing.

Drew gets back under the covers and closes his eyes.

Libby: Honey, before you go back to sleep, will you do me a favor?

Drew looks at her questionably.

Libby: Turn me over.

And Drew helps Libby, now the size of a beached whale, turn onto her side.

FADE OUT.

While the latter exemplified the perfect use of dialogue in combination with the fantasy sequences, some such sequences involved no dialogue at all, as with "Lighter Than Air," the second to last episode of the second year. At the close of "Air," we see Libby turning on the TV, with a 1930s-type dance team doing a routine. She watches with a sketchpad on her lap, her attention divided between the movie and scribbling down ideas. She is charged up, energetic. Suddenly, she looks up to see an elegant dancer type in top hat and tails, as if he jumped right out of the movie. After a moment, she puts down the pad, gets up, movies gracefully and effortlessly, drawn to him as if by a magnet. The moment she reaches him the scene transforms into black and white, and in one motion, they begin to dance. As they glide out of the den, they are suddenly in a '30s-decor ballroom for a few graceful turns, and just as suddenly back into the den, dancing until we freeze frame and fade out.

In all, the fantasy sequences were employed with several different techniques on the show.

In the third season, for example, the fantasy element was expanded into reality with Corky/Libby in "The Fairy Tale." Michael Braverman explains, "We had to shoot it so we could get the drawings made. So it was very difficult to shoot. Because we did match-dissolvers. And the paintings were used as a device to get us into the actors...Or with 'Corky Witnesses a Crime,' from the first season, we see Corky's fantasy of being a sportscaster."

"I loved all the fantasy stuff," concludes Tracey Needham. "I would so love to do a show that did that again. Because it really gave you the opportunity to just be silly some of the time, and not have everything be so heavy-handed. And you got to dress up like a space alien, and do a period piece from the forties.

"I kept trying to get them to do a Western, so I could ride horses, but that never happened."

Corky fantasizes that Becca does a play-by-play from the broadcast
booth with Dan Dierdorf, Frank Gifford, and Al Michaels (then real-life
sportscasters of ABC's *Monday Night Football*) in "Corky Witnesses a Crime"
(from the first season). *THE REGAL COLLECTION*

Bill Smitrovich as Drew suits up in army gear for a fantasy sequence in the
fourth-season episode, "Love Letters." *THE REGAL COLLECTION*

CHAPTER 16

LIFE STYLES

"All I remember is that wig. It didn't fit at all, and it looked ridiculous."

— Bill Smitrovich, on Drew's younger look for a flash-back in "Paige's Mom."

When the details of a television series are not neglected, it's next to impossible to result in anything but a quality product. Such was the case with *Life Goes On*, even with regard to the show's makeup, hairstyles and wardrobe departments, all of which were catered to with astute precision.

When we first met the Thachers in their freshman season, they were an average-dressed, middle-class family, with not too much panache, and just enough frill. As the series continued into its second year, they upgraded themselves in the clothing department. Patti Lupone's Libby and Kellie Martin's Becca trimmed their long locks to a more fashionable style. Periodically, throughout the later two years, the two changed their hair again, as did Tracey Needham's Paige, in the fourth year.

As Martin reported to *Teen Beat*, she initially voted against Becca's last lock transition in the final season, which eventually represented the character's general growth. She had no desire to have her mane sheared. In fact, it was only one week before the show's senior year began, that the producers asked her to do so. She was like, "Okay...an inch or two?"

"No, really short, like Bridget Fonda's in *Single White Female* [1992]," she was told.

"That's what they said," she recalled. "And I'm really bad at saying no to anything that involves work. I always try to do whatever they want me to do, which is good and bad." So she compromised. A few days before she returned to work, she had approximately five-and-a-half inches cut off. Even though she classified that cut as "scary," she was told to go shorter. Finally, she said, "No, that's it." Yet as she later understood, they wanted Becca to come back a different person — new clothes, new hair, new everything. Kellie was glad, but being an actress is "hard in that way," she said, "because they hold your life in their hands." [Martin was later placed in a similar experience while shooting *Matinee*, a feature film she made in 1993. "My hair was a flip and a poof," she said. "I had pink iridescent lipstick, and pink clothes. You have to become the character, and you have to do these things even if it's not you…that goes along with being an actress."]

Becca's hair certainly played into the plot of "Struck by Lightning," when the Thachers actually start behaving odd following an electrical storm, though through it all, Becca was obsessed with her locks looking fine, more than anything else.

Be that as it may, the topic of hair seems to have a pervading presence on *LGO*.

Whenever one of the actors/characters did get their locks trimmed, it somehow managed to become part of the actual dialogue in a given episode. There's an onscreen audio reference, for example, to both Becca's and Jesse's haircuts in "Bec to the Future," the first episode of the fourth season. There's also an inconsistency in this segment, because of her haircut. When Jesse sees her after a summer apart, he's surprised that her hair is shorter. He then gives her a painting he created of her while he was away. But in the portrait, her hair has been shorn. What's more, his completed work looks like the likeness he paints full scheme for the next episode ("Exposed," when Jesse draws Becca in the nude, and her boss purchases the final product and displays it in the bookstore where she works).

If the direct-to-the-audience communication regarding the characters' hair changes weren't enough, it may have been obvious to the more perceptive season-to-season viewer that some of the hair twists also made it into the show's various opening-credit sequences. The Kellie Martin/Becca little-girl-to-young-woman transformation was assuredly represented here with different hairstyles (as well as with new eyeglass frames that replaced the famous red ones). Though, as Michael Nankin recalls, the hair-switch in a roundabout way became the reason for the change-of-credit sequences in the first place, "Patti Lupone cut her hair, and came to us and said, *I'd like a new shot.* And we said, *Sure…great.* And then everyone said, *I want a new shot, too.*"

In real life, different styles of clothing are worn or employed for different types of moments, experiences, or events in the social, family or workplace. To retain authenticity, such also was the case on *Life Goes On*, even with regard to a slightly insignificant plotline. When Drew, for example, went bowling in the first year's "Break a Leg, Mom," he donned a bowling shirt. Or as when Becca frequently threw on her white/color terrycloth robe over the years.

More extravagant garb was employed for a traditional wedding look a couple times as when Paige attempted to marry Kenny in the third season finale, "Consenting Adults." Or when Corky and Amanda got married in "Love Letters" (though they did not have a traditional wedding — they

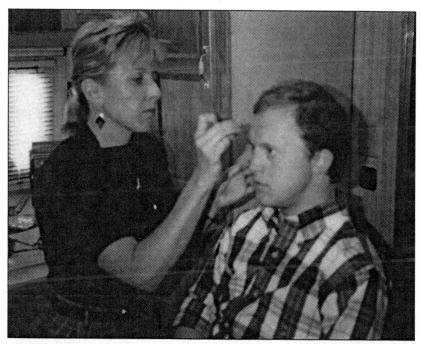

Chris Burke reports to the make-up and wardrobe departments for various guises for the episode "Invasion of the Thacher Snatchers." *KALEY HUMMEL*

Chris Burke adopts various guises: A pirate (with real-life father Frank close by) for the episode "Halloween" (ABOVE), **as a Pilgrim (with acting coach Kaley Hummel) for the episode, "A Thacher Thanksgiving"** (NEXT PAGE, TOP), **and as an alien, for the episode "Invasion of the Thacher Snatchers."** (NEXT PAGE, BOTTOM)
KALEY HUMMEL

eloped). In "Dueling Divas," Patti Lupone played the double role of Libby and her lookalike cousin Gabriella, who had a flair for tacky, flashy outerwear. Certainly, for the second-season seg, "Halloween," the wardrobe and costume changes were important, as they actually became a part of the plot.

There were times, too, when there were more elaborate opportunities to overdo the wardrobe with the fantasy/nightmare/flashback/flash-forward sequences in several episodes. In these instances, the cost for wardrobe, make-up and hair nearly rose to motion picture rates. There were many costume/make-up/hair changes in "Becca's First Love," in which Becca envisions herself as a nun in a habit, in a cryogenic tank, as a homeless girl, or with her brain turning to mush. Or with "Invasion of the Thacher Snatchers," when Corky thinks his family is mutating into space aliens. Or as when Becca and Jesse dolled up in '40s garb for "Love Letters," in the fourth year. Or as hippies in the third-season outing, "The Room." Or when Drew and Libby also dressed like flower children in "Paige's Mom."

Yet "The Room," more than any other episode, is a prime example of how extensively the wardrobe came into play in the show. Here, as previously discussed, the Thacher's represented different eras in time, appearing as families from different eras. Michael Lange, who directed "The Room," explains how the wardrobe for this episode was initially discussed in relationship to the segment's general tone and specific era-changing dialogue. "There were extensive discussions on how people talked and looked in the 1950s and '60s. And we made choices for the episode based on those discussions; how the dialogue was geared toward that approach. And it was comical, because I had to keep reminding Kellie that, in the '60s, everyone was referred to as *man*. I had a lot of fun with having her call Patti, *man*. Kellie was completely shocked by that. She was like, *You mean I have to call my mom, man?*" The costumes for "The Room" were also heavily researched. "We went back and studied magazines from the '50 and '60s," Lange reveals. "We really worked at trying to make it authentic."

Helping the "look-research" along, of course, was Joe Pennella, the Director of Photography, who Lange refers to as a very talented man. "Joe and I watched movies from those periods," Lange explains, "and just tried to match the fantasy sequences with those films. So we ended up filming the '50s sequences in black and white for the '50s, and we used a sort of a desaturated look for the '60s scenes. It was all very, very consciously done, to try to achieve the feeling of the period, and of course we wanted the wardrobe to be in sync with that."

Sometimes, as with "Pets, Guys & Videotape," from the first year, there were subtle shades of wardrobe design that were woven into the show. At one moment in "Pets," Drew steps out of the shower, and is seen in a hunter-green bathrobe, with a red towel around his neck, signifying the colors of Christmas, during which this segment was premised.

Kellie Martin's Becca and guest-actress Christie Clark's Suzanne Westland parade themselves atop one of the larger *Life...*uhm...*props* used for the fourth-season segment, "Udder Madness" (in which Becca enters her high-school's Homecoming Queen competition). *THE REGAL COLLECTION*

Warner Bros., like all the major studios, employs their own wardrobe department, but many times, other rental facilities were frequented by the show. There were also instances when clothes were purchased off-the-rack. "Usually," Michael Lange explains, "the studio tries to encourage their own wardrobe department to utilize what they have in stock, as much as possible. But the reality is, more often than not, you end up going outside."

As to wardrobe expense for each segment, Lange says he hears about the budget when it's "going too far over." That may have been the case for "A Thacher Thanksgiving," when mostly the entire episode was shot in the Pilgrim-era with matching wardrobe. Tracey Needham, who only made her second appearance as Paige in "Thanksgiving," recalls working with the wardrobe in this episode, which was originally envisioned as a comedy segment, particularly where Paige was concerned.

"I was in this low-cut dress. I was like the Pilgrim slut. The present-day man, who was homeless, was the wanderer in the past. Paige was coming on to him. It was all very funny. But all of that got cut, because the comedy didn't work with the homeless issue. It sort of looked like they were making fun of it. Now, I just looked plain ridiculous for no reason in my low-cut Pilgrim outfit that I probably would have been burned-at-the-stake for."

Needham indeed enjoyed the wardrobe for "Thanksgiving," though not as much as she liked the make-up for "Invasion of the Thacher Snatchers." "I must say," she relays of working in the latter segment, "I liked being a green space alien. And I thought Chris Burke was just so funny in that episode."

Conversely, it was not fun in make-up for Kellie Martin in "Armageddon," when she and Tommy Puett were made up as an elderly, miserable married couple: "That makeup took about four hours to have put on. Once they got it on, I looked in the mirror, and saw my seventy-year-old grandmother. It scared me to death. I wanted to get it off. It was awful. I hated filming those scenes because I just wanted to get that stuff off my face. It was really an awful day."

Becca is named the manager of Tyler's band, but finds her shyness to be an obstacle when offered with the opportunity to perform with the group in "Becca and the Band." *THE REGAL COLLECTION/BONNIE COLODZIN*

CHAPTER 17

SONGS IN THE KEY OF *LIFE*

"Life is a cabaret, ol' chum ..."
— from the hit musical, *Cabaret*

Music played a synergistic role in the success and appeal of *Life Goes On*. From scoring high with The Beatles' rambunctious "Ob La De, Ob La Da" as the show's opening credit theme (sung by the cast), to the haunting compositions provided by music maestros Craig Safan and William Olvis.

Various symphonic ties were threaded throughout the series, when other popular songs were utilized for background melody, such as "Joy to the World" (the Three Dog Night version) and "Bad Moon Rising," which are heard in "Thacher and Henderson." Stevie Wonder's "Don't You Worry About a Thing" is played when Corky's first job abilities are put to the test in "The Babysitter."

Several segments secured the music-related talents of the show's main actors and guest stars, and applied them directly to the plotlines. "The music was our attempt to give the show's structure a modern, new-fangled, hip gloss," explains Rick Rosenthal, "which was, in many ways, from another time. Good old-fashioned family drama resonated from a nostalgic standpoint with the Beatles song. At the same time, we would go in other directions." This was accomplished with the spoof of *Hawaii Five-O*'s opening credit sequence, employed in "Vacation from Hell," from *LGO's* second season. Either way, the focus became increasingly teenaged and, according to Rosenthal, "that's what we wanted the music to in some ways reflect."

Or as Michael Nankin explains, "My taste in music always leads me to songs from the '30s and '40s. I was always suggesting some old standard. They used to tease me about my *O.F.* music, which stood for *Old Fart*."

Though nostalgic, sequences such as the *Five-O* take-off, were also very hip, and remain appealing to the modern adolescent viewer. For the *Hawaiian* parody, Bill Smitrovich was placed atop an island hotel, and made up to look very much like *Five-O* star Jack Lord. Helicopters, transporting on-board cameramen, zoomed in with a swift, stuttering, cut-action-cut fashion, while the *Five-O* music played in the background — a near exact replica of the scene that opened the pre-*Magnum P.I.* tropic series.

To create such a perfect panoramic pantomime, Michael Braverman confirms that his assistant, Inness Wei, found it difficult to attain the rights to the *Hawaii Five-O* theme. "Part of the deal," Braverman relays, "was that we had to make commercials for the hotel, in order for us to use their building, and the balcony of the penthouse."

Smitrovich, meanwhile, viewed the *Five-O* sequence as "a great idea." He wanted to make sure that he had the Jack Lord hair and look "just right." "I had a lot of fun doing it," he says. "I had no idea where the helicopters were. All I knew is that there were flying somewhere up in the sky. I had a little walkie-talkie by my feet, and the transmission kept on breaking up, with someone saying, *Okay...here we come. We can see you. Okay...look to the left! Look to the left!!*"

Most of the time, when it came to instilling the sound of music into *Life*, the theatrics were more down to earth, as when the vast vocal variations belonging to Patti Lupone — a legend in the land of musical theatre — were engaged to their fullest degree.

From the get-go, producers took wise advantage of Lupone's harmonic forte, beginning with the first season seg, "Break a Leg, Mom," in which we learn that Libby supplanted a promising career as a vocalist for motherhood. Reinstating her former stage name, Libby Dean, she now auditions for a community theatre production. It seems like old times, as she belts out during the course of this episode a set of four tunes, including "A Wonderful Guy" (from Rodgers and Hammerstein's *South Pacific*) and "Wind Beneath My Wings" (the latter of which she sings to Corky).

As Lupone told *People* in the fall of 1989, around the time "Leg" debuted, "When the producers asked me to sing, I just laughed it off." Taking a non-musical role had not at all saddened her. "After 18 years I didn't regret not singing," she said. "But now that it's been established that the character sings, there will probably be more."

Lupone proved to be right. Several other *LGO* episodes were constructed in which Lupone was granted the opportunity to display her melodic talents. In "The Visitor," from the second year, she performs "I Know a Place Where Dreams Are Born" (also known as "Never Never Land," from Sir James M. Barrie's *Peter Pan*). She closed the show's sophomore season with "More Than You Know" in "Proms and Prams." In semester three's "The Smell of Fear," Libby offers a touching rendition of "Have Yourself a Merry Little Christmas" (from *Meet Me in St. Louis*) to Jesse in the hospital. In each of these segments (and others), Lupone's talent was joyful noise to embrace.

Except, that is, during a moment in "Proms and Prams," when her crooning proved somewhat unsettling for at least one individual: fellow cast member Tracey Needham.

In a subplot to "Prams," Needham's character, Paige, wins a role in a musical, and turns to stepmom Libby for a little coaching. As Needham humorously recalls, "That was my worst nightmare. I have a tiny bit of a singing phobia, which is based on the fact that I cannot sing to save my life. And here I had to sing with *Patti Lupone*. I was mortified. I tried so hard to get out of it, and I remember thinking, *You know…no matter how I hard I try, I'm gonna sound bad next to her.*"

Guest star and island music legend Don Ho with Chris Burke behind the scenes of the second season opener, "Honeymoon from Hell." *KALEY HUMMEL*

Fortunately, Needham's fear and honest appraisal of her vocal talents (or lack there of) suited Paige's predicament in the episode. Then, too, the actress bowed to the philosophy to which many of the *Life* performers yielded: She took from real life and applied it to her craft. "All the nervous energy that I had about actually singing in front of Patti and a cast and crew that I loved dearly," Needham comments, "somehow transferred to the screen. It worked for the character. Because Paige herself was terrified of being in the musical."

When the episode aired, everyone was supportive of Needham's performance. Everyone, that is, except her grandmother. "She made so much fun," Tracey remembers. "She said, *You were so awful in that episode.*"

Another musical non-extravaganza that Needham experienced on the show transpired in "Isn't It Romantic," from the second season, when Paige was serenaded by her motorcycle boyfriend, Kent, played by Craig Hurley, who performed a rousing rendition of the classic rock tune, "Wild Thing," in order to win back Paige's heart. "Oh my gaaawwwd," Tracey states with a gasp. "That was hilarious. Though it seemed like it took days to film the sequence [which included Hurley climbing and body-riding atop Drew's counter in the restaurant], it really only took one. All I can remember is that blue polka-dotted dress I was wearing and [Hurley] crawling on that counter-top. I have to say, he was a good sport about it all. He went all out. But to this day, I cannot listen to that song."

Paige was not the only Thacher woman who was serenaded by unrequited love on the show. Libby refuted the musical flirtations of old boyfriend Frankie Dee (played by Rod McCary) in "Corky Rebels." Becca became hypnotized by the musical charms of Gabe (Andrew) in "Becca's First Love." In both cases, romantic overtures became a little intense for the Thacher females.

In "Love," particularly, Becca goes goo-goo for Gabe when she hears him sing "Whatever it Takes" (with Maxie's brother and his band in their garage). Gabe further entices Becca with a song he writes just for her, "Always Rebecca," which he performs on the Thacher front lawn. On stage at Wylies (a local nightclub — and named for Philip Wylly — one of the show's producers), he sings "Give Me What You Got." Later, he tells her, "You belong here with the music and me" and "I want to kiss you," which became a distinctively historical moment in Kellie Martin's career: It was her first onscreen kiss.

As the actress told *The Hollywood Reporter* in 1989: "[Andrew] tried to make it as comfortable as possible, but he's 23 and I'm only 14. Actually, I think my parents were a little more freaked out than I was. It was an experience. In the end I didn't think it was that hard. When I first read the script, I said, *Oh no!* I was freaked out. When I looked at the script I was on almost every page and I thought, *Oh my gosh, how am I going to do this? This is going to be scary. I don't know if I can handle it.* But I talked to [director] Rick Rosenthal, and he said, *Kellie, I know you're going to freak out.* And I said, *I know.* I did. But he told me to learn it the night before, scene by scene, rather than looking at the whole show."

Today, Martin says "Becca's First Love" remains one of her favorite *Life* segments, because it was one of her "first big episodes. So it's very special to me." At the same time, she adds, "It's hard for me to watch. Because that was really my first kiss. And the scene with Drew [when he catches Becca and Gabe about to lock lips] was so very real. The whole episode was real to me."

There were several music-oriented segments that were characterized on- and off-screen by music mavens, including, jazz legend Leon Redbone ("Corky's Travels"), and Michael St. Gerard ("Head Over Heels"), who was then best known as the star of the critically-acclaimed, though short-lived series, *Elvis*. Industry king Quincy Jones ("Last Stand at Glenbrook"), who was essential in assisting with Michael Jackson's *Thriller* rise to the top; Don Ho (playing himself in "Honeymoon from Hell"), and Donovan Leitch ("The Banquet Room Renovation"), son of 1960s rock guru, Donovan.

While appearances by both Gerard and Leitch were non-musical (and

Kaley Hummel, with the legendary Quincy Jones, who guest starred in the second-season episode, "Last Stand at Glenbrook." *KALEY HUMMEL*

presented yet more love interests for the Thacher family women — Lietch for Becca and Gerard for Gina, Libby's sister), Redbone, Jones and their music connections were more integrated into the storyline. Redbone acted as narrator of "Travels" and appeared on screen, while his music was heard off-camera. In "Last Stand," Jones played a music storeowner who markets controversial recordings that ignite a protest (in which Becca and Maxie participate) about the lyrical freedom of compositions.

Tanya Fenmore shares her memories of working with Jones: "I really don't know a lot about music at all. But I do know that he was wonderful. Such a dear. So humble. He's very soft-spoken and very unassuming. I'm a chatterbox, on the set and off. I loved talking to him. I think he found it refreshing that I wasn't treating him special in any way. I didn't know why. In fact, his daughter used to date a friend of mine. So I knew his daughter before I knew him."

Fenmore recalls her initial feelings: "I mean, like…*Oh yeah…Quincy Jones the record producer. He's So-and-So's dad.* But I had no idea of what a big deal he is. I think he found it amazing that I would just sit in between takes and chat with him. I didn't remember specifically what it was about, but I do remember that he was a very nice, nice man. When I came home and said, *Oh, I worked with Quincy Jones today,* everybody's mouth just dropped. Now I realize, of course, what a big deal it was, and what an honor it was to have him on the set."

Kellie Martin, too, remembers Jones, whom she claims is very much like the role he played on *Life*. In other words, "cool and interesting. Though I wish they would have done more with his character," she says.

Rick Rosenthal, as well, was intrigued by Quincy. "He was a provocative presence," the producer relays, "and it was interesting for him to play the part as well. I spent some time working with him on the weekend. He's a very bright and talented guy, and I told him that acting was listening, and how it's not trying to act. It's trying to be. And I thought he came through pretty well."

It wasn't just the musical vocals that were prevalent on *Life Goes On*. Many times, the symphonic feet took over, as with Kellie Martin and Chris Burke in "Corky Rebels." At this segment's close, Becca and Corky tap into a family tradition. Martin's feet, in particular, were tapping extremely fast. "I have tap danced since I was five or six years old," the actress recalls. "It's funny, because on the show, in general, I had the chance to sing, dance ballet, and tap. But I am not the best in any of those areas. They're like little hobbies that I just happened to have the opportunity to perform on national television."

Behind-the-scenes *Life* scribe Toni Graphia almost had the chance to do just that. She explains: "I never wanted to be a TV writer. I wanted to be a rock star. I came to LA when I was 18 to be in a punk rock band. I wanted to be Chrissie Hynde. Obviously, that didn't work out. But I always missed music, and writing songs. So one of the high points of my TV career transpired during the filming of 'The Blues.' We had a scene in a nightclub where Jesse and Drew were going to catch a blues band. Bands don't perform live when you're filming because it's too time consuming and unpredictable. They record it ahead of time and then use playback and lip sync to themselves.

"I had chosen this Muddy Waters song and we hired the band and booked a couple of hours of studio time to record, which is very, very expensive. The band arrived that night and just as they are warming up, we get word that the song I chose has not cleared. That means we couldn't buy the rights to use it. We're sitting there with a band, studio time, and no song. So I said, heck, I'll just write one. I went outside with a pad and in about ten minutes wrote, 'Last Train to Chicago.' I just hummed it for the guys and they recorded it. We used it in the show. Warner Bros. paid me fifty bucks for the song. I still have it on tape and I pop it in my car once and a while and imagine I'm on the radio. What a geek," she laughs, with self-deprecation.

The Thachers embrace contentment. *THE REGAL COLLECTION*

CHAPTER 18

THE CIRCLE OF *LIFE*

"I think it was a benchmark show. "It changed the way people perceive other people who are different from them. I wish TV had more shows like *Life Goes On*. It had family values. It was well-shot, with good characters. Believable characters."

— *Life* actor Charles Frank

No bones about it — *Life Goes On* was a team effort — without a losing streak. It imbued truth, and embraced optimism, even as it portrayed the direst situations. Such solicitude could have only stemmed from reality. "A lot of our personal values went into the show," claims Rick Rosenthal. "It had great heart and very strong role models. It presented a family that had solid, old-fashioned values. One of the real problems with this country is that parents are not parenting as much as they used to. Some of that is due to the fact that there are a lot of single parents out there. Some of it is due to a general lack of guidance. With *Life Goes On*, we offered some guidance."

"Television has a profound experience on people," Rosenthal assesses. "There are times when it's abused and misused. Then, there are other times, as with *Life Goes On*, when it's incredibly gratifying to see the discerning effect that it may have on people. It took a while for the show to penetrate, but it gradually became a staple."

"The funny thing about this business," adds director Michael Lange of the industry in which he makes his living, "is that a lot of times when you're working on something, you don't realize how good you have it until you leave. Yet pretty much everyone who worked on *Life Goes On* knew how good we had it, even before it was over. It's the benchmark of what television should strive to be always.

"Everyone who does television should look at that show, and say that. Television has an enormous responsibility. You're going into people's homes, and with that you have a responsibility as a television maker to try and strive for excellence. On *Life Goes On*, not only were the stories generally insightful in exploring the human condition, frailties and strength, but also they did so in an

Kellie Martin and Chris Burke smile behind the cameras. *FREEZE FRAME*

entertaining way. It was a very responsible show, and incredible to work on."

Much of what makes a show good and, in effect, long lasting, Lange goes on to say, has to do with the creative dynamics of the production team and the performers. "In order to create real scenes," he explains, "you need to understand what's real. If two characters are arguing, it needs to feel like they're really having an argument. And after four years of those kinds of raw scenes, on a show like *Life Goes On*, you get into some deep stuff, on a fairly regular basis. After a while, it starts to feel like this is really what's happening. For the actor, and in order for them to recreate emotional scenes in a realistic way, they have to feel the emotions [again, to take from real life and apply it to their craft]. Sometimes they forget to do that. With the tension of performing and the emotional vulnerability that goes along with it, it all starts to

Tommy Puett was a good friend to Chris Burke on the *Life* set. *THE REGAL COLLECTION*

become real. It's harder to separate what you're really feeling as the actor, as opposed to the character. But on *Life Goes On*, it somehow all balanced out."

Actor Troy Evans believes *LGO's* theatrical equilibrium was sustained due to the show's encouraging creative atmosphere. "I've done a lot of television and I've been in a lot of series," he says. "Lots of times, I don't want to go to work. Lots of times, it's such a pain in the ass. The people are unpleasant, and the working conditions are so grotesque, that you just don't want to do it. You're making good money, but you're just like every person who has a job that they don't like. The only distinction is that you're making better money than they are."

"But *Life Goes On* was always a good job," he decides. "I was always enthusiastic about it. I spent very little time on that set. I bet a total of twenty days, over a two-year period. The conditions were not opulent by any means, but you were always treated right."

Meanwhile, Kellie Martin believes the various changes in *LGO's* storyline and character developments are what gave the show its longevity. "In the fourth season, especially," she says, "it became a very different show. Certainly once they introduced Jesse [in the third year], it changed. When Tyler died, everything changed. It became something you had to watch every week, otherwise, you would not get your answer. But once you introduce an AIDS storyline, you're not going to have a happy ending. The show became a lot more creative, and took many more risks toward the end."

"I am so proud of *Life Goes On*," Martin continues, "and what it said from the beginning — how it helped to break down stereotypes. Some people who watched it probably began to accept those who have handicaps for the first time in their lives. Maybe now when these same people see someone at the grocery store with a handicap, or someone who has Down syndrome, they don't stare as much. I think that's because of *Life Goes On*.

"For four years, Corky was part of people's lives [and still is] and people are familiar with that — with what went on with him and his family. His life, and life with the Thachers, became not so different a thing from their own. It's just the way it is. People became somewhat less aware of the difference, and viewed Corky as a person, not just as person with a handicap. They came to know and love Corky, while Chris himself went on to make such an impact on the lives of so many people."

Martin feels equally passionate about the AIDS storyline, and the impression it, and Chad Lowe's performance as Jesse, had upon the viewers, as well as the courage it required for those behind the scenes in bringing the storyline to fruition. "There was Chad, playing Jesse, a very young, attractive heterosexual boy who contracted AIDS," she said. "At the time, that was not something that you heard about every day. He wasn't gay, and he wasn't a drug user. He was just careless. The writer's didn't drop the ball. They continued with it to the end of the show. That says a lot for them, and the network. They followed through, even though it was difficult to do. And I was very proud of them for doing so."

Clearly, the powers that be did so, indeed — without the invasion or an overload of network intervention and censorship. *LGO* writer Scott Frost, who was responsible for many great AIDS episodes, adds: "I, by no means, encourage any kind of government censorship, but this industry [television and film] has hidden behind the cloak of the First Amendment freedom, without copping to any responsibility for the direction the country has taken. And that is unfortunate. I don't watch everything that's on, but I think the networks have, maybe over the last few years, made an attempt to at least tone-down, say, senseless violence on TV. But, then again, you see shows that are so off-the-wall ridiculous and violent, and the damage is done."

"At this point," he goes on to say, "let's face it, I mean, we now have weapons that would have not existed back when I grew up watching television.

Today, it's a much more complicated world, and I don't have a solution. I don't know too many other people that do, beyond taking responsibility for whatever your actions, whether you're on TV or not."

Frost recalls a responsible act in his fourth-season segment, "The Whole Truth," that relates to what he's saying. "Truth" has to do with Paige's attempted date rape by one of Becca's teachers, while a subplot involves Corky's fantasy fascination with an attractive calendar girl come-to-life. For Frost, the Corky/girl interplay, in particular, represented, in general, how he believes the media has portrayed women, and its relation to what happens in this country. As he recalls in shooting the episode, "We had to stop tape because the network was freaked out that the actress was in a bikini. They did not want to equate the fact that date rape and violence toward women is very directly related to the way they are portrayed in the media. But what the network was saying is, *We don't want to associate a woman wearing a bikini with rape or date rape.* And that was kind of the whole point."

The entire point of *Life Goes On* seemed to have become moot when the show was cancelled in the spring of 1993. "It was like a wake," Scott Frost recalls. "The writing staff was called into Michael Braverman's office, and he gave us the news. We all felt like we had just been hit in the stomach. It was a unique group of people that got together. It was as generous a creative group of people that I've ever had the privilege to work with. And suddenly, the rug was pulled out from under us."

Although it may be that programs ending abruptly are part of the business of television, Frost, speaking for all of those associated with *Life*, still could not help but feel unsettled upon experiencing the show's demise. "It was not a good day," he states simply.

Still, the cast and crew knew that *Life* was frequently hindering on a final departure, and there were recurrent discussions as to how the series should end. Yet, by the time shooting began for the final segment, "Life Goes On (And On)," Frost was gone. "I missed a few of the parties where they ran clips of the bloopers, and everything. But that's okay, because sometimes it's easier not to look back."

Yet, he does, saying, "It was one of those things that happened and it had its time. Sometimes they should end and sometimes they shouldn't, but they do. Though I do think *Life Goes On* could have gone on. We were all ready for it to. Though it would have been challenging, because by the end of the [fourth] season, we had pretty much said what we needed to say about AIDS, but we would have found other things to talk about."

There is, of course, always the possibility of a reunion film or two-hour movie sequels, either for the small screen or theatrical release. "We never really talked about that," Frost confirms. "But that would be Michael Braverman's call. In the last year, there was talk about moving to cable, or maybe Fox, but nothing came of it. A television movie is definitely an interesting idea, and I don't know if [Braverman] has ever considered that, or if it is something that would interest ABC. God only knows what interests ABC!"

But what about a TV-to-movie feature, *a la The X-Files* or *Twin Peaks*, the latter for which Frost wrote episodes? "Yeah, well," Frost says in a sardonic manner, regarding the possibility of *LGO* as a feature film, "the *Twin Peaks* film was a complete disaster — one of the worst movies ever made."

Notwithstanding, Frost admits his perspective may be somewhat subjective. "It's so different being a writer on the show, as opposed to a fan," he says. "We can't look at things as a viewer would. Because what a show is to the person who is in the middle of it, is sitting down late into the night with someone on the writing staff pounding out ideas, banging your heard against the wall, trying to find an answer to whatever puzzle you've got yourself stuck in at the moment."

Frost also admits, however, that with *Life Goes On*, the pieces came together between the series and its audience. "Something special happened with the show," he says. "It doesn't happen a lot, but occasionally viewers, and writers and producers all get lucky when something like *Life* is created. And we all got lucky."

Frost's colleague, Marshall Goldberg, credits the expertise and encouragement of the show's two Michaels, series creator Michael Braverman and executive producer Michael Nankin, in allowing that something special to blossom so fruitfully for all involved. "They created an atmosphere where everyone could do their best work. They allowed people who were hired for their creativity, to be creative. That attitude was everywhere present in the show. Actors were not told, *Just say it!* Directors were not told, *Just shoot it!* and writers were not told, *Just write it!* People were given freedom. You could ask anyone in any department, and they would have said it was the least stifling show that they would ever have to work on, across the board. That really began with Michael Braverman, and then Michael Nankin took the ball, and ran with it. He put *his* life into that show."

In more ways than one. As others of the *Life* cast and production team have relayed elsewhere in this book, the show has had a lasting effect upon those who worked on it. Nankin, for one, has forever bonded with the viewers, on one level or another. He recalls the lasting effects of one experience, forever connecting him, *Life's* audience, and the show's original network demise.

"As we were winding down the final weeks of the fourth season, as the show was coming to a close and we were in the most intense moments of the AIDS story, I found myself alone in my office. I was about to go home. The phone rang. A timid voice asked if she had reached *Life Goes On*. I sat in my office in the dark for the next two hours talking to a frightened 18-year-old girl who had discovered that she was HIV-positive. She was calling from the airport, about to travel home to her parents, afraid to tell them what had happened to her in college. She didn't know how to tell them. She didn't know what was to become of her. She had no one to talk to and so she called a television show.

"What this says about the impact we were having was completely off-set by the questions it raised about *Who Is Raising Our Children?* I gave the girl names of clinics and counselors — we were in contact with many — and told her what I learned about survival rates and living with HIV. She seemed to take comfort, but what the hell was I doing counseling a troubled teen? Where were her friends and family? How could it be that in the greatest crisis of her life, she would reach out to a TV show? Is making good TV good enough — or is it comparable to being proud of manufacturing the lowest-nicotine cigarette? I sat in the office in the dark long after the call was over."

Yet "in the dark" is far from where TV watchers of *Life Goes On* will find themselves. It employed itself, and the medium on which it was broadcast, for the betterment for all who viewed it.

"There are several categories to television," explains former ABC executive Chad Hoffman. "There is television that is damaging, which is a large percentage of what's on the air. There is television that is purely fun and entertaining, and hopefully not damaging at the same time. And then there are those few shows that actually mean something — that remind people of things in their own life, and touch them in their own ways that hopefully even enrich a few lives, maybe even change a few...and that's what *Life Goes On* was."

Hoffman goes on to say what an enjoyable experience it was to work with *LGO's* creator and executive producer, how the show was a result of Michael Braverman's "passion and commitment to really doing something special, and being involved with a show that matters." "Everyone who worked on the show was like that," Hoffman concludes. "To me the real reward was having the show succeed after early on so many people thought that it wouldn't make it. How years later, it survived to reach a very precise audience. And I think it made a difference."

LGO confirmed a mission Hoffman says he ignited, along with ABC and Braverman: "I really believed that TV could be a lot better than it was. It didn't have to be commercial. We could still do unique projects that people would watch. I felt that we had a great responsibility with forty or fifty million people. That's why I felt we had to be diverse, and to do our best, and go beyond the obvious. And that's one of the reasons I left Hollywood. Because I don't know that if within the Hollywood structure, if there is an opportunity to do that very much. But I do think those opportunities are available with television."

Detailing just what that purpose involved, Troy Evans recalls when he was approached by a non-affluent African-American teenage *LGO* fan at a café in Long Beach, California.

"You're on that TV show, *Life Goes On*, aren't you?" the young man asked.

"Yes, I am." Evans politely replied.

"I *love* that show," the boy returned. "It says that anyone can do what they want to do."

Evans disagreed. "Frankly," he says today, "Anyone *can't* do what they want to do. But anyone can have at least a shot at what they want to do. And I was amazed that he made that connection — that that's what he got from the show. That the show was not just about someone with Down syndrome, or that if you're ill, you don't have to be bedridden for the rest of your life. Instead, he saw it as a metaphor for meeting any kind of a challenge."

Life Goes On, overall, was a collaborative effort between the directors, producers, writers, and actors. After a time, each creative individual became a family member on the series. As director Michael Lange perceives it, the show's general style had been clearly indicated to him by Michael Braverman and the writing staff. "Visually," he says, "they usually let the director do pretty much his or her own thing, in terms of how to interpret a script. And that is a rare thing."

"There was never any show like *Life Goes On* before it, and there hasn't been any show like it since," concludes casting director Dee Dee Bradley. "One that has meant so much to so many. It was more than just a TV show."

Like Ray Buktenica has pointed out elsewhere in this book, Bradley became somewhat unsettled, regarding those who criticized or ignored Burke's talents. "It makes me so angry that Chris Burke never won an Emmy," she says. "He should have won. What's worse, he was never even asked to be a presenter at the Emmys ceremony." She points out that, in total, *Life Goes On* received merely two Emmys for acting [Chad Lowe, guest-actress Viveca Lindfors], which only adds to her fury. "There were some incredible performances on the show," she says, "and some wonderful scripts. But having Chris Burke never even being acknowledged by the Academy — that really upset me."

Fortunately, there is the flipside. As Michael Nankin recalls, "There is a moment I realized that we were changing the world. I was shooting the 'Arthur' episode. One of our locations was an old house in a residential section of Pasadena. Shooting on location always attracts attention and in the afternoon, after school, we had a giant group of neighborhood kids sitting on a wall across the street, watching the shoot. Chris Burke came out of his trailer and began to walk by the kids. The second they saw him, they leapt to their feet and surrounded him. They were gleeful. Their eyes were sparkling. *Corky! It's Corky!* It was a love-fest. They wanted to see him. To touch him. Chris waded through them like Christ walking on water. I watched this and realized that before *Life Goes On*, had Chris walked by this same group of kids, they would have averted their eyes, or stared at the 'retarded' kid, or perhaps said something cruel. But now they loved him. He was a TV star. His Down syndrome had become completely transparent and they saw the person beneath. This was the entire point of the show. There are some jobs that make it easy to get up in the morning."

So there you have it — once pegged a failure by some because it spotlighted a teen with Down's, *Life* instead has sprung eternal. Once misunderstood, those with AIDS and Down syndrome are perceived more clearly today, because of the program's artistic decisions in conveying realistic life choices. According to Michael Braverman, personal experiences of the show's cast and crew frequently grounded them in reality, allowing for such decisions to transpire: "Throughout the show's production, we had twenty-four pregnancies, plus an adoption."

The latter of which specifically transpired during the filming of "Proms and Prams," the final episode of the second season, when Patti Lupone's Libby brought a new life into the fold. As mentioned, by this time, off-camera, Lupone had given birth to a son of her own. Also during production of this segment, Bill Smitrovich needed to leave the set, to pick up his adopted baby girl, just then born. Such occurrences blurred "the line of fictional family," Braverman once decided. "It's kinda nice."

Echoing such sentiment at the end of "The Pilot," Tyler tells Becca, "You've sure got a nice family."

"Yeah I do, don't I," she replies.

A revelation for her.

A confirmation for the audience.

Life **creator and his star inspiration: Michael Braverman and Chris Burke.**
KALEY HUMMEL

THE *LGO* LOG

CENTRAL CREDITS

MAIN CAST

Drew Thacher . . . . Bill Smitrovich
Libby Thacher . . . . Patti Lupone
Corky Thacher. . . . . Chris Burke
Becca Thacher . . . . Kellie Martin
Paige Thacher (1989-1990) . . . . Monique Lanier
Paige Thacher (1990-1993) . . . . Tracey Needham
Nick Thacher (1992-1993) . . . Kevin and Christopher Graves
Tyler Benchfield (1989-1992) . . . . Tommy Puett
Jesse McKenna (1991-1993) . . . . .Chad Lowe
Amanda Swanson (1991-1993). . . . . Andrea Friedman
Arnold, the Semi-Wonder Dog. . . . . Bullet

SEMI-REGULAR CAST

Jerry Berkson (1989-1992) . . . . Ray Buktenica
Sal Giordano. . . . . Al Ruscio
Teresa Giordano . . . . Penny Santon
Gina Giordano (1991-1992). . . . . Mary Page Keller
Zoe (1991-1992). . . . . Leigh Ann Orsi
Mary McKenna (1991-1993) . . . . Dorothy Lyman
Mr. Benchfield (1989-1992) . . . . .Charles Frank
Mrs. Benchfield (1989-1992) . . . . .Fern Fitzgerald
Hans . . . . .David Byrd
Maxie (1989-1992) .Tanya Fenmore
Matt . . . . Adam Carl
Goodman (1992-1993) . . . . Kiersten Warren
Rona Lieberman (1989-1991). . . . . Michelle Matheson
Brian Russo (1989-1991) . . . . Eric Welch

Cousin Angela (1989-1992) . . . . Gina Hecht
Artie McDonald (1991-1993). . . . . Troy Evans
Harris Cassidy (1992-1993) . . . . Martin Milner
Kenny Stollmark, Jr. (1991-1992) . . . . Steven Eckholtd
Michael Romanov (1991-1993) . . . . Lance Guest
Ray Nelson (1991-1993). . . . . Michael Goorjian
Stan Baker (1991-1993) . . . . Barney Martin
Midge (1991-1992). . . . . Mitzi McCall
Mrs. Kneffer . . . . Gloria Gifford
Mrs. Schiller (1989-1992). . . . . Lisa Zebro
Mr. Mott (1991-1993) . . . . Robert David Hall
Paintz Kutner (1989-1992) . . . . Peter Van Norden
Lisa Gallaway (1989-1992). . . . . Karen Rauch
Brent (1989-1990). . . . . Mike Marikian
Kent (1989-1991) . . . . Craig Hurley
Doreen (1990-1991) . . . . Elyssa Davalos

PRODUCTION STAFF

Creator/Executive Producer/Director . . . Michael Braverman
Co-Executive Producer, Director (1989-91) . . Rick Rosenthal
Co-Executive Producer, Director, Writer . . . Michael Nankin
Co-Executive Producer . . . . R. W. Goodwin
Supervising Producer . . . . Liz Coe
Producers. . . . . Phillips Wylly, Sr., William Cairncross,
Thania St. John, Toni Graphia, Lorenzo De Stefano,
Bruce Ettinger
Executive Story Editor . . . . Brad Markowitz
Creative Consultants . . . E.F. Wallengren, Marshall Goldberg
Writers. . . . . Brad Markowitz, David Wolf, Star Frohman
Directors . . . Michael Lange, Kim Friedman, Gene Reynolds,
and several others.
Director of Photography . . . . Joe Pennella
Production Designer . . . . Ned Parsons, Tracy Bousman
Set Designer . . . . Charles Vasser, Eric Orbom
Editors. . . . Jim Stewart, Mallory Gottlieb, Maryann Brandon,
James Coblentz, and several others.
Composers. . . . . Craig Safan, William Olvis
Music Editing . . . . Johnson/Livingston
First Assistant Directors . . . . Louis Race, Mark Bashaar,
and several others.
Second Assistant Director. . . . . Michael J. Pendell
Men's Costume Supervisor . . . . Ed Sunley

Women's Costume Supervisor............Robert Newman,
Sara Markowitz
Make-up .... Pamela Westmore, Kevin Westmore
Hairstylists .... Cheri Ruff, Sylvia Surdie, Steve Elsbe,
Carl Bailey
Script Supervisor.....................Theresa Eubanks
Dialogue Coach................ Kaley Holdberg-Hurrel
Arnold's Trainer....................... Richard Calkins
Set Decorators................ Ira Bates, Bryan Thelford
Property Master ....Jimmy Heron, Jr.
Set Property Master .... John Martinez
Special Effects........................ Abe Hernandez
Sound Mixer....................... Andy Gilmore
First Assistant Cameraman.................. Bob Heine
Camera Operator .... Bruce Pasternack
Key Grip........................... Ted Shinneman
Gaffer .... Robert Deperna
Leadman........................... Ralph Agnone
Sound Mixers .... John Speak, Andy Gilmore
Transportation Captain..................... Jack Grant
Construction Coordinator................. Reggie Foster
Casting ....Dee Dee Bradley, John Levey
Creator's Assistant....................... Inness Wei
Assistant to Executive Producer .... Marilyn Cronkite
Assistant to Co-Executive Producer (Rick Rosenthal) ......
Marti Noxon
Assistant to Co-Executive Producer (Michael Nankin) .....
Mary Margaret Peters
Assistant to Co-Executive Producer (R. W. Goodwin)......
Elpe Villard
Titles & Opticals........................ Pacific Title

The First Season of *Life:* (from left) Monique Lanier, Kellie Martin, Bill Smitrovich, Chris Burke, Patti Lupone and Bullet (who played Arnold). *THE REGAL COLLECTION*

Episode 1: "The Pilot" . . . . [9-12-89]
*Written by Michael Braverman. Directed by Rick Rosenthal. Guest stars: Eugene
Clark, Steven Keats, Art La Fleur, Steve Eastin, David Allyn, Danna Hansen,
Kristin Pearcey, Brian Beery, Ryan Davis, Carla Dorren.*

Libby deals with turning 40 and Drew's too-expensive-gift of a ring,
while Paige moves back into the fold, and Corky attempts to mainstream
into his high school freshman year, alongside an uncomfortable Becca. She's
somewhat concerned that her unique brother may prevent her from being
with Tyler, whom she later learns, has a sibling named Donnie who also
happens to have Down's. Through it all, the "Corkster" imagines he's the
King of the Homecoming Dance, with Queen Rona Lieberman by his side.
In reality, he's accused of looking at Rona's answers during a test when, in
fact, just the opposite occurs. Should Corky mainstream, enter a special education program, or attend a private hall of academia, tuition for which the
Thachers will be incapable of sustaining? Corky, Libby, Drew and Glenbrook
High's principal take a meeting, at which time Corky recounts, word for
word, Edgar Allen Poe's eminent poem, *The Raven,* and quickly disperses
any question as to his scholarly abilities.

 • Establishes that the Thachers are middle class and sentimental (family
photos, knickknacks, personal mementos are spread throughout the house).
 • Co-executive producer Rick Rosenthal "loved" directing this episode,
which he says "has a tremendous emotional catharsis to it. It was also a lot
of fun. There was a trick shot in the end that everyone still talks about. They
wonder how I went from the dog, eating the cake, all the way through the
living room and out the window in just one shot."
 • "Corky's Theme" does not play during the closing credits, though it's
employed as background music when Paige enters the kitchen and breaks
down crying.

Episode 2: "Corky for President" .... **[9-24-89]**
Written by Paul Wolff. Directed by Kim Friedman. Guest stars: Oliver Clark, Ryan Bollman, G. Adam Gifford, Kristin Pearcey, Kevin Sifuentes, Billy Joe Wright

Corky's new school peers mistreat him in the corridors, in the bathroom and on the playing field. In class, Rona and her cheerleading click, that falsely encourage him to run for student council, use him. He seeks support from Lester, the smart, loner student, who initially declines a job as Corky's campaign manager. While Becca worries about her brother and becomes protective, relations are strained between Libby and Paige, due to Paige's breakup with a boyfriend. They eventually reconcile, and though Corky loses the campaign, he delivers a heart-wrenching spontaneous speech — after throwing his notes away.

• Substantial lines regarding the word retard, a term with which Corky finds humor, but which Chris Burke finds offensive. "I hate the word," he says.
• Drew and Libby wallpaper and paint the bathroom yellow, constituting that they do much of their own home improvement.
• Paige wants to serve humanity. When Rona asks Corky, and not Lester, to a party, Paige advises Corky to lie to Lester; to say he's going shopping. But Corky doesn't even know what revenge means, let alone a lie. He seeks only to do the right thing.
• At one point, Corky says, "I have feelings, Lester. Just like you do." And when Libby threatens to give a school bully "a shot right across his lip," Corky says, "Please, Mom. I can take care of myself."
• Drew, regarding Corky: "He loses and gets hurt all the time, but he picks himself up and tries again."
• The following conversation between Tyler and Becca gives good insight into Tyler's relationship with his father, his brother, Donnie (who has Down's), Corky and Becca:

> *Tyler:* You and the Cork are the only kids in school who know I have a Down's brother. And if you don't mind I'd like to keep it that way.
> *Becca:* Why?
> *Tyler:* I'm a private type of person, that's all. My dad's like that, too. We just don't like people knowing our personal business, okay?
> *Becca:* But that's wrong. Tyler, you can't keep a secret like that locked up forever. You're ashamed of a member of your own family!
> *Tyler:* I'm not ashamed!

Becca: Yes you are!

Tyler: Oh and you're totally comfortable with it, right? I don't see you going around announcing to the world: "Hey, guys, I have a special brother!"

Becca: I happen to be proud of my brother.

Tyler: Oh yeah? Then why don't you support him for president?

Becca: Because I don't want him to get hurt. That's why!

Tyler: You don't want to get hurt! The spotlight's on him and you don't like it because it's gonna be on you, too! So don't preach to me, Becca 'cause underneath you're just like me …"

• And then later, Tyler argues with Brian Russo, who wonders why Tyler cares so much about not hurting Corky's feelings: "What's with you, man? You act like the guy's your brother or somethin'?"

He is my brother," Tyler replies.

• Later, Becca defines Corky: "He doesn't even know what revenge is. He just wants to do good."

• In another poignant moment, Libby reminds Drew: "Remember when he was an infant and we didn't know if he would ever be able to talk or walk?…I went to Mass every morning. I wore out my knees. Please, just let him be able to do some normal kid things… So… let him get puffed up! It's normal. Let him lose. Let him win. Let him have his day in the sun."

• Corky's speech: "I'd like to win…But if I didn't I still have some wishes… I wish the kids who tease handicapped people could stand inside our shoes. Then, they would know we have a life. We have dreams…just like you. All we want is a chance to be your friend…Thank you very much."

• The Libby/Paige conflict here comes to a head in the episode, "Paige's Mom."

• The character of Steve is played by Scott Weinger, who was the voiceover for the 1992 film *Aladdin,* starred on ABC's *Full House,* and whom Kellie Martin calls one of her "best friends."

Episode 3: "The Babysitter" . . . . [10-1-89]
Written by Jule Selbo. Directed by Rick Rosenthal. Guest stars: Paul Gleason, Parley Baer (Bewitched), Rebecca Stanley, Jacob Gelman, Kevin Telles, Jr., Jay Saunders, William Barker, Jodi Peterson, Jason Hillhouse, R. Leo Schreiber, Don Maxwell, Kristin Pearcey

Becca's got a hot date, can't baby sit for little Billy Graber, and asks Corky to step in as her replacement. Drew and Libby are apprehensive about this development, as are the Graber parents (she works in the school office; he's a dentist). But after Corky's meeting with them, followed by a test run, and a minor Thacher/Graber conflict, he gets the job. Unfortunately, the evening becomes a nightmare when Tyler's ill-will friends pay a visit to Corky and Billy, and a possible gas leak leads to a lost walk in a wooded area on the outskirts of town.

Corky reads to Billy from The Owl and the Pussycat, while Tyler later wants to borrow The Grapes of Wrath.

• We learn Drew and Libby were married on March 8, 1971, when he plays "First Time Ever I Saw Your Face" on the stereo; when he and Libby are alone for the first time in a long time (though they later check on Corky and bring him some cannoli).

• We meet Mr. Hube, played by Parley Baer, who later appears in "Thacher and Henderson."

• Paige decides to be a vegetarian, while her boyfriend shows up for their date with two motorcycle helmets.

• Becca to Drew and Libby: "I'm always in trouble. I try to do something kind, helpful and intelligent and it turns around and bites me in the butt."

• Drew to Stan Graber: "I'm not saying that all Down's kids are capable of babysitting...I guess what I'm saying is that they're individuals, just like us. There's some things I'm good at, some things I'm not. And I know what my son is good at."

• "I like this episode a lot," says Chris Burke, "because it shows that Corky can have a job, to be a babysitter, which I do in real life. It shows that Corky can handle a situation like this without having other adult people in the house. It gives a message of independence for Corky. The father gave Corky a chance to baby sit for his son, even though they come to not trust Corky in the end. My favorite scene is when Corky admits to the father that he did a good job. And that was a real important moment with Drew."

Episode 4: "Break a Leg, Mom" . . . . [10-8-89]
Written by Michael Braverman. Directed by Rick Rosenthal. Guest stars: Dena Dietrich, Jim Holmes, Greg Kinnear, John Wheeler, Phil Reeves, Mark Travis Fuller, Mary Anne Schafer, Cynthia Mann, Brad Miller, Julie Redford, The Del Rubio Triplets

Corky wants to be like everyone else. That includes learning to drive (from Coach McNulty, who also instructs Driver Education), and doing well in mainstream school, both at which he is failing. He's also feeling even more isolated, because no one ever told him about his mother's past singing career. To top it off, he now feels responsible for her decision to cut short that career. So he makes a deal: He'll return to educational tutoring (with students who are ten years younger) if she auditions for the local community college production of Autumn Follies.

• Becca is both embarrassed and jealous when Tyler sees her in hair rollers and a mudpack, while he also notices Paige (who's washing her old Volvo).

• Becca and Libby go through family memorabilia and old photos of relatives who are obviously Italian and classical musicians.

• We learn that Libby likes to garden, and Drew likes to bowl (he wears his team shirt here).

• With a general concern for health and the environment, Paige complains about the misuse of water, high cholesterol, and Drew's dietary choices. She also goes on a date with a handsome and smartly-dressed man who seems perfect until he opens his mouth.

• Major flashback: To 1971, when Corky was born in the hospital. The doctor explains numerous problems, instructing Drew and Libby to institutionalize Corky. But they will have none of that. In the background, we hear "Blowin' in the Wind."

• At the end of Act One appears one of the most unforgettable moments in the series' history. It takes place between Libby and Corky:

> *Libby:* Corky, are you still bummed out about your accident in driver's ed? ... Hey, we all have accidents. Don't you remember when Daddy slid into the snowplow? Or the fender-bender Paige had at the market last year? Everybody has accidents. C'mon. Don't worry about it.
> *Corky:* You had an accident, too, didn't you?
> *Libby:* No, I don't think so, but...
> *Corky:* Yes you did...Me.

Then, a major flashback to 1971 in the hospital, when Corky was born:

> *Dr. Singleton:* Look, these things happen. It's a quirk of nature, a genetic misfire...nobody's to blame. It happens.
> *Libby:* I want to see my baby.
> *Dr. Singleton:* Libby, please, you don't. Don't put yourself through this.
> *Libby:* I want to see my son.
> *Dr. Singleton:* Drew, please, do her a favor, talk to her... Libby, listen to what I'm saying...It's Down syndrome. Chances are this baby may never walk, never talk, never be able to take care of itself. He'll be nothing but an incredible, unrelenting burden on you and...and Drew for the rest of its life. Don't do it to yourselves.

Drew: What do you suggest we do, Doc. Just walk away
and leave him here? Huh? Is that what you want?
Dr. Singleton: No, of course not. All I'm suggesting is that
there are some pretty terrific institutions that specialize in
caring for these children...Libby, look, you don't have to...
in fact, you shouldn't decide right now. Just think about
it, okay? You asked me the options and I'm telling you...I
think...You should put him in an institution. It's the best
place for him and for you. Put him in an institution."
Libby: Over my dead body.

Later, in the present, Patti Lupone sings "Wind Beneath My Wings" to
Corky, a scene that Rick Rosenthal defines as "very powerful."

Rosenthal categorizes this episode "honest in its assessments of limitations and that's where we got back on track, in terms of more accurately portraying a kid with Down syndrome as developmentally disabled, as opposed
to giving him the ability to leap buildings."

Episode 5: "Becca's First Love" . . . . [10-15-89]
*Written by Jule Selbo. Directed by Rick Rosenthal. Guest stars: Peter Neptune,
Robert Dubac, and "Andrew"*

Becca falls for Gabe, the 16-year-old lead singer in a neighborhood
band, which also includes Maxie's brother. She stays out with Maxie to
listen to the group past their curfew. Backstage after a later performance,
Drew walks in as Gabe is just about to plant one on Becca. Eventually,
Gabe shows his true (selfish) colors, while Becca and her dad bond even
closer.

• Kellie Martin's narrative as Becca is employed here much like Fred
Savage's voiceover as Kevin on The Wonder Years; though it's more apparent here that she's writing her diary. ("How many nerve endings can be in
your lips"..."Why do I have to lose Dad to have Gabe?")
• Major fantasy/literal/visual sequences, via Gabe's mesmerization of
Becca: Becca's hair stands on end, her brain turns to mush, she becomes
embedded in a block of ice, dresses as Benedict Arnold, spontaneously com-
busts, lives homeless in cardboard box and checks into convent, in full nun's
garb and habit.
• When Becca asks Libby what Drew is afraid of, she replies: "sex."
• Great line from Corky: "Girls are pretty weird."
• Becca asks Paige if she ever fought with Drew. "Yes, but he gets over it
quickly."

• Meanwhile, Paige, whose 20th birthday falls on the night of Gabe's concert, gives Becca love advice, and calls Gabe an "octopus."

• Gabe labels Becca his lucky charm, and admonishes her to not "get heavy" or be "a downer."

• There are several heavy laughs, at Drew's expense: He gained ten pounds when Paige started dating. Becca was good for fifteen. In the end, he shines through, when Becca throws her arms around him, and says she sorry. Drew replies: "I just can't keep all the pain away."

• Maxie's brother's name is Ben, and makes his only series appearance.

• There's a warm, climactic scene with family and ice cream, and a nice speech from Drew, at the close. Though an upset Becca has the best line when she tells Gabe, "Everyone else is just Kleenex. You blow your nose and you throw them away."

• Director Rick Rosenthal had "a wonderful time doing this episode. It was interesting for me. Again, it's another example of the show's ability to portray honesty. For example, in dealing with Drew's protection of Becca, his concerns, and his anger."

Episode 6: "Paige's Date" . . . . [10-22-89]
Written by Joe Shulkin. Directed by Jerry Jameson. Guest stars: Johnny Haymer, Steve Eastin, Kenneth Danziger, Ken Foree, Geoffrey Blake, Faye DeWitte, Kirk Scott

Corky and Drew are concerned with economic security and the future. Corky wants money for a new electric train. Drew compares his life and career to those of his peers. In the midst of these assessments, Drew and Libby attend the wedding of a friend's daughter, where Drew meets Larry, whom he believes is an ideal love match for Paige. The date, however, ends up not only being a dud, but a con artist; a discovery that becomes apparent when the young man attempts to swindle Corky out of the hard-earned money he acquired by raking leaves for Drew, and washing and polishing the family's Ramcharger.

• Many comic bits, including: Libby being dumped on by a waiter during a business dinner with Jerry, Drew's carry through from an instruction book to test an abdominal tension exerciser; and his use of a plunger on a kitchen garbage disposal.

• Drew also has an interesting fantasy sequence, when he envisions Paige's wedding and a feast in the Thacher mansion.

• Part of Corky's enterprising: Creating a tag board with a magic marker for his lemonade sign.

• Four different monologues with Paige have her speaking directly to the camera on what was called a Limbo set; the first and only time this technique was used. The first aside involves her trouble with men, and that dating is not pretty; that's how she got involved with Larry, but that's getting ahead of herself. So she starts the teaser with: "Dad and Libby were invited to Kathy Ross' wedding," and the segment segues into the original opening. The second has Paige professing her love with Larry. The third has her wondering why everyone is so down on him. The fourth reveals that she's been crying. "I never saw Larry again…they were right and I was wrong." This concludes with her saying, "…a couple of weeks later, I met Jeffrey. Yep. I think I'm in love again. But that's another story."

• "We broke through the fourth wall," Michael Braverman says of Paige's camera-talk. "We felt we had an extraordinarily bad episode. Some of it was really bad. And by the time we cut out a lot of useless dialogue, we were short nine minutes. So we placed Paige as the narrator on screen of every act. We didn't have the money or the time to write and edit in additional scenes. So it was one of those times where we said, Okay…let's make her a narrator."

Episode 7: "Paige's Mom" . . . . [11-5-89]
Written by Ronald Rubin. Directed by Gene Reynolds. Guest stars: Lisa Banes, Christopher Neame, Wayne Quimby, Jenna Pangburn.

Paige's free-spirited, independent mom (who's now been married three times) pays a short visit. She and Paige share new joyful times together, and make plans for a trip to England. Then the irresponsible mother winds up leaving without her daughter, whose heart is torn and broken, once more, as it had been so very along ago. Paige, Drew and Libby remember almost too well when her inconsiderate mother, who chose the stage instead, left Paige, as a child.

• Several stylish film noir sequences were filmed in black and white, such as when Paige meets her biological mom at a restaurant while it rains, and when the show flashbacks to Paige's past in 1974, in Drew and Libby's old apartment.
• A serious confrontation occurs between Paige's mother and Libby in the kitchen, a battle that Paige witnesses from aside.
• Becca and Tyler rehearse Romeo and Juliet, for which Libby fits Becca with a costume.
• Drew and Libby watch TV (football), and eat homemade popcorn.
• Corky studies math.
• Drew calls Paige "Button," while Paige ultimately reaches out to Libby and calls her "Mom"…for the first time.

Episode 8: "Call of the Wild". . . . . [11-12-89]
Written by Linda Cowgill. Directed by Georg Fenady. Guest stars: Nicolas Coster, Mickey Jones, Ned Romero, Banscomb Richmond, Amy Lemon, Biff Wiff, Michelle Davison

Drew's hired to develop new luxury homes on a construction site that could lead to a big promotion. Problem is, the area is located on the Indian Woods burial ground, where a wolf mysteriously guards the land. While Paige joins a campaign to stop the construction, Corky somehow connects with the animal, on an intuitive and almost spiritual level. As a result, Drew's job future is questioned, while Corky's safety also becomes a concern. hen the wolf rescues Corky from Dobermans, however, everyone's perspective changes.

• One fantasy sequence involves a semi-transparent Corky rising out of a sleeping Corky, running through woods and encountering the wolf.
• Drew straightens tools in the garage, fixes the gate, eats from pizza boxes in the back patio, tries to practice football with Corky, and dries dishes while Libby washes
• Drew later sips beer and eats peanuts in a bar with his boss.
• A film montage at the end illustrates the erosion, pollution and destruction of nature, if we don't watch it.

Episode 9: "Corky Witnesses a Crime" . . . . [11-26-89]
Written by Tom O'Brien. Directed by Kim Friedman. Guest stars: Dennis Arndt (Annie McGuire), Alan Oppenheimer (The Six Million Dollar Man), Michael Bays, Kevin Telles, Dan Dierdorf, Frank Gifford (married to Kathie Lee), Al Michaels, Mel Johnson, Jr., Lance Reed, Matthew Ross, Deonca Brown

Corky tries out for the football team, but only qualifies for the position of water and equipment manager. It's a good thing, too, because the coach abuses his team; one member in particular, quite violently. Corky sees the whole thing, and is compelled to tell the truth. He has his chance when a trial is called. At first, the coach tries to say that he was hit first. But that's not what happened. He even tries to turn the tables on Corky, but fails when other players on the team side against the man they once admired. Now, it's Corky who has their respect.
• Corky works a jigsaw puzzle and listens to music with headphones from a tape deck, while struggling with the situation at hand.
• Flashbacks include present-episode-scenes of the locker room with the coach screaming at Corky, and slamming a student against lockers.
• We learn that those with Down's can't play contact sports (which is also

stated again in "Thacher and Henderson").

• Arnold eats from an overloaded bowl, and barks.

• Bill Smitrovich likes this episode, but regrets "that there was never a confrontational scene between Drew and the Coach. That was unfortunate. Here is where I think we could have seen a little bit more of a who do you think you are type attitude from Drew." As stated elsewhere, Smitrovich "wanted Drew to be less emotional, and more direct. More aware. More assertive. There were times where I would have just loved Drew to corner some jerk, and just lay him out. I wish there would have been just one episode when he did that. He would have suffered the consequences, but he would have felt real good about it."

• Though Smitrovich admits that such a development would have not only distanced Drew from humor, but would have also "run the risk of having your character be unlikable. And they spent a lot of time trying to make sure that Drew was never unlikable."

Episode 10: "Ordinary Heroes" . . . . [12-3-89]
Written by Paul Wolff. Directed by Gene Reynolds. Guest stars: Louis Giambalvo, Jennifer Savidge, Mario Roccuzzo, Earl Boen, Steve Eastin, Apollo Dukakis, James McIntire

After struggling for some time with the frustrations of construction work, and not being his own boss, Drew quits his construction job and goes into the restaurant business. Meanwhile, too, he joins Libby in counseling a couple whose newborn daughter has Down's. As the father finds it difficult to accept his special child, the owners of Drew's potential restaurant refuse to sell him the establishment because of Corky.

• We learn that Hans makes the best french fries.

• Corky and Becca do a take-off of the famous cheeseburger-cheeseburger routine from *Saturday Night Live*.

• Drew eats and hurts his back when stressed out. Libby massages his back twice.

• Drew and Libby sand off varnish of an old chair on the covered kitchen table.

• One late night in a nearby park on swings, Drew talks with his friend, the reluctant father-to-be of a Down's baby, and calls such children "gifts."

• Later, at home, Corky awakens for a midnight snack, and wonders about his dad's friend: "Are you the man who had the Down syndrome baby?" he asks.

"Yes, I am," the man replies.

Corky smiles, shakes the hand of his father's pal, and says,

"Congratulations!"

According to Chris Burke, this dialogue was taken from his real life: "This episode was based on a true story. I have this friend of mine, Jim Bizel, who's actually a very good friend of my parents. I said the same thing to him that Corky did to Drew's friend."

"There were many nice touches in this episode," adds Michael Braverman, who credits writer Paul Wolff, who stayed with the series for approximately one year. "This was his first episode."

As to the particular prejudice shown toward Corky here, Bill Smitrovich concludes: "Unfortunately, it happens, and you have to deal with it."

Episode 11: "Pets, Guys & Videotape" .... [12-10-89]
Written by Star Frohman. Directed by Mel Damski. Guest stars: Whip Hubley (Flipper), Marianne Muellerleile, Mary Pat Gleason, Mary Betten, Vivian Bonnell, Lana Schwab, Jean Speegle Howard, Irene Forrest, Reuben Grundy

It's Christmastime, and Libby, Paige and Becca uncover valuable insight into the challenges faced by modern working women, while Corky obsesses over the film Casablanca. Paige wants to earn money to move out, so she finds a job as a receptionist at the office of a veterinarian who knows how to talk to the animals, but seems to have trouble relating to humans. While she struggles with her attraction to the man (who is divorced with child), as a school assignment, Becca videotapes a chaotic career day in the life of Libby.

• There's an important Hawaii foreshadowing to the first segment of the second season ("Vacation from Hell"), when Paige gifts her parents with money from her first paycheck toward their second honeymoon.

• Drew sings a few bars of "Tiny Bubbles," but Libby makes him promise never to do so again.

• Paige's vet/boyfriend makes another appearance in "Thacher and Henderson." The actor who portrays him, Whip Hubley, later appears as Becca's gym teacher in "Head Over Heels."

• Several comedic bits: Corky does magic. Paige tries to work as a Mary Kay-type cosmetic salesperson and has fantasies of being with her vet (in the operating room and in a "madcap crazy world" film-style of the 1940s).

• We also hear (once again) that Paige is a vegetarian.

• Drew exits shower with wet hair (and later wears his tool belt), while the family watches *Casablanca* on TV, cracking and eating walnuts.

• Corky is seen in bed reading a Casablanca companion book, and wearing a t-shirt of his hero: Casablanca star Humphrey Bogart.

• Restaurant suggestion: Antonio's.

• Also, though this episode takes place during the December holiday, it is not designated as a Christmas episode, but rather an episode that happens to be surrounded by Christmas; a rarity for series TV (and keeps with the show's just-so-happens-to-be general theme).

• We also hear first mention of the extra room above the garage, early on, when Paige's school chum stays over. The room later becomes an apartment for Paige, who later gives the place to Corky and Amanda when they get married.

Episode 12: "Corky's Crush" . . . . [1-14-90]
Written by Jule Selbo. Directed by Gene Reynolds. Guest stars: Shannen Doherty (90210), Cristine Rose, Ryan Bollman

Becca and Corky (both freshmen and sharing some classes) do a classroom exercise in which paired students pretend to be married for a week to investigate issues of marriage and family life. Becca is first partnered with Lester, then switches to Tyler. Neither works out terribly well. Corky, on the other hand, hooks up with the new girl in school, upon whom he develops a crush. But she only has eyes for Russo, and Corky has to make peace with only being friends. Meanwhile, Libby's parents hole up at the Thachers, and continue their love feud.

• Becca fantasizes about being married to Tyler, and later stout-heartily defends Corky: "You're talking about my brother. He's got Down syndrome. Do you have a problem with that?" To Ginny and Russo: "I think you two are the most insensitive people on this planet." She also pictures Rona's face on a dartboard. But that's ultimately why she wins with a new boyfriend (played by Scott Weinger in his second appearance).

• Great speech from Libby to her parents about appreciation: "Don't you see how lucky you are."

• Libby's parents had three children? Who else besides her and Gina (Mary Page Keller)?

• Drew has the birds-and-the-bees talk with Corky, when Corky writes Ginny a poem. "Both people have to want to be kissed"… "Corky, you have to find the right person. Everyone has to find the right person."

• Arnold eats popcorn with the family, who are all drinking hot chocolate, and watching home movies of Drew and a six-year-old Paige playing ball.

• Libby's father, Sal, gives Corky a haircut, and has a nice moment when he encourages his grandson that the right girl is out there.

• "Corky did have a chance to at least dance with Ginny," Chris Burke says, "and I thought that was important, even though she turned out to be not such a nice person. Most of her friends did not like Corky."

• "With episodes like these," Burke concludes, "it really helped teenagers see a different perspective [on romance], from someone like Corky."

Episode 13: "Thacher and Henderson" . . . . [1-21-90]
Written by Michael Nankin. Directed by Rick Rosenthal. Guest stars: James Cromwell, Sherry Rooney, Alan Blumenfeld, Jordon Lund, David Crowley, David Selburg, John Di Santi, Nick Angotti, Udana Power, Anne Wyndham, Steve Hutchins, Leigh Taylor Walker, Marsha Kramer, Bryan Schwarz, Brendan Schwartz

At Drew's high school football reunion game: He finally makes peace with his best friend after a falling out over a business deal that caused him to lose ten thousand dollars; he learns his friend's son died of crib death; Becca watches through binoculars as Paige chooses between Dr. Matthews, the vet, and Kent, the motorcycle man. Becca then gets a crush on one of the football players until Tyler shows up, placing her in the same situation as Paige. Throughout it all, Corky aches to play contact sports, while Libby pains to tell him that such a thing will never be.

• Opens with Drew, working out. Paige says: "Dad's using the bike. Dad's exercising." "Wow," Becca replies.
• Very funny physical comedy episode.
• Mr. Hube (Parley Baer) and Paige's vet-boyfriend, Dr. Oliver Matthews (Whip Hubley) make second appearances. The latter's emergence motivates Paige's Harley love to ask, "What's up, Doc."
• Corky's athletic enough to at least run in this episode, and jump for joy (when he finds Mr. Hube's lost coin). But Libby reminds him. "No physical sports."
• Early handshake between Drew and Henderson represents show's theme: forgiveness.
• Football halftime is called at the episode's half-hour commercial break.
• Libby gets the ball.
• Drew physically battles with Henderson, which is difficult for Libby, Becca, Paige and Corky, who eventually says, "Dad, you don't throw away your friends."
• Of the actual fight, Bill Smitrovich comments, "It was upsetting to both of us [he and James Cromwell] to do the scene. I mean, we got into it...big time. And I've seen Jamie since then, at a basketball game in Vancouver. He's a great guy."
• Smitrovich also makes note that this episode featured "many great actors, including Peter Van Orten."
• "When I was writing this segment," recalls Michael Nankin, "I real-

ized that it all took place in this park. There were sixteen football players
and their families, and they were all in every shot. Just talking about that
with some people on the set made us shiver. We thought it was going to
take forever to do the episode. But we were told, Oh, no ... it's going to
be fine. It ended up being a hugely expensive show to film. Not only that,
it was shot during December, during the shortest day of the year, and
it was always daylight. Then halfway through the shoot, Rick Rosenthal
came down with the chicken pox. And everything was shut down for three
days."

Episode 14: "The Return of Uncle Richard" . . . . [2-4-90]
*Written by Michael Braverman. Directed by Kim Friedman. Guest stars: Rick
Rosenthal, Monique Salcido, Tom Maier, Claire Berger, Dominic Oliver*

Uncle Arnie, husband to Dorothy, and mother to Cousin Angela, dies.
The Thachers go to the funeral, where Corky is apprehensive about seeing the body. Libby's mother empathizes with him, and protests on his
behalf. Drew and Libby, however, decide that he should go to the wake.
Consequently, Corky envisions the dead man's eyes opening and runs out of
the parlor. Later, he becomes obsessed with the thought that his parents will
die and leave him alone. The question then becomes: who will take care of
Corky in the advent of Drew and Libby's death? Becca, Paige? Libby thinks
it would be selfish for either of her children to have to worry about Corky.
In the midst of this, visits Drew's younger brother Richard, a lovable family
black sheep, and with whom he doesn't get along. But the kids love him, so
much so, that they convince Richard to chuck his too-fake-looking toupee.
All ends well when Libby and Drew decide to entrust Corky in Richard's
care upon their demise

• Lots of good lines: Becca at the funeral, "We're all dying to be here."
Later, to Corky: "You're missing the joy of relatives." And, "Everybody
dies."
• Libby to Becca: "Daddy and I will be around long enough to see your
grandchildren." To Becca and Paige: "Goodnight, women."
• Cousin Angela tells Richard's girlfriend, regarding Corky: "Please
stop frightening him with your ridiculous theatrics," and turns to Corky:
"I'm sorry he's teasing you." Corky replies: "I'm used to it." He tells Richard,
referencing his fake-looking toupee, "The hair isn't you. I like the real
you."
• Becca adds later: "You're really very handsome. You don't need a rug."
• Richard tells Corky: "As long as I've got a breath left in this stout body,
you'll never be alone."

• Richard and Becca talk about Tyler:

> *Becca:* Friends are precious. Two different people sharing
> the same soul.
> *Richard:* This Tyler...he sounds kind of young for you.

• And later, during a basketball game, Becca says, "No way." "Way,"
Richard replies.

• Corky, Becca, and Paige visit Richard while packing, and he fesses up:

> *Richard:* I lied. I'm what you call a phony. I'm not like your
> dad. I never quite got it all together.
> *Becca:* It's not what you've done or not done. It's who you
> are.
> *Richard:* I'm a failure.
> *Corky:* Not as an uncle.

• Drew is 43 here (Uncle Ernie is five years older).

• Drew calls Libby's dad by his first name (Sal).

• The dead man's eyes opening is an early nightmare edition of a fantasy
sequence.

• Who is Cousin Angela, and how is she related to the family? Through
Libby?

• Libby's mom, Theresa, is interested in Angela's romance.

• We get a first look at the room over the garage, which will house Gina
and Zoe in the second season, then Paige, and finally Corky and Amanda,
when Paige gives them the place for their wedding, and returns to her
room.

• There's a reference to Bette Davis' death (who had passed away shortly
before this segment aired).

• Michael Braverman "owed" Rick Rosenthal an acting episode. "When
we did the pilot," Braverman explains, "he always harbored the belief that
he'd like to be an actor. I said, Okay, if it ever goes, I'll write you a show.
So I wrote 'The Return of Uncle Richard,' and Kim Friedman directed it.
Though they threw me off the set because I was thinking of directing it. But
I didn't have the time. I used to stand behind Kim, and Rick was a very insecure actor. Kim would say, Cut, Print, and I would just shake my head. Then
Kim would say, Okay, we're going to go again, and he'd come up to me and
say, Okay what's the problem? Apparently, I was throwing Rick off. It got
too crazy for him. So I threw myself off the set. But, overall it was a very
strong episode, with a solid beginning, middle and end."

• "Though Kim Friedman directed this," Rosenthal admits, "I will say that
there were times when I thought that Michael Braverman was directing it.

It was amusing, because I would look over at Kim, and she would get one set of notes, and I would get another set. It was a little confusing."

• Meanwhile, Chris Burke "didn't like this episode because Uncle Richard was a con man, and he lied."

Episode 15: "Brothers" . . . . [2-11-90]
Written by Ronald Rubin. Directed by Jerry Jameson. Guest stars: Alfred Dennis, Michael Griswold, Nancy Stephens, Michael Rankin, Karen Rauch, Brad Silverman, Ellerine Harding, Lisa Fusco, Tara Hutchins, David Bursin

The Special Olympics, a time for warm-hearted competition and fun, also brings love to Corky and a challenge to Tyler, whose father won't permit Donnie to participate in the games.

• Many of the show's stars, including Chris Burke, Bill Smitrovich and Chad Lowe, volunteer their time year round with several charity events similar to those portrayed here.

Episode 16: "Corky Rebels" . . . . [2-18-90]
Written by Paul Wolfe. Directed by Gene Reynolds. Guest stars: Rod McCary, Tony Mangano, John Wheeler, Andy Hirsch, Gina Marie Vinaccia, Beverly Piper, Ruben Santiago Hudson, Nicole Gruber, Howie Lotker

At 18, Corky wants out from under his parents' wings, even if it means just taking the bus to school. He feels he's older than Becca, but she gets to do more on her own. Unfortunately, Corky then ends up hanging with the wrong crowd and, with bad boy antics, auditions for the community talent show with a hip-hop dance routine. The not-so-great crowd eventually turns on Corky, who mends his ways and does his standard tap routine with Becca — and is finally is allowed, after much study with Libby and Drew, to take the bus.

• Corky performs to "Fight the Power" from Spike Lee's film, *Do the Right Thing*.
• Libby sings Gershwin's "Someone to Watch Over Me."
• Corky wonders: "You talking to me."
• Good conversation between Tyler and Becca:

> *Tyler:* Having a special brother isn't so special. Sometimes it hurts."
> *Becca:* I guess I do have mixed feelings about it.
> *Tyler:* Join the club.

• Becca later freaks out about dealing with Corky (and his Down syndrome), or at least not admitting to a problem.

• Drew to Libby, in bed, regarding Frankie: "Why did you date him?" Libby: "Because he was cute."

• The scene dissolves with the added special effect of Drew's glowing green eyes of jealousy. (A fantasy sequence within reality?)

• Drew to Frankie: "Break a leg. And if you don't stop coming on to my wife, maybe I'll break it myself."

• School gang leader asks Corky to steal lunch. Corky refuses, and later defends Becca: "Don't touch my sister."

• Mrs. Kneffer tells Drew and Libby: "Some parents of handicapped kids tend to be confused." Libby replies: "Oh, is that right?'"

• "We had done a couple of episodes where we had the chance to do a show-with-a-show," says Rick Rosenthal. "And those are always fun because you know the actors get to play more than one role."

Episode 17: "It Ain't All It's Cracked Up to Be" . . . . [3-4-90]
Written by Star Frohman. Directed by Kim Friedman. Guest stars: Reni Santoni (Seinfeld), *William Gallo, Dick Patterson, Jennifer Warren, Ami Foster, Ann Walker, Edmund Shaff, James Nixon, Ginger Alden, Dinah Lacey, Loyda Ramos*

With a scholarship as the prize, Becca enters a Miss Teen contest and finds out that she is sharing a room with none other than Rona. Becca gets to see a different side to Rona, whose troubled mother shows up drunk, and embarrasses Rona during her piano solo. And while Drew has problems with the new neighbors, whose young son plays his band's music a little too loudly, Corky fails to make the school chorus because he can't sing. Later, the neighbor boy gives his old set of drums to Corky, who has apparently found his musical niche. Drew and the neighbors then make peace, as do Becca and Rona, and, to some extent, Rona and her mother.

• Libby tries to teach Corky to sing, which she will also attempt with Paige in "Proms and Prams."

• Becca, who really looks like Libby here, says: "Paige is the one with the dates. I'm the one with the grades."

• Tyler makes himself at home in the Thacher kitchen.

• The neighbors here, who are of a Latin descent, would have made good semi-regulars, especially with a prejudice tie-in, but they never made another appearance.

• Good episode theme: the issue of true inner beauty.

• This theme is further explored in "Udder Madness," from the fourth season (when Becca, via Ray's sneaky nomination, joins a Homecoming Queen contest and loses out to a cow).

Episode 18: "Pig 'O My Heart" . . . . [3-25-90]
Written by Michael Nankin. Directed by Michael Braverman. Guest stars: Paul Koslo, Mario Roccuzzo

Drew finally gets a chance to own his own restaurant, but it's Corky who brings home the bacon. He adopts a huge runaway female pig named Jeffrey, who hogs Corky's affections; a development that is evidently helping to fill the void left by the absence of Paige, who moves out.

• Paige gives Becca a watch.
• Drew tells Libby that he will never let Corky experience the kind of hurtful prejudice that the restaurant man's brother relayed in "Ordinary Heroes," a few episodes back. And how Drew attains the restaurant also bears discussion: In "Heroes," he tries to purchase it, but when the brothers who own it discover that Corky has Down's, one of them gets cold feet, saying Corky might be bad for business. The writers then decided to focus instead on the fact that Drew can't get the loan approved to buy the place. When the owner of the pig is finally reunited with the animal, he mentions something about liking restaurants, but not having the time to run them. Drew sees his chance and goes for it, with a Grand Opening of the Glenbrook Grill (with cameos by many friends of the family from previous episodes).

Episode 19: "Becca and the Underground Newspaper" . . . . [4-1-90]
Written by Jule Selbo. Directed by Rick Rosenthal. Guest stars: Georgann Johnson, Brandon Douglas, William Gallo, Jan Rubes, Helen Page Camp, Susan Merson, Danielle Koenig (daughter of Star Trek's Walter Koenig), John Welsh, Steve Jerro, Matthew Ross, Brenda Kay Pope

As a reporter for her school's underground newspaper, Becca zealously pens an exposé of Kominksy, the janitor. The article misrepresents his past, communicating some criminal activity that is only partly true; he had a minor illegal infraction years ago when he broke into a house to steal money to feed himself and his wife. And Becca never interviews him for his side of the story. The scandal breaks, and Becca realizes the irresponsibility of her actions, even though she was pressured into such tactics by her pretentious editor (who also asked her out). She apologizes to Kominsky, publishes a formal retraction in the legit school paper, and Kominksy then gets a job at the Grill.

• "We delved a little bit more into the high-school world here," comments Rick Rosenthal. "Everyone involved was quite good, and I thought that we got everything that we could get from the episode."

Episode 20: "Save the Last Dance for Me" . . . . [4-15-90]
Written by Judith Fein. Directed by Larry Shaw. Guest stars: Viveca Lindfors, Steven Keats, Mark Hutter, Ryan Bollman, Susan Merson, Don Maxwell, Gregory Daniel, Deborah Strang, Joe Stark, Laura Mooney, Steve Jerro

A lover of dance, Becca writes an essay about the art form for English class, while her aged dance teacher (who had once taught Libby), must enter a nursing home — a development that inspires Corky to add to her life his special touch of grace.

• Rick Rosenthal: "We were dealing with the issues of age and aging. It is an extraordinary, fabulous episode. Viveca Lindfors gave a wonderful performance. Larry Shaw's direction was superb; especially what he did with the ghost dancers. The episode, in all, had some of the best imagery that the show ever generated."
• Kellie Martin: "This was one of my favorite episodes. I'm a ballet fanatic."

Episode 21: "With a Mighty Heart" . . . . [4-29-90]
Written by Paul Wolff. Directed by Paul Wolff. Guest stars: Pat Hingle, F. William Parker, Andy Craig, Heather Lind, Peter Stracke

Drew's father has always been somewhat of a vagabond. Now the eldest Thacher stops by on his way to join the Peace Corps in the Solomon Islands. There seems to be more to this story, as Drew senses something is amiss, resulting with an intense confrontation between the two, and the opening — and healing — of old wounds.

• Guest actor Pat Hingle is a veteran performer of the stage, film and television. As Bill Smitrovich recalls, Hingle was "a delight to work with."

Episode 22: "The Spring Fling" . . . . [5-13-90]
Written by Ronald Rubin. Directed by Larry Shaw. Guest stars: Tony Mockus, Archie Lang, Jeff Imada, Karen Rauch, Jodi Peterson, Nina Werman

Tyler finally asks Becca to the dance. Problem is, she had already accepted an invitation from Matt. She goes to the dance with Matt, telling Tyler (who is performing with his band) that she'll meet him there. They both think they are on a date with her. Meanwhile, Libby's at home, contemplating the increasing maturity of both Becca and Corky.

• In the first episode of the following season, this episode is referenced when Becca, Tyler and Maxie have a conversation regarding the dance. At this point in the series, such a reference was unique, as the show had yet to be serialized.

The Second Season of *Life:* (from left): Chris Burke, Patti Lupone, Bill Smitrovich, Kellie Martin and Bullet, with a Paige still missing (as Tracey Needham does not join the series until a few sophomore segments later). *THE REGAL COLLECTION*

Episode 23: "Honeymoon from Hell" . . . . [9-16-90]
Written by Michael Braverman. Directed by Rick Rosenthal. Guest stars: Dennis Arndt, Oliver Clark, Patrick Thomas O'Brian, Ray Bumatai, Don Ho, Lisa Zebro

Corky wins a raffle prize: a trip to Hawaii. For Drew and Libby, it's their dream vacation. Becca, on the other hand, doesn't want to go, but concedes. Things start to turn sour upon their arrival in the hula capitol. Their luggage is lost, their hotel is a decrepit, lizard-filled horror, and their dining and entertainment coupons (part of the raffle prize) have expired. Within hours, the Thachers decide to go home. But Corky runs into famous entertainer Don Ho, who sets them up in a luxury hotel. Ho introduces them to luaus and a range of vacation adventures.

• Guest Dennis Arndt plays the dishonest coach in the first season's "Corky Witnesses a Crime."
• Early on in this episode, the priest from the parish shows up at the door to give the Thachers the good news of their winning vacation. When the doorbell first rings, however, Drew is beat and worn out from a long day at work. So he hopes the doorbell brings news of his restaurant burning down. Yet as the third season commences with "Toast," this development really does take place. Then, it becomes no laughing matter.

Episode 24: "Corky and the Dolphins" . . . . [9-23-90]
Written by Jule Selbo. Directed by Rick Rosenthal. Guest stars: Dean Cain (Lois and Clark), Janet Carroll, Robert Pine, Elizabeth Lindsey, Evan Murakami , Moku Young, Jr.

Corky learns to surf and is asked to care for the performing dolphins at an ocean-theme park. That's where he meets co-worker Kimo, a handsome young surfer boy with whom Becca engages in mild flirtation. When Kimo discovers that she's Corky's sister, the island stud loses interest in Becca, prompting her to give him a piece of her mind in return. In the meantime, Drew and Libby don't get along at all with two bickering honeymooners. Though, Libby's delight with Drew's on-stage "oh, what the heck" singing debut alongside Hawaiian legend Don Ho somehow places everything in a happier perspective.

• Corky exhibits a special bond with the dolphins.
• Guest actor Robert Pine was the sergeant on *CHiPS.*
• The background score when Corky swims with the dolphins is particularly beautiful New Age-type music.
• Of this and the previous season opener, Kellie Martin says: "These were definitely not our best episodes. I thought they were a little bit too fluffy. But that's okay. It was Hawaii."

Episode 25: "The Visitor" . . . . [9-30-90]
Written by Michael Nankin. Directed by Michael Nankin. Guest stars: Adam Carl, Oliver Clark, Stephanie Dicker, Bradley Michael Pierce, Lynn Milgrim, JG Buzanowski , Gregory White, Kara Dennis, Nasslynne Mama-O, Kevin Mockrin, Jake Price, Seth Green

Shortly before she finds out that she's expecting another child, Libby begins experiencing nighttime visions of a young boy. The pregnancy draws a bad reaction from Becca and Corky, both of whom seem to think that they should have been consulted about such a big change. Drew also frets: he feels the family already has trouble making ends meet with only two children. Eventually they come around, and Libby's little vision pays one last visit — at the train station.

• May 17 is Libby's due date. She once had a miscarriage, and is a late-lifer.
• Great lines from when Libby: To Drew, regarding her pregnancy: "Don't be mad. I couldn't deal with it if I thought you were." Concerning the vision: "I already know him"..."I want him to be healthy and perfect. But if he's not, what do we do? I want to be fair?" ... "Can you imagine not having Corky?"
• Drew, who wants to wait to see what sex it is, replies: "Not for a minute."
• Drew wants to wait to see what sex the baby is.
• Becca, after flossing, finds the disposable pregnancy test in the bathroom trash, and says, "Mondo revolto."
• When Corky and Becca offer negative reaction to, and wonder why, about the soon-to-be-new-kid-on-the-block, Libby replies, "There is no why. It's something that happened."
• Becca: "You decide to change the whole family without telling us."

• Corky: "What's so great about being born anyway?" and "Why do we have to have my birthday?"

• Touching scene with Libby and little boy:

> *Boy:* What's it like?
> *Libby:* What's what like?
> *Boy:* Life.

• The Boy later says, "I tried to come before" (re: misty miscarriage scene).

• In the doctor's office, Drew asks Libby: "Did we bond with the kids? I don't know if I'm reading about babies or adhesives?"

• It cost approximately $200,000 to raise a child to 18 years of age.

• The doctor calls Libby, Elizabeth; in "With a Mighty Heart," he calls her Olivia.

• Libby is in the kitchen with the boy. The phone rings. Becca walks in front of the door: Libby's crying.

> *Becca:* Mom, what's the matter?
> *Libby:* He's perfect.

• Later, between Libby and Corky:

> *Corky:* You don't care.
> *Libby:* I do.
> *Corky:* No, you don't. You don't want me.
> *Libby:* You're the first thing I think about in the morning and my lost dream at night. Would you be happy if the baby had Down syndrome?

• Corky later says, "You guys are nuts."

• Libby twice tells Corky the story: "There was a beautiful baby boy..."

• Corky is fascinated with space. Becca gets him a telescope and a pizza with candles that say Happy Birthday, Corky, Charles. When Libby says, "Make a wish, honey," we know Corky wishes for a healthy baby.

• Michael Nankin: "This was my first directorial effort and I wanted to make a splash. We hired out Union Station in Los Angeles, a grand 1920s-era Spanish Revival train station and used it as heaven. We filled it with children, dressed in clothes from every era, every country. These were the spirits of children waiting to be born. Waiting for their time to come to earth. Waiting for the call. Generally, an episode of television has to be shot very quickly — averaging about seven script pages a day. Thank God for Michael Braverman and Rick Rosenthal. They recognized the importance of getting those images right. They fought the studio for me. A first-time director and he's doing a one-page day? Later in the episode I had to do some nine- and 10-page days to make up for it, but I'll always be grateful for my champions. These guys made me a director."

• The announcer at the train station voices in a few languages (Japanese, Italian, etc.)

Episode 26: "Becca and the Band" . . . . [10-7-90]
Written by Susan Wald. Directed by Kim Friedman. Guest stars: Stephanie Dicker, Jeff Silverman, Mark Addai, Susan Angelo, G. Adam Gifford, Matthew Ross, Margaret Howell, Lisa Kudrow, Sarajane Robinson, Joey Sciacca, Steve Jerro, Susan Varon

Rona and Tyler break up because she lied to him and went to a frat party. Becca becomes manager of Tyler's band, schedules a gig for the opening of the new mall, but the band has to have a female singer. Tyler asks Becca, who initially agrees. At the last minute, she backs out and asks a friend to fill in. Tyler ends up leaving with the girl, while Becca gets depressed. In the meantime, Libby is offered a chance to leave the restaurant and return to her old high-pressured, but higher-paying job with Jerry.

• Good line from Libby to Becca: "Sometimes you've just got to put yourself out there or life passes you by," which strings together nicely with two subplots: Becca's fear of diving and Libby's chance at a new job. For example, Becca jumps in the pool, cannonball style, while Libby takes her dive into fresh employment.

• "We had an opportunity to take a different look at Glenbrook," Rick Rosenthal says. "And we gave a tremendous amount of production value to an episode that was somewhat confined by production restraints."

Episode 27: "The Banquet Room Renovation" . . . . [10-14-90]
Written by Wesley Bishop. Directed by EW Swackhamer. Guest stars: George Finch, Paul Koslo, Donovan Leitch, Susan Merson, Paddi Edwards, Charles Champion, Gary Grossman, Gary McGurk, Andi Methany, Tiny Ron

Drew decides to turn the back area of the restaurant into a banquet room in hopes of bringing in more money. Teddy, a young construction worker, helps him out, while Becca falls in love. Drew receives funding from Farmer Jack on the condition that Drew uses his son Teddy as a worker. When Drew agrees, he and Teddy develop a father/son relationship, which makes Corky jealous. As a result, Corky tries to help but causes more damage than assistance, which Drew blames on Teddy until Corky tells him the truth. In the interim, Libby, back at her old job, tries to dig up a canine star for a gourmet dog-food commercial.

• Libby, regarding the dogs: "Two-heads are better than one."
• Jeffrey, the pig from "Pig O' My Heart," makes his second appearance. He belongs to Farmer Jack.
• Good lines from Drew: "You're my son, and I wouldn't have it any other way"…"Wasn't buying this restaurant supposed to make life easier?"
• Many *LGO* crew members were employed for onscreen crew of the commercial.
• "The whole question of guilt and the misappropriation of guilt," says Rick Rosenthal, "were some pretty strong issues and assumptions based on the fact that a person is handicapped. Issues which were explored that we deemed quite provocative. I also thought that Donovan Leitch gave a very good performance as a misunderstood kid, his relationship with Drew, and the jealousy from Corky that it incurred. All of it was complex, and very well played out. And then there was also the sequence with the dog commercial, which was very funny stuff. So this episode really presents a nice mix."
• The late director, E.W. Swackhamer, guided several episodes of *Bewitched*, which featured the advertising business. He died shortly after directing this episode.
• Beyond Swackhamer's involvement, and the general premise theme of prejudice, there are other correlations that may be made between *Life Goes On* and *Bewitched*. Libby worked for a self-absorbed, demanding ad-man boss (Ray Buktenica's Jerry), just as did Darrin on *Bewitched* (Larry Tate, played by the late David White). There were two Paiges (in the guise of Monique Lanier and Tracey Needham), just as there were two Darrins (Dick York and Dick Sargent, both of whom have passed away) on Bewitched. The exterior house and neighborhood scenes from Life Goes On were shot on the same studio street lot where Samantha and Darrin's house resided. In fact, just two doors down. (Others on the lot include the exterior home facades for *The Partridge Family, I Dream of Jeannie, Father Knows Best, Gidget,* and *Marcus Welby, MD* — the latter for which Michael Braverman produced a reunion movie.)

Episode 28: "Halloween" . . . . [10-28-90]
Written by Liz Coe. Directed by Kim Friedman. Guest stars: Lisa Lawrence, Danny Goldman, John Melichar, Aaron Seville, Bonnie Morgan, Dennis Nishi, Ben Pfeiffer, Masami Saito, James Schendel, Adam Wylie and Stephanie Block

Halloween scares up a bad time for all: Libby and Drew at Jerry's masquerade party. Corky at a school gathering. And Becca who, when home alone, gets scared watching horror movies. It doesn't help when the lights go out, and an intruder breaks in. But it turns out to be Tyler. Back at the school dance, Corky falls for a girl he dances with. Thing is, he doesn't take off his mask.

• One of the most poignant scenes in the entire series: Corky realizes he's in love, but can't remove his mask. He goes to bathroom, does so, and looks intensely into the mirror. Chris Burke's acting shines.

• Corky's Dance Partner says: "Sometimes, it's a little hard to understand you. Must be the mask."

• Arnold wears a mask.

• It's the first time freeze-frame is employed, when Becca thinks out loud in the Thacher hallway.

• Great dialogue between Libby and Drew:

> *Libby:* Honey, I know Jerry isn't one of your favorite people.
> *Drew:* That's putting it mildly.

• Corky wore Drew's costume. How could it fit?

• Paige picks up Corky, which proves there was always some plan to bring her back.

• Becca on horror movies: "I watch them. I don't like them."

• Funny scene between Libby and Drew, fighting over a piece of toast.

• Drew says: "Would a chocolate pumpkin make things easier?"

• "We shot this in the [San Fernando] Valley, at a hotel in Reseda, California," recalls Ray Buktenica. "It happened to be during one those colossal heat waves. I mean, it must have been 104 degrees outside. It was excruciating. The air conditioning was overwhelmed by the amount of people and lighting."

• Besides the physical discomfort, Ray remembers what didn't work for him, theatrically. "I had a scene with just one line, which is the most difficult thing to have as an actor. It's like waiting for the subway. You see it down the tunnel. You know it's coming. There it is. It's here. It goes by, and then you're like, Well, what was that?"

• Meanwhile, Kellie Martin "learned how to light a match" in this episode, which "was a lot of fun" for her. "I had to stop my heart every time they said, rolling, because Becca was supposed to be frightened in every single scene. It was kind of like filming a horror movie for me. A very mild horror movie."

• "The use of music and Corky's mask were extraordinary," adds Rick Rosenthal. "It explored the liberation of Corky with a different identity. All of it was quite powerful, and Kim did an excellent job of directing."

• Michael Braverman agrees. "This episode was wonderful. The last shot was just incredible. The whole thing was about masks. Very touching. I loved it."

Episode 29: "Chicken Pox" . . . . [11-4-90]

Written by David M. Wolf. Directed by Chuck (a.k.a. Charles) Braverman (no relation to Michael). Guest stars: Christopher Crabb, Bennet Guillory, Robert Arthur, Steve Jerro, Melora Marshall, Howard Mungo, Debra Sullivan

Becca dreams about figure skating with a man, wakes up with the chicken pox, and stays home sick from school. Tyler comes to visit several times to talk about his problems with Rona. He and Becca become closer until Rona shows up (just when they're about to kiss), stealing him back from Becca. Drew hires a wacky waitress at the grill and comes down with the pox himself, as does Corky, who thinks Becca got him sick on purpose. Paige's vet boyfriend has gone to a conference, and will move back home to Maine, and take over his father's practice. He wants her to go with him. She wants Libby to go to a spa with her to get away and think about the dilemma. The decision is made for her when she finds out the vet wants to get married — to another woman. After all three Thachers get over the pox, Libby comes down with a nervous rash from all her stress, is bedridden for the weekend and left alone to fend for herself.

• Becca says to Libby regarding a new love beyond Tyler, "I haven't really met him yet. But I know I'm going to." Prophetic, to say the least.

• Tyler breaks up with Rona for good, after she lies to him about not going to a college frat party. But they get back together again, to the dismay of Becca, who says: "... I'm eternally doomed to wanting someone who's totally wrong for me. If the man of my dreams came to our front door I probably wouldn't even notice him."

• Soon after, Becca lays it on the line with Libby: "Why does everyone always assume I'm so competent and level-headed? Good old Becca, you never have to worry about her. Sometimes I need you to."

• Act Three opens with several pleas for Libby's assistance:

> *Corky:* Mom, I need you.
> *Becca:* Mom, my soup is cold.
> *Drew:* Libby, do we have any more calamine lotion?
> *Corky:* Mom, my eyes hurt.
> *Drew:* Libby, my fever's back. Could you bring the thermometer?

Becca: Mom, do we have any popcorn?
Corky: Mom, I have to throw up.
Becca: Mom, I can't sleep.
Drew: Libby, there's something wrong with my ears.
Corky: Mom, I think I could eat something now.
Drew: Libby, where are you?
Becca: Mom, where are you?
Corky: Mom, I need you.
Corky/Drew/Becca: …Where are you? … I need you.

• Tyler asks Becca: "Why does everybody think of me as this stupid immature jock dating cheerleaders and reading comic books?" He then tells her he's read A Tale of Two Cities, and explains, "I think it's a perfect description of what it's like to be a teenager."

• Doreen the waitress calls Libby Mrs. T., to which Libby replies, "Mrs. T?"

• Near the close, when Libby feels abandoned by everyone in the family, including the dog, she says, Et tu, Arnold; the show's early nod to Shakespeare, of course.

• Fun ending: Everyone in the Thacher household exits the front door, free from chicken pox, and just as happy as can be, while "It's a Beautiful Morning" (by The Loving Spoonful) plays in the background.

• It's Tracey Needham's first appearance as Paige.

• This episode was inspired by Rick Rosenthal's real-life bout with chicken pox, while shooting the first season segment, "Thacher and Henderson." It was also written by Rosenthal's brother-in-law, and while Rick, who played hockey in college, didn't direct the entire segment, he was called into pinch-hit for some scenes. He explains: "We went for something a little bit lighter with this episode. I thought the opening scene of Becca skating was pretty magnificent, and Kellie did almost all of the skating herself. I also had a great time on the ice myself. I got a phone call in my office during this shoot, and was asked, Rick, we've got to shoot some stuff on the ice and no one could do this except you. Could you come down and bring your skates? So I went down there and put my skates on and grabbed this pogo camera, which is a little bit like a steadicam, and shot a couple of swirling sequences, with the goal set to focus on Kellie's face for a close-up."

• Though we in the audience never got to see the kid that Becca was entranced with, Rosenthal thought the ending made up for it; where Libby mimics Hans, and says, "Don't expect miracles." Rosenthal concludes: "I thought that was terrific."

• Rosenthal also "thought there was a wonderful moment between Libby and Becca in the kitchen when they fall on the floor, after arguing. "The falling just kind of happened during rehearsal," Rick explains, "and they just stayed with it, which I thought was great."

Episode 30: "La Dolce Becca" . . . . [11-11-90]
Written by Star Frohman. Directed by Miles Watkins. Guest stars: Anna Berger, Elizabeth Berkley (Saved by the Bell), Julie Cobb (Charles in Charge), Terri Ivens, Joshua Lucas, Eric Welch, Nick De Mauro, Steve Jerro, Freeman King, Barry Lee, Jordan Liggett, Susan Varon, Claudia Bloom

Becca gets a crush on a French student, while Maxie falls for his friend. Both girls have hopes of getting in with the in-crowd; hopes that are dashed when they visit a bar with these boys who turn out to be from the wrong side of the tracks. Especially when Maxie gets drunk. The next morning, Becca tells Libby, who offers some helps for Maxie's hangover. Libby tells Maxie's mom what happened, betraying her promise to Becca. After an argument with Maxie, Becca ditches school, gets grounded, then sneaks out to seek out Maxi who's been stranded by one of the bad boys. While all of this is taking place, a lady chokes at the restaurant, and Corky runs to get Drew who gives the woman the Heimlich maneuver and the two of them become heroes. Unfortunately, the woman later sues Drew for $25,000, because she claims he broke one of her ribs.

• This episode's title was taken from the director Federico Fellini's 1960 film, *La Dolce Vita*, which starred Marcello Mastroianni as a journalist who is caught up in the high society of Rome.

• Dylan, one of the new hip kids in town, overly expounds on the meaning of his sculpture in art class: "Does revolution create evolution? The world revolves but does it evolve? Always turning, never still. We are forces joined together, one affecting the other. All parts of the same machine...Poetry in motion. Separate units connected together acting as one powerful source. It's about as real as you get...Art is supposed to expose truth, not hide it."

• After art teacher Ms. Stricker reprimands Dylan, Becca comes to his defense with: "Well ... uh...I mean, who's to say what's real and what's not? After all, isn't reality subjective? I mean, even in representational art, the perception of the artist is its own reality."

• After class, Maxie tells Becca: "I don't care what anyone says. You are tres cool and I am proud to be your lifelong best friend." Of course, she also tells her later, in comparing herself and Becca to the cool gang: "Excuse me. Reality check. You and me? We're in the kiddie pool and they're swimming in the deep end."

• When Becca asks her mom if all pregnant women are as emotional as she, Libby replies, tearfully, just "The Italian ones."

• On the possibility of extra restaurant publicity in The Glenbrook Gazette for Corky and Drew helping a choking victim, Corky says, "Please, Dad, I want to be famous."

• Later, Drew gives into a news reporter taking pictures: "You know, I think if you shoot me from the other side, it's uh, it'll look a little better. It's just that I have this bump on my, on the left side of my nose. My wife says from this side I look like Kirk Douglas, you know, with the cleft and all... Hey, what about in front of the clock? Cork?"

• When the woman later sues Drew for breaking her rib, Libby tells Corky: "Sweetie, there's always gonna be some people out there who'll try to take advantage of other people's good will."

• When Corky later helps his mom upstairs, she wants to know how much she owes him. "No charge for pregnant customers," he replies.

• Becca to Arnold: "Expecting any calls?" "Love this," says Kellie Martin.

Episode 31: "A Thacher Thanksgiving" . . . . [11-18-90]
Written by Michael Nankin and Michael Braverman. Directed by Charles (a.k.a. Chuck) Braverman . Guest stars: Diane Bellamy, Robert Costanzo, Sam Vlahos, Susan Merson, John Welsh, Dan Desmond, Tony Salome, Joe Starka, Parker Whitman

Corky pictures the family at the Pilgrims' first Thanksgiving; Drew, opening the restaurant for the holiday, meets an old classmate who's homeless.

• "This is a very well-done episode," comments Michael Braverman. "John Calvin played the homeless man with the music box. He was excellent."

• It's also a "very funny episode," according to Rick Rosenthal, who adds: "It was ambitious to blend a flashback of the Thachers in the 1600s with the homeless crisis, and the character who had been Drew's classmate in high school as the homeless guy."

• Though, Rosenthal also explains it was somewhat problematic to shoot: "Some of the show didn't click when we first saw them. Or we needed to do a little work here, because it was missing something there. In the course of the series, I think there's always a couple of episodes that when you go in and you shoot, and you come up long or short. Sometimes it takes a while to find the right feel. Some shows come together very easily, and others you really have to work at. Then by the end of the shoot, you've hoped you nailed it. This was an episode when we did some rearranging in the editing room. We almost did some rewriting of the script, structurally. We wondered: Do we open in the past, in the 1600s? Or Do we open in the present and flashback to the past? How do we get back and forth?

• "It's the first time that Hans tells his story," says David Byrd about how he got through the war. One of the things he said that just broke my heart was that he never ate with silverware until he was twenty-three."

Episode 32: "Libby's Sister" . . . . [11-25-90]
Written by Liz Coe. Directed by Rick Rosenthal. Guest stars: Heather Lin, Lynn Milgrim, Drew Pillsbury, Allan Haufrect

Tension builds between Becca and Drew, a development which is not helped by the arrival of Libby's sister Gina and niece Zoe. Becca, then hesitant about inviting Drew to a father-daughter dance at school, decides to take the plunge and invite him. And in the end, she's glad she did.

  • Mary Page Keller and Leigh Ann Orsi debut in their recurring roles.
  • Drew says: "Things may be tight, but we've always had enough money for the things that count."
  • Great initial repartee between Jerry and Zoe at the office:

> *Zoe:* ...get this straight. I'll call you Uncle Jerry when it snows in the Sahara.
> *Jerry:* She's got a mouth on her.
> *Zoe:* And watch it. It's got teeth.

  • We learn that Drew went to high with Maxie's dad, when Maxie tells Becca: "My dad said your dad was the life of the party at their last high school reunion." And when Becca tells Maxie she's not inviting Drew to the Daddy-Daughter dance, Maxie returns with: "My dad's gonna be disappointed. He really likes your dad."
  • The truth from Drew about Gina: "It's not that I don't like Gina. I do. She's just so unpredictable."
  • A flashback home movie of Becca dancing with Drew, feet on his, is replicated at the present-day dance. "I loved it," Bill Smitrovich says. "Absolutely loved it. In fact, we did the [present-day] dancing scene in two takes, with the toes. I still can't watch that without crying. Kellie was wonderful in this episode. And [in a fantasy sequence], I got to play this really whacked out, I don't know what kind of character...the guy with the blue tuxedo and the frilly shirt. I just had a great time doing it, and Rick did a great job directing it. He did a marvelous job of the [master] shot of the dancer floor. And it was all done with a crane. You look at that shot, and you'll see that there were no cuts. And we all had to say our lines at a particular time, so that we would be facing the camera, or coming around to the camera. And the camera kept on moving."

Episode 33: "The Buddy" . . . . [12-9-90]
Written by Brad Markowitz. Directed by Roy Campanella II. Guest stars: Nick Angotti, Alan Blumfeld, Peter Van Norden, Marc Blankfield, Julian Dyer,

Rhomeyn Johnson, Ken Kliban, Hamilton Mitchell, Don Stewart, Carlease Burke, Oscar Dillon, Tony Pandolfo, Michael A. Williams.

At first, it looks as though a fun-loving old buddy brightens up Drew's life. But appearances are deceiving, as the man's other shady side surfaces. Meanwhile, Becca and Zoe squabble over room-sharing.

• Director Roy Campanella, Jr. is son to long-time TV and film actor Roy Campanella.

Episode 34: "The Bicycle Thief" . . . . [12-16-90]
Written by David M. Wolf. Directed by Mel Damski. Guest stars: Anthony Addabbo, Peter Iagangelo, Dylan Kussman, Will Jeffries, Robert Rothwell

Corky resolves to enter the 50K bicycle race despite his father's objections, and makes friends with Mark, another bike rider who is epileptic. To enter, Corky purchases a brand-spanking new bike from Brian, a clerk in the bike shop who has a crush on Paige. The cycle is stolen and Zoe, unable to bear Corky's heartbreak, steals him an almost identical one. During the race, Corky's new friend has a seizure, and Drew is proud when his son is there to save the day. Meanwhile, too, the truth of Zoe's intention is made clear.

• Corky has several great lines in this segment, some of the first to Zoe: "It takes time to make friends." Then, "Every time I talk to a boy one of my sisters likes I get in trouble"..."I don't like surprises." To Mark he says, "When people say I can't do something it makes me try even harder. That's what I always do."
• Zoe says to Brian, regarding Paige: "I don't think you should call her anymore...She's through with men. She's decided to become a nun."
• Drew tells Gina: "You don't know the first thing about raising a Down syndrome kid. Keeping him safe is the most important thing I do." To which she replies: "No, it isn't. Down or no Downs, you have to let kids take chances. You have to let them grow up."
• Rick Rosenthal: "I thought [the actor who played] the young epileptic was extremely good. His scenes brought you right up to the television. Very powerful, and very well-directed by Mel Damski, and written by my brother-in-law [David Wolf]."

Episode 35: "Isn't It Romantic?" . . . . [1-16-91]
Written by Michael Nankin. Directed by Michael Lange. Guest stars: Diane Bellamy, Craig Hurley, Adam Carl, Michael Alldredge, Frank Miller, Wilfred

Lavoie, Ken Thorley, Katherine Amrstrong, Josh Wolford, Grant Gelt, Tiffany Sue Mixlow, Lou Briseno

Cupid is shooting arrows at almost everyone. First, Hans gets a crush on a lady that delivers the newspaper, whose husband just died. Kent, Paige's motorcycle man, returns and, at the grill, charms his way back into her life. Becca has to dissect a frog in biology, with Matt as her partner. They have an up-and-down relationship, but end up as more than friends. Tyler catches them smooching in the hall and becomes jealous, and later sneaks into Becca's room. He proclaims his feelings to her only to find out that it's Zoe that's been listening, because Becca's out with Matt. Zoe says to Tyler, "Get a life." Jerry develops a crush on Gina, and they go out.

- *Becca:* I got this strange feeling. *Zoe:* You mean like you're gonna ralph? Later, with Paige, Becca comes clean with: "I feel like throwing up." To which Paige replies (about Tyler), "That's love."
- Paige says about her past love, Kent: "He was the guy I couldn't forget. Totally wrong. Complete jerk. But oh…To this day, every time I hear a motorcycle, I have to take a shower." Then later, she makes a toast: "To the happiest women on Earth: nuns."
- Waitress Doreen shows up.
- Paige turns to Gina for advice.
- Becca and Matt's slogan for friendship/love: "You get outta here."
- Corky is the only single one, at this moment, who is not stung by the arrow of Cupid's love.
- Ben Savage, star of *Boy Meets World* (and brother to Fred *The Wonder Years* Savage), plays Cupid.
- This episode is memorable for Kellie Martin because "Our [promo] ad was one of the frogs in the frog suits, for the fantasy sequence."
- Michael Lange: "Rick Rosenthal thinks this is the best episode television I've done…ever!"

Episode 36: "The Bigger Picture" .... [1-13-91]
Written by Star Frohman. Directed by Jerry Jameson. Guest stars: Andi Chapman, Christopher Carroll, Pierre La John, David Lupash, Nancy Stephens, Karen Rauch, Tai Thai, Christi Allen, Robin Buck, David Bursin

Gina despairs when nothing she does is right in the eyes of her mother, while Corky despairs when his special ed substitute teacher, Amanda, who takes a hands-on approach to teaching that enthralls her students, suddenly takes leave. Also, Paige is a little overwhelmed when her once-again-estranged motorcycle-riding boyfriend attempts to win back her love with a rousing rendition of "Wild Thing" at the restaurant — much to Drew's dismay.

• Corky's special ed teacher has the same name as his fiancée-cum-wife, Amanda, who he meets in the third season.

Episode 37: "Last Stand in Glenbrook". . . . . [2-3-91]
Written by Marti Noxon. Directed by Larry Shaw. Guest stars: Quincy Jones (legendary music producer), Michael Alldredge, Craig Hurley, Judy Kain, Lara Lyon, Robert Machray, Brandi Chrisman, Michael Ciotti, George Ede, Dawn Landon, Matt McKenzie, John T. Olsen, Jimmy Staskiel, Neil Vipond, Jerry Winsett

Becca organizes a 1960s-style protest in support of a record store owner arrested for allegedly marketing obscene material. Meanwhile, Drew goes a little bit over the top in the worry department, upon learning of a food critic's visit to the Glenbrook Grill. Then he really does have something to worry about when he's the one who ends up getting hauled off to the jail — due to Becca's protest.

• Becca to Drew: "I think your generation was right. You can't trust anyone over 30." And later: "Ban the ban." Kellie Martin recalls: "Oh…ban the ban. I love this episode, and Becca's mild rebellion. I think Becca and the Underground Newspaper had the same feel."
• Drew says: "Do as I say. Not as I did."
• Maxie: "I think what the world needs is the spirit of the '60s but the hairstyles of the '90s."
• Paige to Gina: "Men…Can't live with 'em, can't hunt 'em down and shoot 'em like wild dogs." And — "Think Libby is getting sick of listening to me and Daddy…you know, when I try to talk about [Kent] with him, I can actually see some of those curly hairs on his head turning white. A couple more father-daughter talks and he's going to look like Kris Kringle."
• Fantasy sequences: Book burning and a hippie scene
• Paige: "I need a chance to find out who the I in me is."

Episode 38: "Head Over Heels". . . . . [2-10-91]
Written by Liz Coe. Directed by Dick Rogers. Guest stars: Michael St. Gerard (Elvis), Anne Gee Byrd, Julie Ann Gourson, Andrew Tarr

Becca does a double flip for her gymnastics coach — as does Gina over a handyman several years her junior. While Drew complains about Gina's arrangement, Gina has a heart-to-heart with Becca about her unrealistic crush on a much-too-much older man.

• Libby: "Becca, there's a lot of things I'll do for you, but lying is not one of them."

• Gina moves out; only ten minutes away. But never appears again.

• Coach Bradford talks about his craft: "Gymnastics adds to your self-confidence, your toughness, your joy. It's life's best training ground, because it teaches you to strive for perfection and learn from your mistakes. To me, gymnastics is God's ultimate expression of art. I mean, what's more beautiful than a body in motion floating through a routine?"

• Prime conversation between Libby and Gina, defining Gina's past, present and her relationship with Drew:

> *Gina:* Come on, Libby. You're going to the doctor's. You're getting dressed to get undressed.
> *Libby:* Sounds like your old approach to dating.
> *Gina:* Dating...I know the word. I just can't place it.
> *Libby:* Gina, I really appreciate what you're doing for Drew.
> *Gina:* I wish he did. He acts like baking for him is the break of a lifetime.
> *Libby:* Look, he's feeling pressured. With the restaurant not doing so hot and a baby on the way . . .

• But then, Drew makes it perfectly clear what his feelings are for Gina: "I don't like the way you live your life, okay?"

• Becca denies that Matt is her boyfriend, while she refers to Tyler as her pal, claiming, "I'm not hung up on Tyler anymore, honest. I've cured myself of him."

• She and Matt contemplate taking in a screening of The Philadelphia Story at The Film Art Theatre, but Becca stands him up.

• Meanwhile, Matt brings a book over for Libby: *Giving Birth Under Water*.

• We meet Jed, Gina's carpenter boyfriend or, as Zoe defines him, "The carpenter who's making improvements in Mommy's room."

• Whip Hubley played Paige's boyfriend in "Pets, Guys & Videotape" and "Thacher and Henderson."

• Dick Rogers was a first-time director when he tackled this episode, and as Tanya Fenmore recalls, "He was a friend of Rick Rosenthal's from Harvard. His teaching assistant. So this poor guy had to deal with jet lag from Boston, and his first crew. I was supposed to be the one that was okay in gymnastics. They originally wrote that Maxie flipped off the high-beam. I'm thinking, What? I can't even somersault. I'm pathetic. I'm really bad. I'm just kind of born with no flexibility. Anyway, Kellie and her mother Debbie would often tell the writers, that Kellie can do this, and Kellie can do that, and the writers would somehow work those ideas into the scripts. So when Kellie was little, she did do gymnastics. She was excellent. She just had to kind of limber up those hamstrings and everything was great. For me, the poor director said, Okay, Tanya... let's see what you can do. We worked out first in some gym way out in the San Fernando Valley. Kellie did great, and I was so bad. Gosh, was I bad. I couldn't even stand up on the beam. I couldn't walk on it. All I could do was one of the lunges like Nadia Comaneci — those gymnastic positions where they are their back. I could also maybe tumble on the floor. But that was it. The director viewed all of this with a look of horror on his face, and they had to rewrite the entire script. They did some very selective shots of what was not seen of Maxie's lovely gymnastic skills. It was funny, because all I would do is run around. And they hired some legitimate gymnasts, too. One girl was the world champion from somewhere in Eastern Europe, Hungary, I think. All the extras were gymnasts, too. So here I am running around with all these people who are doing back flips like nothing, and I couldn't even walk on the high beam."

• "Oh, my gosh...oy," adds Kellie Martin in mock exasperation in recalling this segment. "I had to train for a like a month before I did this episode, because I had not done gymnastics for a while. I was doing really well, and I was getting everything back, and I was all ready to do all my stuff, and then I hurt my arm before we started filming. So what you see on screen was really as much I could have done, because my arm was killing me. In the scene where Becca gets over that beam, there's like this pained look on my face. Well, that was real. I had hurt my arm so badly, and I could not do it. So that was very real."

• As to Becca kissing her older, much older, coach/teacher, played by Whip Hubley, Martin says: "Of course it was hard to kiss an older man."

Episode 39: "Corky's Travels" . . . . [3-10-91]
Written by David M. Wolff. Directed by Rick Rosenthal. Guest stars: Leon Redbone, Edward Carnevale, Bernie Coulson, Robin Tunney, Sip Culler, Troy Fromin, Jerome Front

Corky gets lost and wanders around the mean streets of Chicago. He meets a kindhearted, young hooker who gives him his first sexual experience — essentially a few long kisses. Corky is shadowed and mystically guided throughout the evening by a semi-mythical blues singer. Becca and Tyler spend a rainy, frustrated evening driving around Chicago looking for Corky, and end up smooching in the car.

• The episode, filmed mostly in black and white, is intentionally vague about Corky's sexual experience.

• Corky sticks up for himself: "I'm not a retard. I have Down syndrome."

• And when Mary asks him, "Do you do everything your parents tell you?" He replies, "No. Almost everything."

• Becca comes clean with Tyler, when they go out to look for Corky, and someone steals his car:

> *Becca:* You've made my life miserable for two years.
>
> *Tyler:* What're you talking about? I haven't known you for two years.
>
> *Becca:* Then that means you made my life miserable even before I knew you. I can't believe how much time I've wasted thinking about you, talking about you, dreaming about you.
>
> *Tyler:* Dreaming about me? I didn't know that.
>
> *Becca:* You liar. You knew. Everybody knows. A person would have to be in a coma not to notice.
>
> *Tyler:* Becca, I swear…
>
> *Becca:* Stop it! I know all your little tricks, that innocent smile and the way you have of looking at me like there's nobody else in the whole world you'd rather be with. I've seen you turn on the charm too many times, pretending to be so nice so I'll fawn all over you…I finally realized we were never going to be together…Can't you understand English? I don't feel anything anymore. It's over, totally and completely over.

• Corky sums it up: "I got lost. And I was robbed. And I met a girl."

• And when Drew tells him: "You should have never left the bus station. If you ever do something like this again, I'll ground you for the rest of your life." Corky replies, "That's fair."

• According to Michael Braverman, "This was an excellent episode which cost us a fortune. It took so long to film. It was all night-shooting. It was extremely difficult to shoot."

Episode 40: "Thanks a Bunch, Dr. Lamaze" . . . . [3-17-91]
Written by Brad Markowitz. Directed by Michael Lange. Guest stars: Georgann Johnson, Bradford English, Leeza Vinnichenko, Patricia Ayame Thomson, John Welsh, James Boyce, Steve Jerro

Drew confronts his feelings about having another baby. He comes through in the end when another woman goes into labor early. Jerry then steps in as

Libby's Lamaze coach because of Drew's lack of interest. Meanwhile, Becca makes much ado in her school newspaper about the unearned grades of athletes.

- Many funny lines here:
- Becca tries to think up a story: "I'm nowhere with this story…I'm less than nowhere. You can't even see nowhere from where I am."
- Becca helps Tyler with a school English assignment, asking, "Remember what irony is?" To which Tyler replies with a grin, "It's what you do with wrinkled laundry?" But in the end, when he proves himself, Becca is stunned: "I don't know what to say." To which Tyler returns, "Becca Thacher doesn't know what to say for once? That's irony…I think."
- Despite the humor between Becca and Tyler, in perspective, we see her initial impatience and frustrations with his low-intelligence; how this will later increase, paving the way for her romance with Jesse. And it's jarring to hear Tyler tell her later: "Maybe your editorial was right. Maybe I am just a dumb jock. Dumb enough to believe you really cared about me." Whoa!
- Then, too, we get more insight into how Tyler views himself: "Ever since I was a kid, I dreamed about being a star. Hear the crowd yell. Make my dad proud of me. Football, baseball, basketball — I live for it. It's what I dream about." He then tells Becca: "School's easy for you. You're good at it. You're smart."
- Becca also caused trouble, via her strong in-print opinions, like in "Becca and the Underground Newspaper," from the first season.
- The newspaper, here, is called The Monitor.
- We learn that Drew was a jock in school, and enrolled in some courses that were a "piece of cake," including one geology class nicknamed Rocks for Jocks.
- Drew also looks to the past and the future: "When I was a kid, I used to think my old man was ancient. When this kid's Cork's age, I'll be, what — sixty-something. Always figured in a couple of years, Becca's away at school, Cork's coming along — Lib and I would have all that free time." Then, later, to a fellow Dad in Lamaze class: "Look. I've been a father three times, and managed it pretty well without people telling me how I feel or how I should feel or what I mean."
- We also see a semi-foreshadow to the third-season episode, "The Room," when Libby says to Drew: "I'm due in seven weeks, and you haven't done anything about our space problem. The baby's going to need a room."
- The phone rings and Corky tells Libby: "It's your jerk boss." But a later conversation between Jerry and Libby in Lamaze class (when he fills in for Drew) almost — almost — proves otherwise:

Jerry: Okay, I got it. The bomb scare. Remember, we evacu-
ated the wrong way and got stuck in the utility room? Just
the two of us . . .
Libby: The bomb scare?! That's your idea of a nice
moment?
Jerry: Hey, it wasn't so bad. It's dark, we're starving. We
break open the vending machine, and all the candy bars
come spilling out...I remember sitting there in the dark,
eating chocolate, thinking if I gotta go, hey, at least I'm in
good company."
Libby: You really thought that?
Jerry: And what hives I'm gonna get from all that chocolate.

• Corky then tells Drew about the baby, "I wish I could help...So I could
be a dad like you...I want this to be my baby, too."
• Names Libby and Drew consider for the baby: Jonathan, Alexander,
William, Bill (first name to the actor Smitrovich), Billy, Joseph, Matthew,
Matt, Zachary, Kate.
• In a conversation with Libby, we learn that Paige is "lousy at keeping
lists."

Episode 41: "Ghost of Grandpa Past" . . . . [3-31-91]
*Written by Michael Braverman. Directed by Kim Friedman. Guest stars: Talia
Balsam, Bert Remsen, John Walsh, James Edgcomb, Steve Jerro, Johnny Lage*

Drew is stressed out. Finances. The mounting responsibilities of the restaurant. The general demands of fatherhood, and his leadership role in the
family. And while Libby talks with the kids about easing up on their dad,
Drew is apparently having visions of, and conversations with, his grandfather — who's been dead for years.

• Libby's in financial confusion over the books for Drew's restaurant, and
the possibility of selling the place, so she contacts her Cousin Angela, a lawyer, who makes one of her last appearances with some witty words: ".... I
think I've finally reached the point in my life when I should accept any man
who can live up to just two of my most important criteria. That he's breathing and has a heartbeat."
• Tyler takes Becca and her learning permit for a test drive:

Tyler: Press the clutch...the clutch! Shift into second. No!
That's fourth...second!

> *Becca:* Where's second?!
> *Tyler:* Back toward you. Shift!
> *Becca:* I am.
> *Tyler:* Clutch. Watch the turn…the turn…now lay off the gas and hit the brakes. Clutch! Clutch!!!

• We also learn that Tyler's dad owns an Austin Healy automobile, something Drew dreamed of owning when he was in high school.

• We also learn the full extent of what Drew sees as his ideal life and his real life, when he has this conversation with the apparent apparition of his grandfather:

> *Drew:* "..I want to be on a sunny beach somewhere. I want to read a book. Any book. I want to stop being so tired all the time. I want Libby and me to be twenty years younger and I want to drive her around in a red Austin Healy, with our hair blowing in the breeze…How'd I get here, Gramps? I'm almost forty-four years old and I've been working like a dog all my life and what've I got to show for it, huh?
> *Gramps:* You got a pretty terrific family. You love them, they love you…so what's the problem?
> *Drew:* Gramps. Open your eyes. I'm in debt to her and if I don't sell the restaurant, I'll probably lose it. We've got a new baby on the way that we didn't plan and can't afford. What if it…he…she's not healthy, then what? It's already happened to us once. What if it happens again? Gramps, I don't think I can handle it. I'm tapped. Drained. Burned out…and Libby, the kids. They expect me to be the strong one all the time. I'm supposed to have all the answers, solve all the problems, pay all the bills, fight all the fights. I can't do it anymore, there's nothing left in me to give."

• Then, after Drew feels "like the biggest fool on two legs" after hyperventilating and scares everyone in the family into thinking that it was a heart attack, he has a revealing conversation with Libby, who talks about his grandfather and a whole lot more: "…You're human…you finally reached your…stress limit. Babe, there's only so much a person can take. Including you. You have to learn to accept that, Drew…you have to slow down. Nothing is worth this…I want you to sell the restaurant. Sell it. Take the offer. In case you've forgotten, we're going to have a new baby in a few weeks and this baby needs a father. I'm not raising this family alone, Drew. I want you to sell…Your grandfather was never around. He was never home. I'll bet in your whole lives you and your brother never saw him more than a dozen times outside the restaurant. Didn't you tell me he even worked Christmas and Easter and every other holiday? He worked himself right into an early grave. Is that what you want?"

• Finally, Drew confronts the ghost of his past, head on: "Gramps...all my life I've been trying to live up to your expectations. I can't do it anymore...let me go."

• As to the spirit visions of Drew's dad? Was it actually taking place or was it only in Drew's mind? Braverman said the double read was "intentional. But at the end, his grandfather disappeared from the diner. So we took away the ambiguity."

• "I love this episode," adds Bill Smitrovich. "Bert Remsen, who played Drew's grandfather, is a great guy. He loved doing it, and he was wonderful to work with."

• "It was one of the episodes that, in the beginning, was written by someone else," recalls Michael Braverman. "Then I took over. I ultimately wrote it."

Episode 42: "Arthur" . . . . [4-7-91]
Written by Michael Nankin. Directed by Michael Nankin. Guest stars: Ryan Bollman, Talia Balsam, Frances Bay (Seinfeld), David McFarlane, Walter Olkewicz, Annabelle Weenick, Greg Alper, Andrew William Chamberlain, Steve Jerro, Bruce Prescott

Corky befriends Arthur, someone older with Down's who leads the kind of independent life that Corky would like to lead. Libby, Drew, and Corky soon have dinner with the man, and his mother, Eleanor, who, while her son is out of the room, reveals that she has never told him that he has Down's. Soon after this dinner, however, Eleanor dies, and Arthur is left alone, with nowhere to go but a group home for those with Down's. Meanwhile, Corky contemplates what his life would be like when Libby and Drew die.

• Becca, commenting on Corky's frustration with homework the night before: "Boy, Corky really went nuclear last night, didn't he?" Corky, coming down to breakfast: "Hi, everybody. Sorry I went nuclear last night."

• Upon meeting Corky, Arthur asks, "Are you an angel, too?," a statement based on the fact that his mother has told him that those with Down syndrome are indeed angels in disguise; or as she tells Libby and Drew when they come over for dinner; "He knows he's different than normal people. But he's better. He's an angel. That's what we've told him. That God saves the sweetest souls for himself. He sets them apart so they don't get lost. And when he misses them so much he just can't stand it, he sends down a pair of wings so they can fly home."

• In the beginning, Arthur looks to be the one in control, and Corky the man without a country. After Arthur's mother dies, the roles reverse, as evident when Arthur stays with the Thachers until he can be placed in a group home. Corky tells him: "It's okay to be sad."

• Then Libby comes in and ends up telling him, in very essential terms, about the birds and the bees: "The man...loves the woman...and sometimes he loves her so much that the love inside her comes to life...And that's the baby."

• Arthur, thinking about his mother, then asks, "But where does the love go when you die?"

• All of this causes Corky to speak with Becca about what would happen when their parents pass away; and Becca comforting Corky with: "I know you think [Arthur's] cool and so adult and everything, but you're the one, Corky. You're the one that's been out in the world, that's had the challenges and done the hard stuff and...that's grown up."

• Drew's following reprimand of Corky, after he's late for work at the restaurant, is an ideal example of how he and Libby treat him as equal with Becca and Paige: "...if you're going to work here, you have to take the responsibility that comes with the job. If you're not here, someone else has to do your work."

• After Paige helps him with his English class, Corky says, "Do you ever diagram sentences in real life?"

• Recalls Bill Smitrovich: "This is a great episode. Frances Bay [who played the mother] was wonderful. And we had employed a lot of kids with Down syndrome [for the group home where Arthur moved after his mother died]."

• David McFarlane, who plays the episode's guest-lead, is a Canadian actor who had worked with Michael Braverman on TV's *Quincy*, which Braverman co-produced. McFarlane was also originally considered for the role of Corky.

• According to Michael Nankin, this segment was another *LGO* first: "This episode contains a scene in a group home with 12 Down syndrome actors."

Episode 43: "Lighter Than Air" . . . . [4-28-91]
Written by Dick Lochte. Directed by Michael Braverman. Guest stars: Ana-Alicia (Falcon Crest), Tom O'Rourke, Alfred Dennis, Christine Kendrick, James P. Hogan, Caitlin McLean

Libby cooks up a great ad for a line of diet frozen foods. Meanwhile, Corky and Zoe play Sherlock Holmes and snoop into Tyler's secretive behavior. But there's really nothing mysterious about it: He's just taking ballet lessons to help him be more graceful on the football field.

• We learn that Corky's voice cracks every time he tries to humor Becca.

• Jerry tells Libby: "I know I don't always say it, but I want you to know I'm always thinking, 'What would I do without my Libkins. She takes care of all the little details of my life and leaves me free to concentrate on being creative.'

• Corky tells Zoe: "They don't have cars in Holmes' stories." Zoe's reply: "No shine-ola, Sherlock."

• Gina says Zoe's favorite dinner is "spaghetti-and-a-meat-balls."

• Libby's campaign: "Eat Friedkin Diet dinners and you'll be so light and graceful and thin you'll feel like dancing."

• Libby says Shanna Gray was giving her "free rein to do something new," Jerry tells her: "Let me tell you about reins, Libs. They're always free until someone yanks 'em."

• We don't see Drew until the end of Act Two.

• When Libby seeks advice from her sister, Gina tells her: "You must really be desperate."

• Libby turning down a business offer from Shanna Gray: "My idea of heaven isn't Jerry in an Anne Klein suit."

• Gina defines Tyler as ". . . one of those sincere guys who can't wait to tell the truth."

• When personal philosophies change at the end, Gina tells Libby: "Whoa. Is this one of those bad sci-fi movies where our brains get switched?"

• We learn that Libby is 41 years old, here.

• Last appearances of Gina and Zoe.

Episode 44: "Proms and Prams". . . . . [5-5-91]
Written by Liz Coe. Directed by Kim Friedman. Guest stars: Ben Murphy (Alias Smith & Jones, Gemini Man), Jonathan Prince, John Apicella, Zack Phifer, Vali Ashton, Montrose Hagins, Annie Korzen

While Becca's expectations run high as she awaits Tyler's invitation to the prom, Paige wins a role in a musical and seeks singing lessons from Libby. But the expectant mother Thacher has many other things on her mind, including a past love, Jordon Parnell, who just so happens to be directing the play Paige is auditioning for. Does Libby regret abandoning her acting career to raise a family? Can Paige sing? Will Becca and Tyler go to the prom? Who will win the room above the garage, to make room in the house for the new baby?

• Libby has a lot of great lines here, though this is one of the best: "I won't be alone. I'm a mother. I'm never alone." She also summarizes the TV soap, Forever and a Day, for Paige:

> *Libby:* Daryl has a fatal illness, so they're spending his last days at Ashley's mother's summer cottage. But Ashley doesn't know that years ago Daryl dated her mother.
> *Paige:* So Daryl's gonna turn out to be Ashley's father?!
> *Libby:* Bummer, huh?

• Drew mentions his father (who's having cataract surgery) and his brother Richard. And we never hear about them again.
• Dr. Sylvia Tabouri is Libby's doctor, who's out of town, and usually covered by Dr. Odess, who's unfortunately at a golf tournament. So it's all up to Dr. Ettinger, which was taken from one of *LGO*'s associates, Bruce Ettinger.
• At the hospital, after Libby gives birth to her new son Nicky, and after she realizes with joy that her life with old boyfriend Jordon Parnell was destined not to be, she turns to Drew and says, "We've got a great relationship… Not a good one, a great one. Let's never let anything get in the way of that."
• And then Corky and Becca lose out to Paige in living in the room over the garage.
• Drew tells Corky how beholden he is to his son for being there at the hospital, when he could not.
• Near the end, Tyler fears telling Becca that he's failed senior year, and he has to repeat. "Tyler," she offers, "I'm not disappointed in you, I'm disappointed for you."
• "The great thing about Becca," Kellie Martin comments, "is that she was a smart girl, and she wasn't afraid to be smart. And she didn't think because she was smart, she was a nerd. I mean, she was not the most popular girl. She never was. But she knew what she wanted, and she went after it. I think she was very admirable, and compassionate. She didn't really care what people thought about her. But at the same time, she did. Sometimes, she was too smart for her own good."
• While filming this episode, Bill Smitrovich was called off the set to the hospital awaiting the birth of his adopted daughter Maya Christina (named for Maya Angelou whom he met in graduate school). Upon returning to the Life set, he recalls, "The first scene I filmed was Drew looking at Nicky Thacher through the nursery. And that was so incredibly, divinely serendipitous that was. But it was the easiest money I ever made in my life. Talk about sense memory."

The Third Season of *Life:* **(from left): Tracey Needham, Chris Burke, Patti Lupone, Bill Smitrovich, Kellie Martin.** *THE REGAL COLLECTION*

Episode 45: "Toast" . . . . [9-22-91]
*Written by Michael Nankin. Directed by Michael Lange. Guest stars: David
Selburg, John Ingle, John Welsh, Alfred Dennis, Curtis Peek, Karen Salkin, Biff
Yeager*

The Thachers reopen their renovated restaurant, but their dreams go up
in smoke, when Corky is given more responsibility, specifically, cooking
french fries. After closing one evening, he fails to properly turn off the fry-
ers. In reality, he's turned them up to as high as they can go, which causes the
fire. Fearful of telling the truth, and after several guilt-ridden visions of live-
burners coming to the front door, Corky finally fesses up to Drew.

• There's a lengthy, opening sequence that expresses the passage of time,
as well as the alterations that were taking place behind the scenes. And it
was the only teaser with no dialogue. "It was the visual representation of the
show's changes," explains Michael Lange.
• Also, Lange says he received a nickname here: "Backdraft…because I
really got into the whole fire aspect of it."
• A takeoff on the George C. Scott 1970 feature film, *Patton,* was cut.
It was to showcase Drew and his restaurant, with a parody of the movie's
opening sequence, which displays a huge American flag and Patton's initial
oratorio. "We actually paraphrased that speech," explains Lange. "We even
went so far as to build a huge menu. We built the platform and everything.
But it never came to be." Essentially, the Patton satire would have been
similar to the *Hawaii Five-O* mimic that opened the second season with
"Vacation from Hell."
• Meanwhile, David Byrd "was a little surprised that the restaurant burned
down, as they left me out of the next few episodes, although I was reassured
that he would rebuild it."
• Michael Nankin makes his sole on-air appearance here as the fireman
who stops Drew from running into his burning restaurant. And he recalls:
"In a way, this episode started as a joke. During the second season, I kept

threatening to write an episode called The Knob, in which Corky accidentally breaks a knob off a cigarette machine at his dad's restaurant. As his
guilt grows, so does the knob — until its twelve feet tall and fills his room.
I wasn't really joking — I was intrigued with the idea of visualizing guilt
as a growing thing. It's just that no one else took that giant knob seriously.
Also, it's a funny word – 'knob.' Anyway, the idea of a show about relent-
less secret guilt wouldn't go away and I ultimately made it as big as possible.
What does it feel like to burn down your dad's restaurant and get away with
it? Worse than being caught because when you keep it inside it grows. I still
got my knob in. The knob of the fryer that Corky turns the wrong way (and
starts the fire) grows with his guilt. We made five or six knobs of different sizes, culminating with the big 12-footer that appears at the front door.
Of course, you have to be careful what you joke about — we used to tease
Chuck Pratt about his soap opera work. 'Models by day, crime fighters by
night!' Ha ha. He went off and created *Models, Inc.*"

Episode 46: "Armageddon" . . . . [10-13-91]
*Written by Charles Pratt, Jr.. Directed by Michael Lange. Guest stars: Michael
Alldredge, Alan Blumenfeld, Judith-Marie Bergan, Pamela Segall, Alfred Dennis,
Lisa Dalton, Sean LeSure, Frank Novak, Rusty Schwimmer*

New roles with Libby as the primary breadwinner and Drew as the
homemaker, create friction in the marriage.

• The opening segment: Due to the additional stress in the house —
caused by Libby and Drew's life exchange, Paige wonders, "When am I
supposed to shower?" To which Corky replies, "Soon, I hope."
• Libby says: "I had this fantasy that I might have some quality time
with my family." (An onscreen, in-character reference to one of the show's
staples?)
• When Drew breaks good crystal by playing ball with Arnold in the
kitchen, Libby asks, "What have you done? Our only crystal. The only
thing we had left that was worth anything"; kind of a cold statement from
someone who has grown to appreciate what really matters in life. And
though she redeems herself at the end ("We're a family. We're not about
glasses and rings. We're about [those] four beautiful kids"), she should
have known better than to even make such a nasty initial statement.
• Lost Plateau is playing at Corky's theatre; as is *It's a Wonderful Life*.
He reads the poster for the latter in the lobby and, while thinking of his
parents recent disagreements, Corky comments, "Uhm," as if to say, "Yeah,
right."
• *It's a Wonderful Life*, of course, also is a play on the title *Life Goes On*.

• Outside the theater, on the marquee, Corky has misspelled, Gone With the Wind, with Wndi; a sequence that segues into his conversation with Becca, who says, "You got it backwards, Corky," regarding his understanding of Drew and Libby's quarrel.

• Corky is later motivated to ask his dad: "Are you and Mom getting a divorce — like you did before with Paige's mom," the latter two words of which are a title of a first season episode about Drew's first wife.

• Through it all, Corky dabbles with his telescope, which intricately plays into the plot: An eclipse of the sun eventually brings Libby and Drew together (in the sewer, next to Drew's burned-down restaurant — that's where they went to look for Libby's engagement ring, which fell off while she was thinking about life without Drew).

• When Corky is upset about his parents fighting, he walks outside in the backyard. Paige tries to comfort him. "Thought we had a burglar?" she says. This almost seems like a foreshadowing to the fourth season's "Loaded Question," which is about the Thacher home being burglarized.

• After Becca breaks up a major girl fight in school, she says to Tyler: "I swear...civilization is doomed." Then also: "Movies, burgers, concerts... that's not serious." To which Tyler replies, "No...but it's fun." Later, Becca says that "Men are unreasonable...women are specious." When Tyler wonders what the heck that means, she pops back out from a school doorway and tells him, "Look it up!" Then, after she tells him that her "...whole family is mentally self-destructing," Tyler wonders, "Man...where is this coming from?" As if to say, "What's with you?" And later: "Why are we doing this?" [arguing]. Then later, regarding Jesse: "Who knows with the mystery man?"

• The little boy on a bike riding by Drew and Libby when they enter the front gate is reminiscent of the show's opening credit sequence. It's here, too, where Drew pretends to hit Libby, a la Jackie Gleason on The Honeymooners toward Alice Audrey Meadows.

• The character, John Casadorian (from "Thacher and Henderson") returns. He and his wife invite Drew and Libby over for dinner. Drew somehow blabs out over the meal: "Hey, there's nothing wrong with being a housewife." To which Libby replies, "Sure beats bringing home the bacon." Libby later tells him to quit (being a housewife) if he doesn't like it. "You've done it before" (quit — a reference to leaving his previous job as a construction worker).

• Becca's upsetting realization to Libby, regarding her mom and dad's quarrel that she believes may lead to a breakup of the family: "This is everything I've ever believed in — and now I see it doesn't work."

• Back to the Arnold/kitchen/crystal destroyed scene: "There was a big argument with the dog's trainer," recalls Michael Lange. "He said he couldn't get to hit the dog in the nose with the ball. He sort of really didn't know how to do it. So I just heaved the ball right at the dog, and it was perfect."

Episode 47: "Out of the Mainstream" . . . . [10-6-91]
Written by Brad Markowitz. Directed by Kim Friedman. Guest stars: Michael Rankin, Meagan Fay (Roseanne), Danielle Koenig, Lisa Lawrence, Bodhi Elfman, Devin Kamienny, Troy Shire

   Corky is nearly swamped when he tries to help Donnie, Tyler's younger brother, mainstream at Marshall High.

   • Donnie's fantasy of Marshall High: lush green foliage, a beautifully manicured floor. Lockers spruced with fresh paint. A little fawn pauses to drink from a pool of crystal water. Everything's dappled in golden light. It's very different from Corky's Blade Runner-type nightmare of Marshall High in "The Pilot."
   • Libby's Uncle George and Aunt Maria send the Thachers tomato sauce to soothe over the destruction of Drew's restaurant. "They're Italian," Libby tells him. "You have a fire, they send tomato sauce." Drew then wonders, "What do they send for a flood? Seafood?"
   • Becca's first view of Jesse: "He is on the gorgeous side. In a smoldering kind of way." Tyler's thoughts? "What a geek."
   • Jesse's first take on Becca: "...you're the cute one with the special brother at school."
   • Jesse to Tyler in a double-meaning, foreshadowing kind of way, regarding a football paper wad and Becca's decision to go with her friends and not be with Tyler for the night: "You dropped the ball, man."
   • Becca to Paige about Tyler's new distance: "...it's like I've contracted a social disease..."
   • The whole interplay with Becca and Tyler and how he's distant and she thinks she's not pretty enough for him and just too young felt forced, and just not the way things should have gone. Ditto for the frequent Becca reference that she's ugly, too skinny and goofy in glasses. Don't buy it.
   • Becca's friend Julie calls Tyler the "Ty-meister."
   • Corky to Donnie: "People think we can't do things. But we can. You have to show them, too."
   • Donnie decides to write about Christopher Columbus for a school report. Corky tackles Abraham Lincoln.
   • Guest actor Bodhi Elfman is married to actress Jenna Elfman (*Dharma & Greg*).

Episode 48: "Hello, Goodbye" . . . . [9-29-91]
Written by Bryce Zabel. Directed by Jerry Jameson. Guest stars: James Harper, JW Smith, Mark Phelan, Gina Schinasi

The Thachers rise from the ashes of the restaurant: Exchange student Becca prepares to take wing for Paris, and Paige and Corky go hunting for jobs. But Maxi goes off to Paris, and Becca stays because she feels her family needs her.

• Corky, asking for a job from Stan, the theatre manager: "I want to be in show business. I need to make a lot of money." Then, when Baker speaks too loudly, thinking Corky needs a special volume, Corky comes back with: "I have Down syndrome. But my ears are okay."

• Jerry says about Nick: "Sheeesh...the kid opens his mouth, he's like the Exorcist or something...what's his real name? Barfman?"

• Paige gives her passport to Becca for Paris: "Here...I bought it when I was going to tour Europe with Katherine," which is a reference to "Paige's Mom," an episode from the first season when Monique Lanier played Paige.

• Then, in defending herself to Artie (who she meets here for the first time), we see some of Paige's honesty: "No. I'm not real smart. If I was, do you think I'd be doing this kind of work?" Then to Becca, in the car, to the airport: "...one of us Thachers has a chance...a real chance to eventually...dig out from...all of this. I mean, like it or not, you're the designated digger."

• Becca's reasons to stay at home: "I want to see Nick take his first step... to be here when Paige breaks the three-month barrier on her job...Corky to take my ticket in his tuxedo...and the grand opening [of the restaurant]."

• Becca doesn't go to Paris, which means that Maxie can, because she's next in line. But Tanya Fenmore, who played Maxie here and in the first two seasons, really decided to take a sabbatical from acting, and entered college not in France, but in Florence, Italy.

Episode 49: "Sweet 16" . . . . [10-20-91]
Written by Toni Graphia. Directed by Michael Lange. Guest stars: Judi Aronson, Terri Ivens, Judith Jones, John Prosky, Jared Murphy, Kristine Blackburn, Paige Pengra, Karen Rauch, R.D. Robb, Maggi Shelton, Craig Stepp

Becca wakes up and Paige, Corky and Libby are at the breakfast table, discussing her 16-year-old birthday party; a development with which Drew is less than thrilled. A package arrives in the mail from Maxie in Paris. It's a sexy negligee, denoting Becca's coming of age. The entire family blushes.

Later, Becca begins a videotape-letter to Maxie, while Libby and Drew discuss the nights, which ends up inspiring them to schedule a romantic vacation. Then Becca falls asleep on the sofa with Tyler at his house, while Corky opens a checking account with his first check from working at a local theatre. He buys Becca a beautiful leather jacket for her birthday, but does not fully understand the concept of money.

• Some bad kids at school find out that Corky has checks and fool him into giving them a $100 check to join the fictional Plebian Club. One of the troublemakers is Ray, played by Michael Goorjian. I guess the Thachers forgot all about this little incident later in the series. Or forgave him.

• On waking up on Tyler's sofa, Becca says: "This isn't happening." And later, after a fight with her parents about it: "Happy Birthday to me."

• During a question-and-answer period at school, Becca and Jesse answer in unison with: "Passion."

• Becca and her friends in the bathroom, discussing sex: "Has Becca done it? What do you think it's like?"

• When Becca asks Corky how he ever picked such a nice gift as the leather jacket, he replies: "I have excellent taste."

• Corky videotapes Becca's party and Jesse looks into camera and says, "Hi, Mom."

• Jesse talks with a sad Becca outside on the curb: "It's my party and I'll cry if I want to?"

• As to the Sweet 16 label for her party, Becca says: "Kind of a contradiction, isn't it?"

• Celine Dion's "Where Does My Heart Beat Now" is playing in the background.

• Fantasy sequences dissolve into films shown at Corky's movie house, the new girl who works with him, played by a different actress with the same character. The character's name is never given.

• Out of ignorance, the banker talks to Corky in slow motion. Later Libby tells the banker, "Money is a difficult concept for Down's kids."

• On opening a checking account, Corky says, "Becca's only 16. She gets lots of things I could never get. I wanted to do something for myself."

• In the end, Becca points the camcorder toward herself, and opens her robe to reveal her negligee, saying to Maxi, via the video: "Is this hot or what?" "I had a video camera," recalls Kellie Martin, "and I actually shot the scenes. I got to do everything. But I didn't get camera pay. Just the honor of doing it."

• The cast and crew celebrated Kellie Martin's real-life Sweet 16 party on the set.

Episode 50: "Life After Death" . . . . [11-3-91]
Written by Thania St. John. Directed by Larry Shaw. Guest stars: Terri Ivens,
Judith Jones, Caraloe Ita White, Emily Kuroda, Judith Drake, Lin Shaye, Richard
Penn, Kaley Ward, Mina Kolb, Robert David Hall, Bradley, Mott, Christine
Joan Taylor, Lindsay Price, Bodhi Elfman

Becca is devastated to learn that Jesse has tested HIV-positive and, during a scuffle between him and Tyler, she blurts out in front of everyone that
he has AIDS.

• This episode marks an important turning point in the series; as everyone
learns of Jesse's condition.
• Michael Nankin: "If you notice, this rather ground breaking episode is
followed by two bizarre comedy episodes and a show about guns. We did
this intentionally. The whole idea about the AIDS story was not to make it
an 'issue' episode, but to create a continuing primetime character that was
HIV-positive. Jesse shows up for a number of episodes before we reveal his
secret. Then we just leave it hanging for a few weeks. Then slowly reintro-
duce it into the fabric of the show. It wasn't for shock value. It wasn't disease-
of-the-week. We wanted the audience to experience the reality of the episode. It happens when you least expect it. It isn't fair. It happens to people
you know. It doesn't go away."
• "We writers have a saying and that is 'Steal from yourself,'" says Toni
Graphia. "If you have a scene that you love, you can use the essence of it on
any show you do. Thania and I have worked on several projects since *Life
Goes On.* We did a pilot for NBC, a sci-fi drama, VR.5 and recently the
WB series, *Roswell.* We always go back to *Life Goes On.* One of my favorite
scenes she wrote was where Jesse screams at the train in 'Life After Death.'
So now when we're working, we'll need a scene and we'll say, 'How about a
screaming at the train scene?' I think both of us did some of our best work
there, and it never hurts to go back and mine the gold."

Episode 51: "Dueling Divas" . . . . [11-10-91]
Written by Charles Pratt, Jr.. Directed by Kim Friedman. Guest stars: Dan
Gauthier, David Lascher, Eck Stone

Libby's vivacious cousin Gabriella (a.k.a. Gabby) breezes in from Sicily like
a whirlwind, touching everyone's life — and turning Libby green with envy.

• Patti Lupone plays Gabriella in a similar way that Barbara Eden played
Jeannie and her sister and mother in later episodes of *I Dream of Jeannie,*
Elizabeth Montgomery played Samantha and Serena on *Bewitched,* and

Patty Duke played Patty and Cathy on *The Patty Duke Show*. In each case, the double film technique (employed also in 1998's new feature film edition of *The Parent Trap*) was employed.

• *Becca:* I finally get my own room and another relative shows up. Anyone get a whiff of the perfume? All night I'm breathing, like, scented chlorine.

• Jerry introduces himself to Gabby: "Jer-by. I mean, uh, Jerry Berkson. Junior. Libby's boss. The Godfather."

• Drew says to Libby, explaining the ups and downs: "Know what I think happens? Sometimes one of us is comfortable with the way things are when the other isn't, and vice versa. It's all a question of timing."

• Probably the most tasteless line in the entire series comes from Gabby to Hans. After he suggests they "set the night on fire," Gabby returns with: "You Germans. Always setting things on fire."

• We learn that "any artistic touches" on Drew's restaurant came from Paige. "The etched glass windows, those columns," so says Drew himself.

• In a serious moment, Becca calls Libby "Mommy," after she rescues her from the all-too-frisky clutches of school pal Josh.

Episode 52: "Invasion of the Thacher Snatchers" . . . . [11-17-91]
Written by Michael Nankin. Directed by Michael Nankin. Guest stars: Josh Clark, Jeffrey Combs, Timmy Eyster, David Graf, Michael Earl Reid, Will MacMillan, Caroline Williams, Elizabeth Lambert, Melora Marshall, Louise S. Race

Corky imagines that his family is turning into Venusians after seeing a B monster movie, Body Snatchers from Venus, while Paige learns to be a welder. Drew is trying to stick to a new diet and exercise regime. Becca is applying for college. Upon learning in the film that Venusians don't like dairy products or other antacid material, Corky attacks the family with baking soda and milk.

• Libby offers insight to Corky and the audience: "...this is a real difficult time for all of us. We all have different schedules...everyone's working really hard...Things are changing and I know that's hard for you."

> *Corky:* I liked it the way it was. It was good.
> *Libby:* Change is good, too. That's how you grow.
> *Corky:* I don't like it. We never do anything right anymore.

• Between Becca and Paige:

> *Paige:* I think I know how Corky feels. Always the outsider.
> It makes sense that he thinks everyone's an alien. Better

than thinking that you're the one that doesn't belong.
Funny thing is, he belongs more than I do.
Becca: That's not true. Don't say that.
Paige: It is true. You're the big shining hope of the fam-
ily. Corky's got his special little niche carved out, and
I'm just...living over the garage. Here's the killer: I was a
Thacher first.

• And later, Paige clarifies: "I mean we all live in our own worlds, don't
we? So separate and strange. Do you think if any of us really sat down
with Corky and spent five minutes, he would have gone this far? [into alien
fantasy]"
• Then Libby comforts Corky: "...Sometimes...when the real world is
getting us down, when things are getting difficult, sometimes we reach out
for a fantasy. We reach out and hold on to it because it's less confusing than
the real world."
• All's fine, and then Corky closes with: "The name is Bond...James
Bond."
• Corky's nightmares and fantasies: Paige builds a spaceship; Paige and
Becca have a falling out over a malfunctioning answering machine, a long-
distance communicator; Drew's friend says a new exercise machine will
make him "a new man," and Corky freaks; the Illinois State University representative calls and wants to make Becca "one of us," which Corky takes
for Venusian-rule.
• Kellie Martin: "That was not fun putting on that green makeup. It was
like yeacckkk."

Episode 53: "Loaded Question". . . . . [11-24-91]
*Written by Brad Markowitz. Directed by David Carson. Guest stars: Tony
Burton, Steve Rankin, Harold Sylvester, Frank Como*

The Thacher house is burglarized. Suspicions center on an African-
American welder named Marquis, an acquaintance of Paige's who taught
her how to weld. Drew and Libby debate over whether having a gun is
the best thing to do. Corky and Arnold are alone watching a police detective show. Corky hears sounds from outside. He gets the gun, goes outside
in that sneaky cop fashion, emulating the show and fires. As it turns out,
Marquis was meeting Paige to give her a welding lesson, and the family realizes how much they overreacted.

• Some of the items stolen: Libby's dangle earrings (handed down from
her grandmother), Corky's Hulk Hogan watch, Paige's silver music box —

the one that played "Getting to Know You," the only thing she ever kept from Katherine, her birth mother.

• Corky asks the police (who are impressed with his use of jargon), "Are you going to catch the perps?" and "Are you going to do a stakeout?" He also later watches Burt Reynolds in Sharky's Machine on TV.

• Those the Thachers consider as the culprit: According to Libby, it was "the guy from the messenger service. He delivered a packet from Jerry...I knew there was something wrong with him. He was greasy-looking."

> *Drew:* I had subcontractors in, delivering bids.
> *Becca:* I let in a lady with a petition...[from the]... Neighborhood Watch Group. Paige thinks it might be "...that guy Marquis...the one I had over from work to help me with my welding...He came into the house to use the bathroom. I don't really know him — but I have this weird feeling..." Then everyone mistakenly believes it may be Lorenzo, the diaper-service guy.

• When Drew changes Becca's curfew back to nine o'clock, she protests with, "...that is so unfair...The Russians are free, the Poles are free, but I'm still under totalitarian rule." But Drew is just paranoid about recent events, because he also tells Paige that he even wants her, a young adult, in at "a decent hour."

• Drew on fatherhood, and keeping the gun (after Libby protests): "A man protects his family. At all times. At all costs. That's job number one, and it has been from the beginning of time." While Becca calls the gun "sick," Corky doesn't like it either. "We need a bigger one," he says.

• Fortunately, for everyone, Drew finally comes to his senses: "I'm the one who made the mistake. I brought it in the house. I got carried away and it got in the way of my better judgment."

• Tracey Needham: "A very heavy episode."

Episode 54: "Triangles" . . . . [12-1-91]
Written by Toni Graphia. Directed by Kim Friedman. Guest stars: Betty Carvalho, Megan Gallivan, Judith Jones, Karen Rauch, Alison Guffe

Corky takes a tumble for the new assistant manager at the theatre, Michelle, who at first appears to be a flirt. Later, she confesses her attraction: He's like her son, with Down's, whom she was forced to give away at birth. Meanwhile, Becca is torn between Tyler and Jesse; Tyler says he isn't over her; Becca can't break the news to him because deep inside, she wants to commit to Jesse. Becca helps Jesse search for Allison, the girl who infected him with HIV. When they come to the house where she lived, Becca learns Allison died — three months before.

• Math teacher Mrs. Schiller opens Act I with "Triangles. Three sides. Three angles. A yield sign. A piece of pie. Arsenio Hall's haircut… Circles are based on equality — all points are the same distance from the center. A square always has four equal sides. But triangles are based on inequality. The sum of any two sides is always greater than the third side."

• Corky, says about his movie-theatre tux: "It's kind of hard to figure out the bow tie part, but the rest is easy."

• A fortune teller at the carnival relays to Jesse: "…You are a very old soul. A kind man who is generous and sweet and doesn't want anyone to know it. I see creativity. An artist. One who works with his hands. A painter. This line…the path of your life. So far, many curves. Your road, rough, jagged. Yet it has not broken you. It has sharpened you. Like a knife. But sometimes, you turn it on yourself." Then she stops abruptly after seeing something dark in his future.

• Paige readies herself for the worst when Corky needs to talk to her. But all he wants to know is, "Do you put bleach in before or after the spin cycle?"

• Libby to Michelle: "All I know is…when I see a truck coming, I pull my kid out of the street."

• Becca tells Jesse regarding Allison: "Tyler's not the one who came between us. She was. One night, Jesse! She didn't know you…didn't care about you. Not like I do. And in one night, she took everything. From you. From us."

• Corky become angry with Michelle: "Don't be nice. Don't say something when you don't mean it…You could never love me. Because I'm not normal. I'm not perfect." But once he understands the truth about Michelle's life and son, he returns to his more compassionate self, saying: "You gave him away because it was better for him. Even though you loved him."

• Jesse, walking through a cemetery during a particularly low point, tells Becca: "Do you know that no matter how much I want you, I can never have you?" Becca answers: "Yes! Yes, I do. Because I feel the same way about you."

• "I love this episode," says Kellie Martin.

Episode 55: "The Smell of Fear" . . . . [12-15-91]
Written by Thania St. John. Directed by Michael Lange. Guest stars: Don Amendolia, Katherine Cortez, Bradley Mott, Andrew Berman, Jim Hudson, Ernestine Phillips, Phil Forman, Professor Toru Tanaka, Sebastian Massa, Great John L. Gabe Green

Christmas brings anxieties to all. Drew, who's down due to a lack of customers at his new eatery; Libby, who's frantic, because she's just been named
the fill-in director of the community theatre Christmas pageant; Paige,
because she feels more lost than ever; Corky, who's still questioning the existence of Santa Claus; but most of all Becca and Jesse. She fears the worst,
when he's hospitalized with pneumocystis pneumonia. And then Libby's
inspiration to bring the Christmas spirit — along with the pageant — to
Jesse's hospital room saves the day, warming everyone's heart, and restoring
Corky's faith in Santa.

• Much comic relief including this interplay between Eric and Midge, the
Waitress at Drew's restaurant:

> *Midge:* The theatre'll break your heart every time.
> *Eric:* I only work commercials. The theatre is dead.
> *Midge:* So's Elvis — but he keeps popping up everywhere.

• And when Midge helps Libby out at the pageant:

> *Midge:* We got problems. The seven swans-a-swimming
> and the six geese-a-laying are arguing over the size of their
> beaks.
> *Libby:* The swans get the longer ones.
> *Midge:* You tell that to six angry geese. And another thing,
> nobody ever told me to put eyeholes on the snowman cos-
> tumes.
> *Libby:* Well, get a scissors. They have a hard enough time
> dancing when they can see.
> *Midge:* And nobody can find the goat?
> *Libby:* One of the maids-a-milking is an animal rights
> activist.

• And when Santa Claus pays a visit at the restaurant:

> *Drew:* Eric, I need a setup for Mr. Claus by the window.
> But he doesn't want to eat. He just got mugged and all he
> needs is to use the phone.

• Santa then sparks a conversation between Corky and Tyler, who says: "I
think anybody who gives presents to strangers on Christmas has gotta be
pretty cool, don't you?"

> *Corky:* I guess.

• And later, Hans gives his more cynical view of the Man in Red: "...I didn't want to live in a world where there were no miracles, Charles."

• Drew feels depressed about his lack of customers. Paige tells him that Rome wasn't built in a day. Drew replies: "Does that kind of sage advice sound as stupid when I give it to you?"

• But he comes through with Paige later:

> *Paige:* What's my life about, Dad? What makes me special?
> I'm twenty-three years old, shouldn't I know by now?
> *Drew:* I'm forty-four and I spent most of my life doing
> something I didn't like before I decided to open the res-
> taurant. And even though it might not make me a fortune,
> I wake up every day, looking forward to going to work...
> You'll know your dream when you find it. And until then,
> just do the best you can at whatever it is you're doing."

• Libby has the best lines of sentiment: "To me, Christmas has always meant sharing. Not just gifts, but family and friends getting together, having a good time, being happy that they have each other and hoping that they always will. That's what the holiday spirit is all about. So tonight, I'd like to think of ourselves as one big family and this is my wish to all of you."

• And Becca gives it to Jesse, after he tells her, "I don't need your pity, okay?" To which Becca replies, "Just because you're sick doesn't give you permission to be a jerk."

• We learn Jesse's address: 3150 Oakwood Avenue.

Episode 56: "Struck by Lightning" .... [1-5-92]
Written by Charles Pratt, Jr.. Directed by Larry Shaw. Guest stars: Alan Blumenfeld, Kerrie Keane, Jordan Lund, Ed Evanko, David Correia, Joe Ochman, Marc Epstein

The Thacher house is struck by lightning. As a result, Corky predicts the future, Arnold runs away, Becca gets a major static problem with her hair, Drew becomes attracted to another woman, someone from his past shows up for a school reunion, and Paige enchants the boss's son, Kenny Stollmark, Jr. Nothing returns to normal until lightning strikes the house once more.

• We learn that Drew once wanted to be an architect.

• Paige on Drew: "Reunions are tough at Dad's age. Like sit-ups...and diets." She tells Artie about "The rites of a passage of a woman welder," and that ". . . someone should write a book," He replies with, "I am...but it's called Zen and the art of the y-joint," and then hands her a large tube of industrial glue. Soon after, she meets Kenny for the first time.

• Paige on love: "How many chances do we get? ...One...two...six? When do you strike out for good?" Drew answers, "When you give up, I guess."

• Midge the waitress makes an appearance. We learn that "lady luncheons" at the restaurant are her "personal favorite." And on meeting Drew's old school friend, she says, "Bimbo. Someone get me an aspirin."

• Artie's initial suspicions about Kenny: "What'd he talk about on the date? The factory, right? The family business? They need someone on the inside, princess. They always do. Last time, it was me, but instead of champagne and flowers it was perks and days off...This is the wrong time to makes those kinds of friends."

• Drew confesses that he secretly met with Beverly (though nothing happens), and Becca wonders what's going on. Libby replies: "Your father's moving out." Drew begs Libby: "I'm sorry. I'm sorry I allowed this to happen. I don't know what I was thinking...But when I was there, in her apartment, all I could think about was you and this family...our lives together. I was out of my mind...risking it all that way...It was stupid...I love you, Libby. I could never love anyone else. You gotta know that." Corky later adds, however, that "Dad's in the dog house."

• When the lightning strikes again, Libby calls Drew an "impossible... jerk," then dashes into his arms, holding tightly.

• Michael Braverman, categorizes this segment as a Bill show, as in Smitrovich, and further explains: "This was another episode where we said, What would happen if? It was another one of the fun shows. There was one terrific scene where they were sitting in the emergency ward and someone asks for the time, and they all have different times. I also thought it was funny when they kept walking past the elevator and it kept opening and closing."

Episode 57: "Jerry's Deli". . . . . [1-19-92]
Written by E.F. Wallengren. Directed by Larry Shaw. Guest stars: Sandy Baron, Michael Earl Reid, Alfred Dennis, Rick Simone, William F. Kramer

Jerry's dad shows up at the ad agency and starts pushing his son around. Jerry quits and offers to help run the grill, much to the annoyance of Drew, who's decided that he and Corky should be closer; that Corky should inherit the grill. So when Drew asks Corky to work with him at the grill, Corky quits his job at the theatre. Jerry then tells him to lead his own life and stop letting his dad make his decisions, a reflection of Jerry's own situation. Corky quits the grill, and learns that his old job at the theatre is no longer available. And while Drew persuades the movie-house owner to let

Corky be the apprentice projectionist, Jerry's dad, Sam, pays a visit and then suddenly dies. Corky persuades a reluctant Jerry to go to the funeral, after which he loses his car keys in the snow and breaks down. Fortunately, Corky is there to comfort him.

• Jerry's father heard one of Jerry's radio spots for the Glenbrook Daily News. But Sam wasn't too impressed with Jerry's slogan: "Out with the old, in with the news."

• Meanwhile, Drew has father-son aspirations of his own, regarding the restaurant. "A real father and son operation — that's what this place was meant to be. Maybe we'll even open a few more someday...get a whole chain going..."

• We also learn that Jerry had an idea to open a gift shop with souvenirs, trinkets, and postcards, near the entrance of Drew's restaurant. Thus, this episode's title.

• We learn that Jerry's father owned 51% percent of the company.

• Libby sticks up for Jerry to his father. "Jerry's whole life is wrapped up in Berkson and Berkson. Since the day you left, this company has belonged to him. Then you show up out of the blue and take it back...and you're surprised that he quits...He's confused. He's in pain."

• Becca and Paige go at it:

> *Becca:* ... you should automatically leave every job that doesn't make you happy?
> *Paige:* Why not? Why spend your life being miserable?
> *Becca:* I hate to be the one to say it, but that attitude cost you your last apartment.
> *Paige:* Thank you very much — as if you even know what you're talking about. You haven't had a real job in your life.
> *Becca:* I suppose you think advance placement classes aren't real work.
> *Paige:* Try using a welding torch sometime. Or a drill press. Or a fork lift.
> *Becca:* No thanks. With a little hard work I think I can do better than that.

• Drew bosses around Corky just as he would any other employee, let alone someone who has Down's or one who happens to be his son. Good. Let's hear it for equality and the lack of nepotism.

• In one moment, in the graveyard, Jerry has not yet cried over his loss. Dazed and confused, he loses his car keys. Corky finds them, and hands them to Jerry, who then finally breaks down: "We did that scene at the graveyard on the second day of shooting," explains Ray Buktenica. "This episode was very unusual to shoot, in that, outside of maybe one or two scenes, the entire episode was shot, for me, in reverse. The last scene, of Jerry driving up in the car, was the very first thing we shot." As to Jerry crying, Ray adds: "I had to make clear what had transpired."

• "This was an episode that was really written specifically for Jerry," Ray goes on to say. And though Ray believes Jerry was the "main thrust" of this segment, he also had some "unresolved issues" with it. "You get the rewrites," he states, "and they kind of fix things, and some of the things kind of fall apart. And you hope that by the time that you're actually in front of the camera, that all the loose ends are tied together. But they weren't really tied together for me, even though they kind of appeared to be here."

• Still, Ray adds, "This was really the best dramatic opportunity that I've ever had a chance to play on film, with the graveyard scene and all."

• This was also the first time that Jerry had any major scenes with Corky, who was the one who convinced Jerry to visit his father's gravesite and go to the funeral. "It was the first time we really had some in depth opportunity to work together," Buktenica says of acting with Chris Burke. "And we both loved it."

• Jerry had previously noted that his father was deceased.

Episode 58: "The Room" . . . . [2-9-92]
Written by Tony Graphia, Michael Nankin, Charles Pratt, Jr., Thania St. John. Directed by Michael Lange. Guest stars: Udana Power, Laura Waterbury, Patrick O'Connell

Becca, Libby and Paige have entered the Man Zone. They tear down a wall in the Thacher house to reveal another room, which is then redone (mainly by Paige) to be baby Nick's new room. Libby decides to leave Jerry's advertising firm to deal fulltime with Nick, while Paige discovers her true calling after finishing Nick's room: She wants to be a builder.

• Mementos from the old room lead to flashback fantasy scenes that reveal the changing roles of women in American society: Jesse and Becca as '60s hippies, Libby becoming an Avon lady in the 1950s, et al. At one point, in one of the first such instances in the series, two different fantasy sequences follow one after the other. From the '50s to the '60s.

• This segment is filled with great comedic lines, and pop culture/sci-fi references from everyone. The aforementioned Man Zone is a play on The Twilight Zone. Upon first finding the room, Corky says, "This is like Indiana Jones..." "And the Closet of Doom," Becca adds. Then, too, she says: "It's like our own private time machine." Later: "Maybe we should have called Geraldo" [because he was once into finding lost places...like Capone's tomb].

• When Paige makes a first break into the room's outer wall, Becca is shocked. "Wow...did you learn that from Dad?" "No, from dating," Paige replies, as Libby laughs.

• When Jerry comes to make a home delivery to Libby of some work, she opens the front door, and he says: "Look at you...Rosie the Riveter." She returns with: "Look at you...Woody the Woodpecker."

• Regarding Drew and the new room, Libby later says: "He'd lift his leg and leave his mark on this stud if he could."

> *Paige:* The face of power...shaves.
> *Becca:* It's the '90s. Wake up and smell the estrogen.

• In the '60s fantasy sequence, Jesse makes reference to Becca's zodiac sign: Libra. He's a Taurus. (Kellie Martin and Chad Lowe's real-life astrological symbols).

• Corky says about Nicky: "He's not sleeping with me. He makes me psycho."

• There are also serious speakings, of course — As with one of Jerry's lines, stated twice with a different sentiment. At first he says, "Take care of my godson," in a jovial way. Then, after Libby decides not work for him anymore and stays home and takes care of Nicky, he says the words with melancholy.

• Jesse, upon noticing a Make Love, Not War button Becca's holding (one she found in the room): "I always thought the '60s should have been my time. I've just been misplaced."

• Nicky says "Momma" for the first time. But he does so in Paige's arms, in front of Libby, which makes Libby feel distraught. She has spent too much time at work.

• Libby to Becca: "Once you give up a dream, you never get it back. I know," which is a reference to Libby's decision to leave her life as Libby Dean, the stage singer, to raise a family (from the first season's "Break a Leg, Mom").

• Patti Lupone sings a cappella, "Do I Want You?" to little Nicky in the closing scene, in which the child is really sleeping.

• "This is probably my favorite episode," comments Tracey Needham. "I had such a great time doing it. I learned a lot. And it was the first time that I really had the chance to work with Patti and Kellie for any extensive amount of time. I learned so much from them. However much younger Kellie was than I, she had a lot more experience than I did. And just to do the different time periods was challenging for me. Overall, it just made it a very special episode for me."

• "I had the chance to work with Patti and Tracey a lot," adds Martin, "And I loved it. It was like doing a little feature film inside our episodic television show."

• Director Michael Lange thinks this segment is "interesting because we were able to express what was going on in the present by illustrating it with the mores of the past," for example; in the present Jesse had AIDS. In the 1960s, he was drafted for Vietnam. "It was a death sentence, either way," says Lange.

• Becca and Jesse, however, finally got to kiss onscreen, albeit in the "fantasy-past," when the hippie-Jesse did not have AIDS.

Episode 59: "The Wall" . . . . [2-19-92]
Written by Brad Markowtiz. Directed by Michael Lange. Guest stars: Michael Cudlitz, Amy Moore Davis, Sheila Larken, Steven Mushhond Lee, Carol Locatell, Michael Earl Reid, Carol Swarbrick, Toni Attell, Liz Georges, Scott Campbell, Tisha Putman

Jesse, Becca, and Tyler and some friends go turkey bowling, and are ordered to repaint a graffiti-covered wall. In the interim, the wall becomes a symbol of the future for Jesse, who's awaiting his medical test results, while Tyler has had it with Becca's mistreatment of him. Also, Corky feels that finders should be keepers when he discovers an abandoned baby in the theatre.

• Jesse says to Becca: 'Carpe turkem.' Seize the bird."

• When Becca gets a strike, Jesse says, "Way to go, Becster."

• Tyler bleeds his heart to Becca: "Seeing you with Jesse. Thinking about you with him. Knowing you're with him…I know that's wrong. I know it sounds crazy. But you know what makes me craziest? I can't even hate him. I want to. Do you know how much I want to hate him, Becca? For taking you away? If he was anyone else, I'd fight him, I'd hit him. I'd punch him out, or he'd punch me out — but I can't fight him. How do you fight someone who's gonna die? How can you beat that? I can never win. I can't even play. Even after he's gone, you'll just love him more."

• "Becca's a fighter," says Kellie Martin, "and she really had the chance to really vent in this episode." Though Martin was upset about the turkey sequence: "I thought it was disgusting. When I first read the script, I was like…Turkey bowling? They're bowling with turkeys?"

• "This was a weird episode because I think everyone hated it," adds Michael Lange. "And with all due respect to [writer] Brad Markowitz, this episode was saved in production, by the actors and me. I just have memories of a lot of discussion in pre-production about. I went into Michael

Braverman's office and said, I really only have one note on the script: 'Throw it out!' which he didn't. But he didn't throw me out, either, so that was good. But it turned out to be actually kind of exuberant. And we might have all been wrong, because when it all came together, it turned out to be a fun episode."

• Mark Bashaar was Lange's assistant on *Life*, and then *Beverly Hills, 90210*.

• As to Tommy Puett's moving speech of defense to Becca, Lange says: "He had something to play. A lot of times, jock-type characters are not really given challenging dialogue to play. But here, I think Tommy's talent really shined."

Episode 60: "The Blues" . . . . [2-23-92]
Written by Toni Graphia. Directed by Michael Nankin. Guest stars: Megan Ashby, Justin Duso, Don Perry

Jesse gets hired to work as a waiter at Drew's place, but declining patronage forces Drew to let him go. They become real close because they share a love of the blues, so Jesse is upset when Drew tells him of his decision. In the end, Drew offers the job again, but Jesse declines. Meanwhile, Corky and Becca share an interest in stargazing.

• "Face it," Jesse tells Becca, about Drew, ". . . a boyfriend is to a father what a snake is to a mongoose."

• Then, when Drew and Jesse talk, Drew says: "Death. Misery. Poverty. Betrayal. We've all gone through it." Jesse replies: "Some of us have perfected it to an art."

• Jesse tells of his real dad: "Died when I was six. Ice on the road. That's all they ever said. Not that he was killed, or it was a terrible wreck. Just 'ice on the road...' over and over like a weather forecast." Then when he asks Drew to "tell me something depressing," Drew replies: "My father never left. He stuck around and drank. Cheated on my mother. Ignored my brother and me. But he never left."

• Becca said about her boyfriend and father: "...it's kind of weird. Turns out they both like [the] blues. God knows how anyone could listen to that depressing stuff, but hey, whatever works . . ."

• Hans quits because Jesse's always in the restaurant, now, around food. And business is not good. A similar plot device that was used in another episode, when Drew first tried to buy the restaurant, and he was having trouble because Corky was discriminated against.

• Features a poignant scene where Drew watches as Jesse sleeps, something that Jesse's own father would do.

• Becca, Libby and Mary McKenna tell Drew to butt out of Jesse's life, and not get so close; that he has his own family to worry about.

• Corky: "Sometimes people say they're okay, when they're not." And later, referring to Jesse, he says: "...I think he needs you more."

• Libby says to Becca: "I've known your father a long time. He's always been like this. He can spot them a mile away, the wounded ones. The drowning ones. And he won't stop until he's dragged them kicking and screaming to shore and pounded their chests and breathed into their mouths and made them live...They say you can't do it. They say you can't save a person who doesn't want to be saved. But your father will never believe that. And neither will you. You're just like him."

• Drew to Jesse: "...people are so ignorant. If there was a way to explain it to them so that they wouldn't be afraid of you...But people just don't change overnight."

• Bill Smitrovich says he suggested the storyline for this episode: "I asked the producers to write an episode about the blues, which I love, along with jazz. I mean, the Thachers did live in the outskirts of Chicago [a blues capitol]...so I figured, let's get real."

• Also (as Chad Lowe has previously assessed), there was some distance between Becca's parents and Jesse, and Smitrovich believes this episode helped to bring the two parties closer. "Drew had some very strong feelings about Jesse," Bill explains. "And it was tough [for me as an actor] to say a lot of the things that Drew said. I never thought that he would be taken to that sensibility. I struggled with it. I fought it, actually, but didn't win. I thought that Drew should be a little more understanding when it came to Jesse and Becca, but the show needed that conflict. Though I thought it was a little strong, and a little ill-informed of him. But that's showbiz."

• Still, however, this episode does not ring true. All of a sudden, Drew and Jesse are pals? Doesn't work.

Episode 61: "The Fairy Tale" . . . . [3-1-92]
Written by Thania St. John. Directed by Michael Lange. Guest stars: Greg Kean, Wallace Langham, Caitlin Dulany, Cosie Costa, Steven Hack, Wil Albert

Libby writes a fairy tale about Corky, and Corky enters it in a literary contest, and Jerry becomes the family's agent. Libby then gets an offer to get it published as a children's book, but in a rewritten form. Libby turns down the offer, staying true to the story, which has so much to do with Corky. Becca doesn't like this because she would have wanted the money for college.

• At the beginning of each act in this episode, there is fancy narration and illustration, which fades into the scene in real life. At the end, we see an illustrated bunch of daisies, tied to a beautiful ribbon. The camera follows the vines that come out of the stems, which lead to the words "The End."

• Libby's story is called The Tales of Prince Fearless, which Corky submits to *Tell Me a Story* magazine.

• A subplot features the love triangle between Paige, Michael and Kenny.

• Corky watches *Oprah,* and tells Paige she gets "more mail than Ed McMahon," and when the doorbell rings, he says, "I pity the fool behind the door."

• Drew to Jerry: "Did you move in and not tell us?"

• Ray Buktenica looked forward to Jerry being Libby's agent. He thought, "Oh, good, they're going to open him up to different areas." And though we never got to see Jerry's house, he was given a $60,000 Audi, prompting Buktenica to say, "Oh…baby…all right!"

• "Actually," Buktenica further recalls, "one of my favorite pieces of film is at the very end of this episode, where Libby turns down the money, and in the background, Jerry's talking to the publisher, going through his gesticulations of his idea for another story, when he's hopping around like a chipmunk. I tell you, I must have watched that scene ten times in a row with a couple of my friends, and we just absolutely howled. And I remembered the cameraman saying, You know, I didn't think it was possible for an actor to be forty feet in the background, and steal the scene."

• So were Jerry's antics an idea that came from Ray, the writer or the director? "Well, they held me into the shot," Buktenica explains, "and they saw what I was doing, and they all laughed and got a kick out of it. Then I ran out of the shot, and [the potential publisher of Libby's next book] drove out of the shot, and Jerry chased the car. Then, at the very end, I come back into the shot. It was very farcical."

• Ray figured, "Hell, the Thacher's gave up a twenty-thousand-dollar advance for a book deal; they might as well believe this, too" [that Jerry would be so extremely silly].

Episode 62: "Hearts and Flowers" . . . . [3-15-92]
Written by Charles Pratt, Jr.. Directed by Larry Shaw. Guest stars: Joe d'Angerio, Brian Drillinger, Lorna Scott, Michael Kearns, Neil Tadken

Inspired by her grandparents' upcoming 50th wedding anniversary, Becca proposes to Jesse, and he agrees. Then they have to think twice. Part of the problem: there is a dying man with AIDS at the hospice, and he doesn't want to have anything to do with his wife; he doesn't want her to see and suffer through his agony.

Consequently, Jesse breaks up with Becca, saying she deserves to live the life of a regular teen. Afterwards, the man dies and Jesse speaks with his wife, who makes him realize that maybe Becca is strong enough to handle the same situation. With Becca by now having her doubts, she turns to Libby, who tells her about finding the strength that she needed to raise Corky. So a compromise of sorts is reached: Jesse and Becca reunite, but their marriage is postponed. Meanwhile, Paige, too, is considering marriage — to Kenny, who wants very much to be her husband. But Paige isn't so sure, especially when Kenny makes a disparaging remark about Corky's ticks. She then turns to Michael for counsel (and comfort?).

• Teresa explains how she met Sal: "The Elk's lodge. Only eleven months I'd been in this country...The two of us, we barely know English. He comes to me, the barber from Third Street...on one knee...I know his mother better than I know him."

• On hearing from Becca about her intended nuptials to Jesse, Tyler says: "Congratulations!"

• Kenny asks if Down syndrome is hereditary, and Paige returns with: "My family's dealt with a lot of prejudice over the years. We can see it coming a mile away...Good night, Kenny."

• Sal repeats vows he made to Teresa when they got married — in Italian: "Io, Sal Giordano, prendo te, Teresa, come mia sposa, spose e prometto di esserti, fedele sempre nella gioia e nel dolore, nella salute e nella malattia e diamanti e onorarti tutti i giorni della mia vita..."

Episode 63: "Corky's Romance" . . . . [3-29-92]
Written by E.F. Wallengren. Directed by Kim Friedman. Guest stars: Melendy Britt, Drew Snyder, Gregg Daniel, Paul Eisenhauer

With Corky along for the ride, Drew runs his sport utility vehicle into the back of an automobile that is driven by Amanda, an attractive young junior college student with Down's. A romance blossoms between Corky and Amanda, but is soon nipped in the bud by her parents. Meanwhile, Jerry sponsors Becca in a need-based scholarship contest, and Becca doesn't know it's need-based until the day before a banquet at which she's supposed to make her presentation.

• We meet Amanda for the first time, and Corky becomes smitten, inspired and ignited with enthusiasm for further independence. As he says, "If she can [drive], so can I...I want a driver's license...and a car...a sports car...no, a Jeep...a van . . ."

• Amanda to Corky: "I like the way you mow...Straight."

• Drew visits the church gymnasium/cultural hall where the Hi Hopes singers are rehearsing "Ave Maria." They are all challenged. Drew says, "That was sensational! Those are the Hi Hopes?" Amanda nods and says, "They call themselves the gifted mentally retarded." Libby later defines them as "Savants — people with learning disabilities who are very gifted in an area like music or art."

• Drew allows Corky to use the restaurant all to himself on his date with Amanda, with Hans and Midge, the waitress, lending a hand.

• Amanda: "Most people are afraid of me. Normal people are afraid because I have Down's. Down's people are afraid because I'm too normal."

• Libby and Drew discuss their very unpleasant discussion with Amanda's parents, one in which Amanda's mother and father decide that their daughter should not see Corky:

> *Drew:* Every time I drift off to sleep, Amanda's parents swoop down on broomsticks and wake me up.
> *Libby:* I keep replaying that conversation in my mind. I want to go back and have it again.
> *Drew:* Why?
> *Libby:* So I can strangle them.

• Libby says to Jerry, regarding his assistance with Becca, "For somebody I used to hate working for, you're an okay guy."

• Paige calls Amanda's parents "Meatheads."

• A breath of fresh air from Becca to Corky: "I know that sometimes I get so wrapped up in my own problems that I don't pay much attention to anybody else's, but I'm sorry about Amanda — I really am...." and "I know what's it's like to want someone so badly but not be able to have them. I went through that with Tyler."

• And finally, Becca's speech at the Advertising Council turns into a tribute to Corky: "Without his help, I never would have made it this far. He knows how to lift my spirits when I'm down. He knows how to make me feel loved, and he knows how to make me laugh. He's taught me the meaning of hard work, because nothing comes easy for him. And he's showed me what integrity is all about. But more than anything else, he's taught me that you never, ever, ever give up without a fight."

• Corky meets up with Amanda at the Hi Hopes Concert and:

> *Corky:* May I have this dance?
> *Amanda:* I still don't know how.
> *Corky:* I still don't care.

Episode 64: "More Than Friends" .... [4-26-92]
Written by Brad Markowtiz. Directed by Bill Smitrovich. Guest stars: Micole Mercurio, Matthew Walker, Michael Rankin, Page Leong, Rick Peters, Nicholas Johnson

Drew and Libby leave Paige, Becca, and Corky to house-watch, and a host of disasters begin. First, Becca and Jesse decide to throw a party, which an inebriated Tyler and college frat troublemakers crash and take over. Then, Michael crashes a stuffy gathering at the country club that Paige is attending with Kenny and his parents. But each is over with quite different results. First, Becca kicks a drunken Tyler out of the house and her life, saying she can't be friends with him anymore. He goes to leave, and Corky tries to stop him from driving while drunk, but he can't convince him to hand over the keys. So Corky rides with him. They crash into a tree, leaving Tyler near death and Corky mute with a broken arm. By this time, Paige has returned with Kenny from the country club calamity, and he proposes to her; a precious moment that is disrupted when Paige hears the rumpus from the house. Drew and Libby return, finding one last drunken teen who tells them that Tyler and Corky are in the hospital. There, Becca, baring guilt over Tyler's plight, views the once love of her life, now in a coma, for the last time, while Paige consents to Kenny's proposal, with a dejected Michael leering on from the side.

• Libby explains Uncle Luigi: "He was married to my Aunt Antonia. When I was little, he always used to sit me on his lap and say, 'Sing to me, Eliza-beta. You'll be a great Diva one day.'"

• Corky says about Michael: "I made him wait outside. He looked pretty scuzzy."

• Michael brings Paige a copy of The Architecture of Chicago, by Frank Lloyd Wright, who, according to Michael, apparently grew up about fifteen minutes from the Thacher household.

• Paige confesses, "I just have this tendency, when I'm nervous. I turn into a real klutz."

• Becca helps Tyler study, and he says it's "just like old times."

• Tyler meets Amanda for the first and only time.

• Then, it never got more heavy duty between Becca and Tyler than this:

> *Tyler:* I thought we had something special, Becca. And one day, outta' nowhere — boom! No warning, no reason. You dumped me. Like some old book you already read.
> *Becca:* You dumped me.
> *Tyler:* Only because you already loved him. Did you try and stop me? No. You were glad — it was just goodbye. Not even, 'I'm sorry.' Not even an 'I'm sorry,' Becca!"

Becca: I am sorry, Tyler. I'm sorry you're having trouble in school. I'm sorry your dad doesn't understand you. I'm sorry you're not playing basketball. I'm sorry I met Jesse. I'm sorry I fell in love with him. I'm sorry I can't fix all your problems for you. But you know what I'm sorriest about? That we can't be friends anymore ...You were wrong. You weren't out of my life — until now. Get out of my life, and get out of my house...Go home, Tyler."

• The segment's director was star Bill Smitrovich, who comments on his experience behind the camera: "I kept on bugging them. I had wanted to direct an episode for a long time. Then, Kellie decides to get sick the one time in the history of the show, and it had to be the one I directed. That boned me a little bit on the budget. I also had a few tiny scenes that took longer than they should have, and they boned me a little bit, too."

Episode 65: "Confessions". . . . . [5-3-92]
Written by Toni Graphia. Directed by Michael Lange. Guest stars: Donna Hardy, Michael Rankin, John Apicella, Ron Ross, Brady Bluhm

Corky, somehow rendered mute by the accident, does not speak up until Becca bares her soul to him. Corky then says that Tyler tried to swerve around a boy on a bike. Becca still feels guilty over Tyler's death as she and Jesse place flowers at his grave. Meanwhile, Paige and Michael go looking for a wedding cake, and get locked in a refrigerated room.
  • There should have been more mention of the fact that Tyler drove drunk. He also should have had better reflexes to help him stop hitting the boy on the bike, a storyline development which, as Chad Lowe has previously addressed, was to some extent, a copout.
  • In a flashback to the night of the accident, Tyler talks to Corky about Becca: "She wants me out of her life? I'm out, dude. I'm gone...she really knows out to jerk a guy around. She never wants to see me again? I never want to see her again. This is it. Let her change her mind someday. Let her even try to come around...It'll be too late."
  • Michael tells Paige: "I know the timing is strange, with the accident...I know it seems right now like everything is sad and awful. But Tyler's going to get better and we're going to have our wedding and things will be good again."
  • But things never are. Drew tells Corky: "...There's no easy way to say this, so...Tyler...died last night...he never woke up...we don't think he was in any pain... and it was quiet...I'm going to miss him. We're all going to miss him ..."Then, Drew adds "...I don't know how Jack Benchfield is going to

handle this...because I couldn't. If anything ever happened to you...I would die right with you, because you're everything to me and I'm so afraid...of losing you."

• Becca and Jesse talk about Tyler's death:

> *Becca:* He used to pick me up from school every morning... when we were going together. I used to stand in front of the mirror, rushing, getting ready, putting on makeup...listening for his car. It had a particular sound, and I always knew it was him coming before he even rounded the block...He'd honk his horn and I'd look out the window and he was always there in that awful blue car. I hated that car and that goofy grin and always wearing the same worn-out letterman jacket...I thought he was the greatest thing that ever lived.
>
> *Jesse:* I'm going to miss him, too. I feel like we were just getting past everything. Like we were just starting to really be friends.

• Later, however, Jesse comes down hard on Tyler with: "...that night he was stupid and immature and out of control. And he blew it." To which Becca replies, "You have no right. No right to talk that way about him"

• The only scene between Becca and Tyler's mother, Robin, takes place here.

• Rare insight into the Becca/Paige association: When the series began, the age gap kept them from relating on some level. Now with Becca almost officially an adult, her relationship with Paige changes. Their family ties are somewhat more even; as when Becca overhears Drew answering the phone and learning of Tyler's death; how she then climbs in bed with Paige for comfort.

• In a flashback, Corky tells Tyler: "All I ever wanted since I came to Marshall [High] was to be like you...You're the best friend I ever had."

• More of the Becca/Paige extended relationship may be viewed in "Choices."

• There's a touching scene when Jack Benchfield visits Tyler in his hospital room and, almost in denial of what's transpired, screens home movies of his dying son's athletic achievements. "There was a very technical way in which we shot that scene," explains Richard Frank, who played Mr. Benchfield. "There were specific marks for the projector and the screen, where I was to stand, in proportion to the background, and my body. They pinpointed exactly where each would be placed."

• As to the scene in which Paige is locked in the fridge with Michael, Tracey Needham says: "That was such a fun scene to do. I had such a good time doing it. And I loved [the actress who played the cake lady]. She was the cutest thing that there ever was. On film, for the last take, the last shot, we actually attacked Michael Lange, and it ended up being this huge cake fight on film."

Episode 66: "Consenting Adults" . . . . [5-10-92]
Written by Charles Pratt, Jr.. Directed by Michael Nankin. Guest stars: Micole Mercurio, Allan Royal, John Ingle, Jason Ryder, Alec Murdock

Paige's heart-to-heart talk with Drew about her upcoming marriage with Kenny motivates Drew to take matters into his own hands, convincing Michael to get to Paige. Without telling anyone, Drew then hires Michael's band to play at the wedding. And while Paige breaks up with Kenny at the altar and runs off with Michael instead, Corky proposes to Amanda. Jesse, too, is involved with a heavy transition: He leaves for Arizona with his mom, then later decides to return, saying that Becca is his family now.

• Libby's cousin Gabby from Italy (played by Patti Lupone in a dual role) sends Paige tacky Italian oil as a wedding gift.
• We meet Jesse's stepbrother, Ted, and stepfather, Ben, the latter of whom Jesse calls "a jerk...The guy's got about as much compassion as that sink." Becca then starts to help him understand him better: "He's your mother's husband...Paige and my mom..." But she stops there, as she was going to refer to the conflict that initially occurred between Libby and Paige in the first few episodes of the first season.
• Paige hates "kitchen appliances in general...coffee makers, in particular."
• Amanda says: "Goodnight, Charles," and Corky replies, "No. Corky. Get it right."
• Libby's sweeping observation: "Paige is getting married. Becca's grown out of her glasses...and just about everything else. Nicky's walking...and Corky's feeling...what is Corky feeling? Left behind. That's it."
• Corky's cry for growth: "I'm a man. I'm not a little boy anymore. I need to grow up. I need to grow up now...Paige has her wedding. Becca's going to college. I have to have something, too."
• Drew's the perfect dad when he tells Paige: "Look...button, honey...as much as I've got invested in this wedding, you can't marry Kenny if you're having these feelings. You've got to go out, find this Michael and talk to him. Tonight."
• Then, later, Drew says to Michael himself: "I have this problem... Sometimes it's a real handicap. Other times...a lifesaver. See, I hate it when my kids make mistakes. I do anything to prevent it. Get downright

meddlesome at times."

• Corky asks Amanda to marry him.

• This may be interpreted as an attempt at a series finale, as the show faced cancellation in 1992. It received a major reprieve when *Day One,* ABC's Forrest Sawyer newsmagazine, failed to get off the ground and needed an overhaul.

The Fourth Season of *Life,* (from left): Chad Lowe (now securely in place as a regular, after joining the series in the third season), Kellie Martin, Bill Smitrovich, Chris Burke, Tracey Needham, Patti Lupone. *THE REGAL COLLECTION*

THE FOURTH SEASON
1991 TO 1992

Episode 67: "Bec to the Future" . . . . [9-20-92]
Written by Thania St. John, Toni Graphia. Directed by Michael Nankin. Guest stars: Pamela Bellwood (Dynasty), Frank Muller, Ned Vaughn, Drew Snyder, Charlotte Stewart, Jeanne Mori

A 40-something Becca, a married radiologist, looks back on the summer of '92. In the present, Jesse returns, but the reunion is bittersweet. Becca is avoiding Jesse to be with her new friends who don't know Jesse is HIV-positive. He then lectures Becca about the fact that she didn't tell them the truth about him.

• A future realtor approaches the adult Becca, who she thinks is a potential buyer for the Thacher house. The pitch: "The house has four bedrooms, two baths, and a loft over the garage you can rent out. And one of the bedrooms would be fine for a nursery. But I would knock through the wall, and make it a closet." The last line is a reference to the third season episode, "The Room," in which Becca, Libby and Paige knocked through that closet, and made it a nursery.

• Amanda and Corky are obsessed with "sleeping together," which is all they end up doing, literally, as this episode closes: Laying next to each other on Amanda's bed in her apartment, and falling asleep in each other's arms — with their clothes on. Though, before that happens, they flirt with each other. Corky even asks Jesse for advice, who tells him: "Sometimes it's better to wait" and "This kind of sounds like a dad thing...maybe you should ask him about it?" But Corky replies: "I want to make up my own mind."

• Becca gives Jesse (who spent the summer in Phoenix) her journal from the summer. It explains how she felt every day without him. She later burns it.

• When the future Becca's husband says they missed her at the cardiology seminar (in Glenbrook, that's why she came back to visit the house), Becca replies: "You've seen one broken heart, you've seen them all."

• Meanwhile, the present Becca still has her own way with words: About

301

a special kind of soda: "We get them at the bookstore. They're really good. They're from France."

• Kiersten Warren, Ned Vaughn, and Martin Milner debut in their semi-regular roles. All present nice comic relief, in general, while Milner's Harris Cassidy has a very funny line, in particular, here, when Becca and all invite him to Goodman's for a pool party: "Once I took a dip in Ava Gardner and Jack Warner's pool," Harris replies. "It was so perfect; I swore I'd never swim again."

• At that same pool party, Jesse later arrives, and discovers that Becca has told her friends about him, but not about the fact that he is HIV-positive. "You didn't tell them," he says. "I don't need you to protect me." "I like talking about you like it didn't matter," Becca tries to defend, "... I mean...it doesn't matter." Jesse then screams to her: "From AIDS...there is no break...I don't need you." Becca later says, "I get so sick of you acting like you're already dead." Jesse returns with: "And I get so sick of you acting like I'm never gonna be! Do you really think that we have a future?" "No," Becca says. "I want to remember me and tell people about me"; which future Becca finally does, with her husband, David, with whom she's been married for ten years. But she never mentioned Jesse.

• The future Becca also tells her husband: "Life isn't fair" (which is something Jesse once told her — in this episode).

• Drew looks at picture of child-Paige, and Libby clarifies, "She's not gone. She's just married." "I know," Drew returns, "but it'll never be the same." He then asks, "Remember when it just used to be you and me?" "Barely," Libby replies.

• When Paige comes home, Drew calls her "Button."

• During a talk with Becca, Paige divulges that she and Michael have broken up: "Michael's not coming back," she says. He's too free-spirited, and Paige was "finally getting some order into my life."

Episode 68: "Exposed" . . . . [9-27-92]
Written by E.F. Wallengren. Directed by Michael Lange. Guest stars: Thomas Ryan, Billy Kane, Ben Lemon, Stephen Rowe, Michael Arenz, Ryan Jarvis, David Listman

Jesse paints a nude painting of Becca, Harris Cassidy purchases it, and it's displayed in the Nevermore bookstore, all of which leads to somewhat of a scandal. And endless date proposals on her answering machine are just the tip of the iceberg. Drew buys his paper there, sees the portrait, and goes ballistic, even lecturing Becca at school in front of her French class. He offers to purchase the image from Harris, who declines. Drew, Corky and Jesse then conspire to steal the painting back, but get arrested. Meanwhile,

Paige, still hurting from her breakup with the irresponsible Michael, shows Becca and Libby a tattoo Michael painted on her shoulder. Back at the police station, Harris bails out the three art bandits after selling the painting to the proprietor of a biker bar, and after Drew comes to terms with the fact that Becca is maturing, and Paige agrees to have the tattoo removed.

• When Ray Nelson, Jr. returns, with a list of guys who want to pay Jesse to have their girlfriends painted nude, he remarks to Jesse, "You've got HIV. What could happen?"

• It's never determined if Becca posed nude or if the nudity was solely the product of Jesse's imagination.

• Corky was the mastermind of the thieves, inspired by the Pink Panther Film Festival at the theatre. In reference to the portrait, Corky says to Becca: "You're in your birthday suit."

• Paige sulks to very sad music (including "Stormy Weather" and "Lover Man"), prompting Becca to comment: "That's the most depressing music that I've ever heard."

• Meanwhile, Paige has some very funny lines, including: "Artists should be lined up against a wall and shot."

• When Paige thinks she hasn't yet hit bottom, Libby corrects her with, "You are a wreck."

• Jesse and Drew also have a comical banter as they're lifting the portrait off the wall:

> *Jesse:* At what point did it become uncomfortable to see your little girl naked?
> *Drew:* Let's just get the painting, down, okay?

• We find out that artist Carlo Santiago painted a portrait of Harris Cassidy when he was young.

• Drew meets the eccentric Harris for the first time here, and wonders, "Do you always get this way when you drink cappuccino?" The two almost get into a fistfight over the painting, which both Drew and Jesse attempt to purchase from Cassidy.

• The Police at the station study the portrait with the eyes and critique of artistic connoisseurs ("It definitely suggests spring time or fall...").

• Becca questions her brother's involvement in the attempted paint stealing. And after Corky deviously replies with, "It was my idea," he and Jesse break up into uncontrollable laughter.

• Intense Drew/Becca conversation:

> *Drew:* ...it seems just like yesterday you had pigtails and those red glasses...
> *Becca:* I guess I'm not your little girl anymore.

• Very conscious statement from Jesse to Becca regarding the show's changes: "Things are really different, aren't they...I'm living on my own. You've got all these new friends...this new self-image."
• A favorite for Bill Smitrovich.

Episode 69: "(PMS) Premarital Syndrome" . . . . [10-4-92]
Written by Toni Graphia, Thania St. John. Directed by Michael Braverman. Guest stars: Drew Snyder, Charlotte Stewart, Diana Castle

Corky toils but finds it difficult to save enough money to purchase a diamond engagement ring for Amanda. Consequently, their trial marriage gets off to a rocky start, which is more than noticeable to Jesse and Becca, who come over for dinner.
• Interviews with couples who have Down syndrome are interwoven, a la *When Harry Met Sally...*
• This episode smartly conveys Corky and Amanda's relationship as two people who have a relationship, instead of two people with Down syndrome who have a relationship. For example, during the dinner party with Becca and Jesse, Amanda and Corky argue, loudly. Becca and Jesse turn to each other, as if to say, "Should we leave?," instead of "Oh, we better do something. They shouldn't argue with each other. They have Down syndrome. Something could happen."
• Toni Graphia recalls, "This is one of the most special episodes we did, because we featured couples with Down syndrome. We had this idea to have a round-table at the beginning of the season and invite those with Down's and other challenged people to share their stories. There's nothing like talking and doing research with the real people so that we could accurately portray and do justice to their stories. So we had this big dinner where the writers just chatted with this wonderful group and then we thought, 'Hey, let's put them on camera.' They were so charming and heartfelt. I found myself thinking about them for days. A sentence or impression haunting me.
"And we found that many of them were in couples, real romances, and that they had the same problems as everyone else. So we decided to do this *When Harry Met Sally...*-style piece and write a story around it where Corky and Amanda try to make it work."

Episode 70: "The Whole Truth" . . . . [10-18-92]
Written by Scott Frost. Directed by Michael Lange. Guest stars: Leigh J. McCloskey (Dallas), Juanita Jennings, Shari Shattuck, Michael Dempsey

Still depressed over her breakup with Michael, Paige attempts to break free with a date with Becca's English teacher. Unfortunately, the evening turns into a nightmare, when she fends off an attempted date rape. But Paige and the teacher have different perceptions on what transpired during the evening. At first Becca believes her teacher, only to confront him when his story gets a few holes in it. Meanwhile, Corky imagines that a swimsuit model has come to life. The fantasy calendar girl turns out to be quite wise; she explains how men tend to see only the bodies of women, and not what's inside their heart. Through it all, Libby confronts her own memories of a rape that transpired in college.

• There's a cute adlib scene between Patti Lupone and one of the Graves twins who plays Nicky.

• Great lines from Harris: "Did I ever tell you about the scavenger hunt at Jayne Mansfield's house?"

• When Libby asks Becca who it was at the door, she replies, "Paige's date," which is a phrase that was used as a title from one of the show's first episodes. Later, during a confrontation with the teacher, Becca says she wants "the whole truth," which is this segment's title.

• Corky to Becca: "Paige wouldn't lie...she's your sister."

• Between Drew and Corky, regarding Corky's movie house job:

> *Drew:* So what's playing tonight?
> *Corky:* Lolita.
> *Drew:* Figures.

• Between Corky and the calendar girl in the men's room:

> *Girl:* I know you're in there.
> *Corky:* No, I'm not.

• Later, Libby says: "Silence is much worse than fear...Silence becomes your companion — your ally...it's difficult to let go of it."

• Music: "Would I Lie To You?" by Charles and Eddie.

• We also learn that Libby loved to listen to Janis Joplin, which she, Paige, and Becca end up doing at this episode's end. They are later joined by Drew and Corky.

• Tracey Needham: "I remember thinking it was a little bit odd the way this episode was presented, though I loved how they went through all the different perspectives and all the different points of view; how different women deal with it."

• As with "The Room," from the second season, there are extensive scenes between Libby, Becca, and Paige, which granted Patti Lupone, Kellie Martin and Tracey Needham the opportunity to have their characters relate on an equal basis. Whereas in earlier seasons, Becca was simply Paige's little sister, or the two girls were merely Libby's daughters. "Unfortunately," Tracey Needham says this kind of interplay "didn't happen very often."

Episode 71: "Love Letters" .... [11-8-92]
Written by Michael Goldberg. Directed by Georg Fenady. Guest stars: Frances Bay, Warren Frost, Paula Marshall, Charlotte Stewart, Ned Vaughn, Hector Elias, Ralph Meyering, Jr.

Becca and her friends discover old World War II letters at the bookstore. Eric gets cozy with Becca, and Jesse does the same with a woman named Jill from an art gallery. Becca returns the letters to the woman who wrote them. Corky and Amanda get officially hitched, on the sly.
   • Goodman on romance: "It's not real. It's voodoo…" And then: "…people who write letters…that's romance. People who ignore them…that's reality."
   • Jesse to Becca: "…I moved away from my family for you. I live in a strange town, and I go to a school I can't stand. I've changed my whole life because of you. What more do you want?"
   • Jill on Jesse's art talent: "I'm not sure you're ready for a show, at least a solo show. But there is something. An anger, a voice, that people will respond to." Jesse's return: "Well, if you like dark, you've come to the right place."
   • Becca and Eric sing to "Nice Work If You Can Get It," which plays on his car stereo:
   • I never cared much for moonlit skies, I never winked back at fireflies, But now that the stars are in your eyes, I'm beginning to see the light.
   • After Drew buys Libby an expensive gift, she asks him to return it: "… We aren't kids anymore. We're middle-aged parents with bills and carpools and meetings and customers…This is our life now, not midnight movies or watching the sunrise."
   • Eric and Becca talk more about the woman and her man in the letters:

> *Eric:* I don't envy her. She's this terrific girl, who's latched on to a guy with whom there may be no future. It's not his fault he's got himself into this, but what does she do? She's in a tough position.
> *Becca:* But she's in love. She doesn't want to be with anyone else.
> *Eric:* Come on, Becca. She's only human. You read her letter. She's lonely, hurting. How much can you expect of her?
> *Becca:* So you think she should give someone else a chance?
> *Eric:* I don't know. But I wouldn't blame her if she did."

• Drew and Libby watch Casablanca, and Paige, in a stupor of breaking up with Michael, comments, "Michael and I went to Casablanca. It doesn't look anything like that."

• Becca finds the woman who wrote the letters. Her name is Sara, and she gives Becca her opinion on love: "It has to be the most important thing in the world to you, more important than your friends or your work or even your own heart. If you love someone that much, you find a way. It may bring you pain, even destroy you, but you find a way."

• Drew asks Hans if he's still with Bea, the woman from "Isn't It Romantic," in the second season. Hans, who's preparing a cake for his beloved, replies: "A day does not go by without her Hansie making her feel special. And she does the same for me."

• Then, later, as Corky and Amanda stand before the Justice of the Peace:

> *Amanda:* Charles, are you getting cold feet?...If you don't want to go through with it, it's all right...I love you, Charles. I want to spend the rest of my life with you. I don't need a ring or a ceremony to do that.
> *Corky:* It scares me...That I won't be a good enough husband for you...You will be the best wife I could ever want.
> *Amanda:* That's how I feel about you. The day I met you was the most wonderful day of my life. Whether we get married or not.

Corky then asks Amanda to marry him, and the judge complies.

• Kellie Martin, Chad Lowe, Bill Smitrovich, and Chris Burke, read selected letters while playing double parts: a solider and his factory-employed girlfriend; a soldier working a machine gun in a trench; another soldier longing for his family in a tent.

Episode 72: "Windows" . . . . [11-22-92]
Written by Toni Graphia. Directed by Michael Nankin. Guest stars: Paula Marshall (Chicago Sons), Drew Snyder, Charlotte Stewart, Val Bisoglio (Soap), Mark Bramhall, Owen Bush, Fred D. Scott, Jim Delgado, Robin Skye, Kale Ward, Ed Wasser, Nitza Wilson

Amanda's angry parents vow to annul her marriage to Corky and try to regain her custody. The young lovebirds then run off to a motel, further angering the Swansons, not to mention their attorney. Amanda's father also falsely tells Corky that it was his daughter that initially desired the annulment. Meanwhile, Becca and Jesse are upset with one another. He's angry because she's unable to attend his first gallery show (which doesn't go well) due to the Corky/Amanda debacle; she resents his growing involvement with Jill, with whom she later has a confrontation. Jill says Becca is too much in control, and acts like the only one who can take care of Jesse, so Becca backs off. Later, Jesse speaks with Corky about his honeymoon, and Corky satisfies Jesse's artistic need for approval by interpreting one of his paintings in a window. Then, too, the Thachers and Swansons go to court, and the judge lets Amanda make the final decision: She will live with Corky; they inherit Paige's old loft above the garage (when Drew and Libby's eldest child decides to move out…again).

• Corky has a touching speech (given in voiceover) about "windows."

Episode 73: "Babes in the Woods". . . . . [11-29-92]
Written by Thania St. John. Directed by Sandy Smolan. Guest stars: Judith Jones, Paula Marshall, Jared Rushton

Becca, Goodman, Ray, Jesse and two other students from their English class go on a weekend camping trip, chaperoned by Harris, which turns near treacherous. Becca gets sprayed by a skunk, and then knocks over a kerosene lantern that starts a fire in the barn where everyone is staying. Making matters worse is the rain, and the troop's discovery of a note from Harris who says they must fend for themselves.

Though some good does come out of the experience: Becca admits that she may be somewhat of a control freak when it comes to Jesse and Goodman, the latter of whom had been questioning her place in high school.

• Becca reads a note left by Harris: "Your only assignment is to survive on your own. Time for you kids to get some real experience. You won't learn that from any book. See you tomorrow night. Harris."

• Becca tries to get Goodman to go to Marshall, via checking transcripts with Goodman's mother, which surprises and irritates Goodman, who later comes clean about her mom: "She's an alcoholic, Becca. I spent seventeen years trying to work things out. Ands then one day I decided to have my own life instead of trying to save hers all the time."

> *Becca:* So you just ran away from home?
> *Goodman:* Home is a family. Someplace where you feel safe.
> You can't run away from something that never existed."

Then Goodman slams Becca with: "…it's your fault that Jesse missed that art scout, and it's your fault that we're all stuck out here so maybe you should concentrate on your own problems for a change and stop causing everybody's else's."

Harris corners Becca: "I didn't leave you to die; I left you there to learn something about yourselves. I figured you'd be the first one to crack. Nice going with the lantern, by the way. I always wanted to get rid of that shack."

Then Harris gets really heavy: "You know, there was a time in this country when certain people thought they knew what was best for everyone. After awhile these people in charge began to make decisions based on what they thought was right. They created a blacklist and ruined a lot of lives. Mine was one of them...Helping is a noble thing. But just makes sure [they] want it before you give it to them."

Harris delivers even more later: "You know, you kids think there's a solution for every problem. You think life is going to miraculously embrace you and then spit you out again at the other side and in between everybody's going to play fair and everything's going to go the way it's supposed to?... Well, you're wrong. Life is what you don't expect and most of the time you have no control over any of it. The sooner you figure that out, the better off you'll be."

• Drew and Paige have one of their heart-to-hearts:

> *Drew:* I wish I could set you up in an apartment, or buy your Mom a new car, or send Becca to college without any student loans...but I can't. So I try to make up for it with little things.
> *Paige:* Like providing a home for us? Making us feel loved? Always being there when we need you? Are those the 'little things' you mean?
> *Drew:* Yes, those things.
> *Paige:* You've got Corky and Amanda to think about, now. And Nick. This kid's got to start taking care of herself.

• With reference to Becca and friends left at the cabin, pal Ziggy says: "Wow...this is very Lord of the Flies."

• Corky suggests that Paige return to welding, because she was "happy there." Paige replies with just a bit of sarcasm: "Graveyard shifts and grease under my nails? Five-minute breaks and four-hour union meetings? Me and six hundred steel workers...?" Then sincerely, "You're right. I was really happy there."

• Becca's bout with control was first referenced by Jill (Paula Marshall) in "Windows" (the previous episode).

Episode 74: "Udder Madness" . . . . [12-13-92]
Written by E.F. Wallengren. Directed by Kim Friedman. Guest stars: Christie Clark, Casper Van Dien, BJ Jefferson

Ray nominates Becca (against her wishes) for Homecoming Queen and Goodman nominates a cow in protest of beauty pageants in general, while the third contestant is a cheerleader in need of a serious attitude adjustment. Also, Artie and Paige form their own construction business, Darlin' Construction, and redo a restaurant with a bovine motif.

• Goodman says to Becca on the whole Homecoming thing: "It's a stupid, sexist tradition…Six thousand years of oppression and you haven't learned a thing."

• Regarding a visit to the Thachers and seeing Drew and Libby, Artie says, "It's the Cleavers — Ward and June!"

• Ray says about Suzanne Westland (Becca's apparent rival since sixth grade): "She hasn't been the same since she fell off the human pyramid at opening game."

• Jesse comments on Becca's running: "What's next — Drill Team? Glee Club? Usherettes?"

• Drew mentions Donlan's Family Restaurant: "…I ate a bad chili dog there right before your Uncle Albert's funeral. I think it almost woke your Uncle Albert up."

• Corky says the final score of the game: "We got killed. Forty-two to six."

• Corky tells Paige about her relationship with Artie: "He's too old for you." But later, he tells her: "You have to go to him…You can't leave it like this" (Paige doesn't return Artie's affection).

• Artie to Paige: "I want to get you out of my system, Blondie. It doesn't help to have you standing in front of me in a pair of tight jeans . . ."

• Drew referencing Artie: "He's abusive, irritating." Paige, in defense, says: "He's my friend and my partner. I like him and that's all that counts." Still complaining: "I'm twenty-four years old, I'm still living at home, my life's going nowhere."

• The cow's name is Mary Lou. Goodman says she got her from her aunt, who "happens to feel the same way I do about things like homecoming."

• Crossed wires between Becca and Libby:

> *Becca:* I'm running against a cow . . .
> *Libby:* I wish you wouldn't talk like that.
> *Becca:* Her name's Mary Lou. She has these huge udders.
> *Libby:* Becca!
> *Becca:* They're so big; she kicks them when she walks.
> *Libby:* Enough.

• Paige is then inspired in her craft by the cow, and says to Artie: "I've got it. A farm motif for the restaurant...you know...cows everywhere."

• We learn that Michelle Ross is the Action News Anchorwoman of Glenbrook.

• Darlin' Construction was so named due to Artie's nickname for Paige.

• The episode ends with the "moo" of the cow (which adds to the show's heavy pull from the animal kingdom — pigs, dolphins, dogs, wolves.)

Episode 75: "Happy Holidays" . . . . [12-20-92]
Written by Marshall Goldberg. Directed by Randall William Cook. Guest stars: Drew Snyder, Charlotte Stewart, Jo deWinter, Erika Cohen

The holidays take on a whole new meaning for Corky, who's celebrating his first Christmas as a married man. But the situation turns sour as he and Amanda decide to spend Christmas with her parents, which upsets Drew and Libby. In the meantime, Paige reunites with Michael.

• As Chris Burke has voiced elsewhere, he believed Corky got married too soon. Here, he's forced to choose a family location for Christmas. If an episode had been produced solely dedicated to his first Christmas away from home, minus the marriage angle, it would have been more believable. It was all simply just too much at once.

Episode 76: "Choices" . . . . [1-3-93]
Written by Toni Graphia. Directed by Michael Lange. Guest stars: (None)

Paige discovers that she's pregnant with Michael's child. At first, she's delighted, as is the entire family. But when Michael returns from Spain, he decides he doesn't want the child. Paige considers abortion as an option, while Corky and Amanda seek to adopt the child. By this time, Artie has accompanied Paige during a visit to the doctor, and has expressed his true romantic feelings for her (at one point, serenading her with a flute, from outside in the snow). Fate then takes a deadly turn, when Paige loses the child to miscarriage.

• This touching exchange takes place between Libby and Corky:

> *Libby:* There's a lot of things you can do. But fathering a child, I'm afraid that's not one of them.
> *Corky:* Because of Down's.
> *Libby:* Yes...It's not impossible, but it's only happened once

that a man with Down's got a woman pregnant. Chances
are one a million.

Corky: I thought maybe that could be me.

• Later, Paige says to Drew: "...for the first time, I feel like everything's
under control. Artie and I are doing great with the business, and Michael's
got his new job at the Art Institute."

• Includes a rare scene between Paige and Jesse, discussing Paige's possible pregnancy.

• Paige suggests that, if it's a girl, the name should start with an "R," as in
Rebecca Romanov. If it's a boy, Michael suggests Ralph.

• Meanwhile, Libby feels she's too young to be a grandmother, when she
was "just getting used to being a mother again" [re: little Nick].

• Then she and Drew do some figuring: He was Corky's age when Paige
was born, and she was Paige's age when Becca's was born. And they'd do it
all over in a minute, "except the diapers," clarifies Drew.

• Meanwhile, Paige tells Artie about the new baby, and she feels he'll be
upset. Instead, Artie calls infants "angels on earth." He also tells her: "Don't
worry, darlin'. You go and have your baby. I'll hold down the fort. Take however long you need, and I'll be waiting right here when you get back."

• And there are many touching words between Corky and Amanda,
when they discuss Paige's baby and the fact that they can't have one of their
own:

> *Amanda:* I feel so lucky to be part of your family. I never
> had brothers or sisters and now I'm going to be an aunt.
> I'm happy, Charles. I don't need a baby.
>
> *Corky:* We could still try.
> *Amanda:* But your Mom said we probably couldn't. And
> what if it wasn't okay?
> *Corky:* What do you mean?
> *Amanda:* What if it was like us? What if it had Down's?
> *Corky:* It would be like us, Amanda. It would be strong and
> beautiful and kind like its mother.
> *Amanda:* And have blue eyes like its father.

• Michael's reasoning for not having the baby: "You're living in a dream
world, Paige. We've only been married four months. We've already been
separated. And now we're just getting back on track. We've got a new place;
I've got a new job. We have no money...Look at this place. It's one room.
Where are we going to put a baby?"

Then he suggests, "There are other options," as in abortion.

Then he backs down a little with: "But, if you don't want to...I'll be here for you both. We'll have this baby and we'll do the best we can. I love you, Paige."

• Libby's take on the situation: "...Having a baby is not exactly a stabilizing factor in a relationship. Especially one that's a little shaky to begin with. It's a responsibility and a bond between two people that never goes away, no matter what happens to a marriage."

• Becca makes it clear just how much she loves Jesse:

> *Becca:* I would in a second, you know.
> *Jesse:* Would what?
> *Becca:* Have your baby...if we could.
> *Jesse:* I know.

• Corky lays it straight with Paige, on the possibility of abortion: "Please don't do that, Paige...Please let the baby be born. If you don't want her, I'll take her...Amanda and I really want a baby, but we can't have one. We would be really good parents...That way, the baby can stay in the family. You can visit her and see her grow up."

• As Toni Graphia explains, this scene is "really powerful and hard to watch because essentially, that could have happened with Corky. His mother could have chosen not to have him. And many people do, and that's their right. But it makes for great drama because you are hitting on some pretty heavy duty stuff. No one expected such hard issues on this 7:00 P.M. show, but we kept surprising them and sometimes surprising ourselves."

• And, later Corky really lets Michael have it: "You don't care about my sister. You don't care about anyone but yourself."

• In the end, Paige tells Michael that he's "not wrong," "just wrong for me." Then when Paige loses the baby, in a miscarriage, Drew softens the blow to Corky: "...some things can survive no matter how bad things are for them. They can have the worst conditions and the worst of everything, and still they make it...Some things, no matter how good they have it, just don't make it. And it's not anyone's fault. It's just the way things are."

• Artie's story: "I spent six years in Southeast Asia. And what I can tell you is that they believe that a soul comes when it's ready and not before. When a child dies in the womb or during birth, they wear white for mourning. The village women burn sandalwood, while the men play music to open the heavens and let the child's soul back in. That way, it can be born again later."

• "When Paige says goodbye to Michael," comments Tracey Needham. "That was probably the most heart-wrenching scene I ever did on the show."

• "By far," Troy Evans says, "my favorite moment in the series for Artie.

There's just no question, especially with him in the snow, outside playing that flute. I just thought it was brilliantly conceived. It was so audacious." Audacious enough to keep the audience wondering whether it was a real or fantasy sequence, though Evans clarifies it: "I think it was real. Artie did it." [Unfortunately, however, director Michael Lange "felt bad…because Troy got a piece of plastic caught in his eye, during the shooting of the snow scene."]

• As to the Asian story Artie tells in one sequence, about the spirit's journey to heaven, Evans says, "That was something one of the writers pieced together from various sources. I don't know where exactly. It was very unspecific. It was like Star Trek and Kung Fu, where they sort of spin a pseudo-folk tale to support the thesis of the moment."

Episode 77: "Incident on Main". . . . . [1-10-93]
Written by Scott Frost. Directed by RW Goodwin. Guest stars: Dan Butler, Juanita Jennings, Paul Collins, Mariangela Pino, Jack Black, Marcia Magus, Marilyn Bradfield, Hill Harper, Lindsay Riddell

A band of gay-bashing, Neo-Nazi youths gang up on Jesse as he exits a hospice where he is volunteering. The consequences are doubly devastating when Becca gets his blood on her hands after the beating. She's tested for AIDS, but the results prove negative (though she is instructed to be tested again in six months). Meanwhile, a battered Jesse renders from memory a sketch of one of the skinheads. When it's displayed near the cash register at Drew's restaurant, the drawing is trashed by a lethal band member. Then later, Jesse struggles with identifying the gang member in a police lineup.

• Becca is never tested again for HIV, but it was assumed she never was infected.

Episode 78: "Lost Weekend" . . . . [1-24-93]
Written by Thania St. John. Directed by Lorenzo DeStefano. Guest stars: Diane Salinger, Vincent Ventresca

Becca and Jesse ache to be with one another, once their intimate evenings end. To break routine, Becca suggests they go with Goodman and a friend on a double date. The evening turns out to be less than relaxing, as Goodman's indiscretions prove uncomfortable. Shortly after, Jesse and Becca test the limits of their passions and attempt to have safe sex. The results are less than satisfying, especially after Becca tells her parents that she spent the night in Jesse's arms, and they become alarmed. Drew then expresses to Jesse his concern that he and his daughter have crossed the line of good judgment. Meanwhile, Paige believes she may have feelings for Artie when she becomes jealous of his new friend, and Libby's parents' argument once again results in an overnight visit from Teresa. This time, her husband breaks the furnace at their house; though she does return to Sal "because someone has to keep his feet warm."

• Jesse: "The word, blast, and the name, Goodman, makes me nervous."

• Jesse wonders about the name of Goodman's date, and Becca says: "Bates."

Jesse replies: "As in Norman?" (Anthony Perkins' moniker from the Psycho films).

• During Becca's sleepover at Jesse's, she says: "I used your toothpaste, and my finger."

• On hearing a fire engine, Becca asks: "Think there's a fire?" To which Jesse responds: "Something's always burning somewhere." (As in their passion for each other). Then he wonders: "Where were you two years ago?" Becca: "Looking for someone like you."

• Drew talks with Jesse. "I would give anything if this disease hadn't happened to you...I've grown to love you as a son." Then, regarding Becca: "I love my daughter more than life."

• Also, Jesse and Goodman really talk for the first time, in depth, while Becca dances with Goodman's date.

• Libby's mom first left her husband in "Corky's Crush," from the first season.

Episode 79: "Visions" . . . . [2-14-93]
Written by E.F. Wallengren. Directed by Michael Lange. Guest stars: Tom Wright, Michael Cade

Shortly after his 18th birthday, Becca agrees to a date with Ray while a feverish Jesse, in excruciating pain, collapses at school and is rushed, unconscious, to the hospital. His condition has progressed to full-blown AIDS. Then, at Marshall High the next day, Jesse is incapable of presenting a talk about AIDS to a class, so Becca reads his thoughts, which break her heart. Through it all, Jesse has nightmares mixed with his realities, and can't tell the difference.

• Drew gives Jesse a CD of the Carmel Jazz Festival for his birthday.
• *Becca:* "Jesse, you've been a major yawn lately."
• Little Nicky comes down with the chicken pox.
• Goodman calls Bates, the last guy she went out with, "the dustbin of history."

• Ray asked Becca if she's interested in seeing Hoffa, the film, when the Phish concert is cancelled. But Becca nixes the movie and they go bowling.

• Ray creating computer games: "My goal is to help millions of teenagers squander their lives and irritate their parents...and part with their quarters."

• Dr. Jeffries' diagnosis of Jesse: "His T-cell count is far below normal, and he's manifesting early symptoms of pneumocystis carinii pneumonia...He has AIDS."

• Becca reads Jesse's notes for an AIDS Seminar from his yellow pad:

> "Hi. I'm Jesse McKenna. Most of you know me already. I'm a senior here, and just like you, I can hardly wait to get out of this place...The only problem is, I don't know what to do after I finish. There's a time bomb in my bloodstream, waiting to go off. It's called HIV and it's a killer. Once it gets into your system, it never lets go. I got it by having unprotected sex with an HIV carrier. She didn't know she was sick then. She's dead now...It's only a matter of time before this disease kills me, too. Everything I had and everything I hoped for was taken from me because of one night of passion. A condom might have made the difference, but even condoms aren't foolproof. If they were, half of us wouldn't be here. The safest sex of all is no sex. That's a drag, but it's the reality...Becca Thacher is the love of my life...Never before have two people been more perfect for each other. She's the reason why I get up in the morning. She's the reason why I'm still in school. She's the reason why I'm still alive...I can't begin to tell you how painful it is to know that we'll never..."

Becca stops reading and Goodman takes over...

> "I can't begin to tell you how painful it is to know that we'll never be able to share our love the way it was meant to be shared. We'll never marry, we'll never make love, we'll never have children. We'll spend a few precious moments together and then say goodbye...All because of a single night of passing pleasure. That's my story. I hope there's never another one like it at Marshall High. Thanks for listening."

• Jesse's dreams/nightmares: Ray kissing Becca at Jesse's funeral, and a healthy, nicely dressed Jesse and Becca having a toast in an idyllic setting.

Episode 80: "Five to Midnight" . . . . [2-21-93]
Written by Scott Frost. Directed by Michael Nankin. Guest stars: Scott Jaeck, Tina Lifford, Artur Cybulski, Sarah Kim Heinberg, Gene Keller, Alberto Barboza

Jesse's insurance runs out, and he's transferred to the less-than capable County Hospital. Becca goes with him, and he nearly dies of AIDS-related cardiac arrest. The doctors apply shock therapy at five to midnight. Becca delivers a haunting self-portrait of Jesse that he doesn't remember painting.
  • Jesse dreams of his and Becca's plans of a Paris trip, but the taxicab stops at the hospital with a tab of $11.55 — another interpretation of 11:55 or five to midnight, when his heart stopped.

Episode 81: "Bedfellows" . . . . [2-28-93]
Written by Marshall Goldberg. Directed by Michael Lange. Guest stars: Richard Frank Raye Birk, Rona Canada, Yvette Freeman, Kathryn Graf, Lawrence A. Mandley, Judy Berkowitz, Barry Cutler, Jill Holden, Andrew Philpot, Cynthena Sanders

A fellow AIDS patient named Chester encourages Jesse to learn to live rather than give up and die. He holds game shows with other patients, makes fun of the sugarcoated remarks the doctors make every time a new patient comes in, and sings, too. Jesse objects to Becca's inclination, both to go to Brown University, saying that he would be too much of a burden. Chester dies when he rescues Jesse up on the hospital roof.

  • After Mrs. McKenna buys her son a TV, a patient in the hospital tells Jesse that "Days is on in ten minutes," apparently referring to the NBC day-time soap opera, *Days of Our Lives*. Interesting, because *Life Goes On* was an ABC show, and networks don't usually cross-promote, even in a subtle way.
  • Jesse to Becca: "You don't belong here...This is not your world. You live in your world, I'll live in mine. Although mine won't last as long as yours."
  • Then, Reardon, the Director of Admissions for the school that Becca has applied to, tells her: "...you belong here. We're delighted to have you."
  • Chester nearly blind-sides Jesse with a proverbial *one-two* punch of honesty in how not to give up the good-fight — against AIDS — and for Becca's love:

> *Chester:* You're giving up, aren't you? That's the reason you're pushing her away.
> *Jesse:* It's all pretty inevitable, isn't it? Why bring everyone down with me?"
> *Chester:* Because it's a war, don't you understand that? Us

against the disease. And you have to fight till your last
breath. You can't let it beat you.
Jesse: I'll leave the fighting to you.
Chester: Coward.

Later, after Jesse and Chester race on the roof, connected to their IVs,
Chester tells him, "Maybe you were right after all. It is easier just to stop
fighting."

"No," Jesse replies, "I was wrong."

• A major revelation from Becca, when she tells Drew: "Jesse asked me
if I felt relief at getting into school. I said no, but the truth is, I did. The last
two years I feel like I've been with two people: Jesse and his disease. It was
always with us. And when I was at that luncheon yesterday, seeing pictures
of the school, it felt so good to be away from it...All my life I looked up
to you and Mom. You love Corky completely. There's no pity, no complaint.
It makes me so proud of this family...and so ashamed I can't love Jesse the
same way."

Drew ups the ante: "Let me tell you something, something I don't even
talk about with your mother. There are a lot of times I see Corky and I want
to run...It's more than the responsibility. I don't mind helping him with the
same homework for four years, or driving him everywhere because he can't
get a license. But sometimes I wish...You know how I love Cork. I would
die for him, in a second. But sometimes I see him and say...why can't I have
a normal son...Pretty lousy father, huh?"

Becca returns with, "Yeah...just terrible," and not meaning it.

Still, we can't help but feel that this is not the Drew we knew in the
show's first two years.

• Later, Jesse tells Becca: "It would be great to be regular eighteen-year-olds,
wouldn't it? Go to college, party, be completely dumb whenever we want."

• This was the episode that Chad Lowe submitted for the Emmy, which
he won.

• Marshall Goldberg: "When you shoot a filmed show, you don't shoot
chronologically; you go according to economic convenience. If your show
were to open in the kitchen, and close in the kitchen, and you have seven
days to shoot, and even though they're taking place 45 minutes apart on
screen, you would ordinarily shoot them the same day, and the actors would
have to adjust. You're there; you might as well shoot it. That's the attitude.
It's cost-effective. It's the assistant director who decides the order the scenes
will be shot in. The AD on 'Bedfellows' waited to the last day to schedule the
dying scene. He's a smart guy who kind of did it for a reason.

"And Richard Frank was new to the show, just a guest role. But after
seven days, people had really fallen in love with this character. He made the
character so appealing, they liked the actor. And people really got into the

show. And when we did the dying scene, everyone on the show was crying. And Jesse was comforting him. And when Michael Lange said cut, everyone cried. And Chad, who was supposed to be crying as Jesse, couldn't stop crying as Chad, once Michael Lange yelled cut. And Chad said, 'could we hurry through this, because I don't want to do this many more times. I don't want to go through this again.' It was just so painful for him, and I don't know what he was thinking about, his manger or what not. But he was genuinely grieving. The only time I saw him hesitate emotionally the whole year is when he had to comfort Richard Frank. And we finally convinced him that he had to get into bed. Jesse's too close with this guy. He wouldn't allow any distance. And it was really difficult for him to face that pain, on a personal level. But the professional side of him prevailed, and he deserved the accolades that he received."

• Guest actor Richard Frank, who played Chester, died shortly after had appeared in ABC's sitcom, *Anything But Love.*

Episode 82: "Last Wish" . . . . [3-7-93]
Written by Toni Graphia. Directed by Joe Pennella. Guest stars: Raye Birk, Ed Evanko, Yvette Freeman, Jill Holden, Rosemary Brown

Becca and Jesse journey to see the ocean, after Jesse says that it's something he's always wanted to do. He's not exactly on top of the world, however, as he's jealous of Ray, who's been seeing a lot of Becca lately. It's Ray, too, who purchases the plane tickets they needed to get there.

• During an argument, they flashback a few Glenbrook weeks, not from previous episodes, but stuff that would have occurred during the course of other episodes.

• Toni Graphia: "I was most proud of this episode, partly because I got a Writer's Guild Nomination for it, which is considered even more prestigious than an Emmy because your peers actually read the script to vote as opposed to just watching the tape. I'd never received any award. It's always the big profile, 10:00 dramas. That year, when they made the announcements, it was people like David Kelley for *Picket Fences*, Paul Attanasio from *Homicide*, Tom Fontana from *Homicide*, Barbara Hall from *I'll Fly Away*, and Toni Graphia from *Life Goes On*. I was stunned. I received all these congratulations calls because it was like the Little Show that Could. It was especially cool since the gimmick I'd used was to write the show backwards. The plot started at one point and then we'd have a card that said, "earlier..." and it told what happened previously. I was inspired by a Harold Pinter play, and an episode we'd done on *China Beach*. People at the network had read it and almost threw it out, saying it was way too confusing to follow. In fact, after it was shot, they had the editors do a forward cut, where the story was told in chronological order. They were too afraid people couldn't follow the backwards one. But then we screened both versions and overwhelmingly, the backwards one worked. I knew that, because I wrote it to work that way. It was actually quite awful running forward! So when I received the nomination, it was sweet revenge."

Episode 83: "Life Goes On (And On and On)" . . . . [5-23-93]
Written by EF Wallengren. Directed by Michael Lange. Guest stars: John Ingle, Leslie Ishii, Jonathan Gibby, Spencer Klein

Approximately ten years into the future, Becca graduates from college and marries Jesse, whose AIDS goes into remission. He eventually succumbed to the disease, Becca remarries, and has a son she named Jesse. She tells her son a story about what happened after graduating from high school. Meanwhile, in the present, Corky doesn't graduate, Ray's the valedictorian of Becca's class, Jesse leaves for Europe, breaks Becca's heart, and then returns four years later.

• Corky on high school: "I'll be back."
• It's not determined whether Becca's son was fathered by Jesse or not, but Becca expresses a desire to have Jesse's baby, saying that new treatments could make it possible. The question of who fathered this child is hard to answer as Becca says the final words of the series: "I love you, Jesse."
• Not wanting to give false hope to HIV/AIDS carriers, Chad Lowe said in *Entertainment Weekly*, that Jesse McKenna did not father the child.
• *Life Goes On* never set out to beat viewers over the head with the idea that Corky was a dear lad. The portrayal of the character was of necessity a compromise. It would have been irresponsible to make him either too distressed or too unaffected.
• The three students mentioned with Becca as exceptional students during the graduation ceremony were the names of three fans of the show that coordinated letter-writing campaigns to save the show.
• Are the future scenes fantasy sequences, or did it really happen within the logical arena of the show? And was that child Jesse's child?
• Even though most viewers may not have perceived that Jesse was the little boy's father, Michael Braverman explains: "That was Jesse's child. And it was not a fantasy sequence, as much as a flash forward to the future cannot be a fantasy sequence. I mean, if a flash forward cannot be a fantasy, than it wasn't. It was projecting into the future that Jesse and Becca got together and that at some point, it became possible for them to have a child."
• This episode, too, delegitimatizes the first segment of the fourth season, "Bec to the Future," in which there is no mention of Becca and Jesse's son; in

which there is no mention of Jesse; only in the end, when the future Becca tells her husband David about her past love.

• Libby to Corky: "The world is a better place because of you," and few would disagree. Says Michael Lange: "I'm getting a chill hearing that line now, and talking about this."

• Speaking for everyone involved with this episode, and the show in general, Chad Lowe says, "We wanted to prove that life does go on."

EPISODES IN ALPHABETICAL ORDER

Armageddon (#46)

Arthur (#42)

Babes in the Woods (#73)

Babysitter, The (#3)

Banquet Room Renovation (#27)

Bec to the Future (#67)

Becca and the Band (#26)

Becca and The Underground
   Newspaper (#19)

Becca's First Love (#5)

Bedfellows (#81)

Bicycle Thief (#34)

The Bigger Picture (#36)

Blues, The (#60)

Break A Leg, Mom (#4)

Brothers (#15)

Buddy, The (#33)

Call of the Wild (#8)

Chicken Pox (#29)

Corky and the Dolphins (#24)

Choices (#76)

Confessions (#65)

Consenting Adults (#66)

Corky For President (#2)

Corky Rebels (#16)

Corky Witnesses A Crime (#9)

Corky's Crush (#12)

Corky's Romance (#63)

Corky's Travels (#39)

Dueling Divas (#51)

Exposed (#68)

Fairy Tale, The (#61)

Five To Midnight (#80)

Ghost of Grandpa Past (#41)

Halloween (#28)

Happy Holidays (#75)

Head Over Heels (#38)

Hearts and Flowers (#62)

Hello, Good-bye (#48)

Honeymoon From Hell (#23)

Incident on Main (#77)

Invasion of the Thacher Snatchers
   (#52)

Isn't It Romantic (#35)

It Ain't All It's Cracked Up to Be
   (#17)

Jerry's Deli (#57)

La Dolce Becca (#30)

Last Stand At Glenbrook (#37)

Last Wish (#82)

Libby's Sister (#32)

Life After Death (#50)

Life Goes On [And On...And On]
   (#83)

Lighter Than Air (#43)

Loaded Question (#53)

Lost Weekend (#78)

Love Letters (#71)

More Than Friends (#64)

Ordinary Heroes (#10)

Out of the Mainstream (#47)

Paige's Date (#6)

ABOUT THE AUTHOR

Herbie J Pilato was born on October 9, 1960, in Rochester, New York, on Erie Street, across from where now stands Frontier Field. He graduated from Aquinas Institute in 1978, graduated with a BA in Theatre Arts from Nazareth College, studied TV & Film at UCLA, and served his Internship in Public Relations at NBC Television in Burbank, California.

Today, he is an author, actor, TV producer and singer/songwriter who has appeared on and/or helped to produce hundreds of radio and TV shows, including Bravo's hit five-part series, *The 100 Greatest TV Characters*, E! *True Hollywood Stories* on *Bewitched* and David Carradine, A&E *Biographies* of Elizabeth Montgomery and Lee Majors, TLC's *Behind the Fame* specials on *The Mary Tyler Moore Show, The Bob Newhart Show, LA Law* and *Hill Street Blues*, the Sci-Fi Channel's short-lived but critically-acclaimed *Sciography* series, and *Entertainment Tonight*.

The author of several highly-regarded TV tome companions, including *Bewitched Forever* and *The Kung Fu Book of Caine*, Herbie J (no period after the *J*) has also contributed to many magazines, such as: *Starlog, Sci-Fi Entertainment* and *Sci-Fi Universe*. He has served as a Website Editor for PAXTV.com, UPNTV.com and TV-Now.com, and MediaVillage.com (the latter for which he penned a daily classic TV blog).

Herbie J has worked as a Consultant for the special DVD releases of *Kung Fu, Bewitched,* and *CHiPs*, as well as for Nora Ephron's *Bewitched* movie. As an actor, he's appeared on *General Hospital* and *The Bold and the Beautiful*. He's also directed mainstage productions of Leonard Melfi's *Birdbath, A Phoenix Too Frequent* and the musical *Little Shop of Horrors at RAPA* (one of Upstate, New York's most prestigious theatrical centers), where he also taught courses in acting and writing.

Herbie J offers *TV & Self-Esteem Seminars* to schools, colleges and community and business organizations, has served as the Creative Director for the *Arts & Academic Program* at Rochester's Historic German House, and is the former Executive Director of Public Relations and Communications for the *Mercier Literacy Program* (which services the educational needs of Rochester's underpriveledged youth).

BearManor Media will publish several of Herbie J's new books, including *The Bionic Book: The Six Million Dollar Man* and *The Bionic Woman Reconstructed*), *NBC & ME: My Life As a Page in A Book* (a mock memoir of his *Big '80s* days as a Guest Relations Representative for the Peacock network), *Twitch Upon a Star: The Elizabeth Montgomery Story*, *Kung Fu and The First Journeys of Caine: A Traveler's Companion to TV's First Eastern Western*, and *Trek's Saturday Morning Star Guide: The Colorful Companion to The Animated Edition of The Original Star Trek Series*.

At present, Herbie J is developing ideas for several television shows (scripted and non-scripted) and feature films.

Chris Burke rides the waves of *Life*. *KALEY HUMMEL*

Printed in the United States
200135BV00011B/11/A